WITHDRAWN

AMERICAN LITERATURE

COMPARATIVE LITERATURE series

Italian Literature: The Dominant Themes
French Literature: In the Nineteenth Century

In preparation

American Literature: The Twentieth Century
The English Novel: The Twentieth Century

Comparative Literature

AMERICAN LITERATURE
NINETEENTH AND EARLY
TWENTIETH CENTURIES

Scott Donaldson and Ann Massa

DAVID & CHARLES
Newton Abbot London Vancouver
BARNES & NOBLE
(a division of Harper & Row Publishers Inc.)

British Library Cataloguing in Publication Data

American literature. – (Comparative literature).
Nineteenth and early twentieth centuries.
    1. American literature – 19th century – Criticism
and interpretation   2. American literature – 20th
century – Criticism and interpretation
I. Donaldson, Scott   II. Massa, Ann   III. Series
    810'.9   PS201

ISBN 0–7153–7612–8

ISBN 0–06–491741–X (United States)
Library of Congress Catalog Card Number: 78–52628

This edition first published in 1978
in Great Britain by
David & Charles (Publishers) Limited
Brunel House Newton Abbot Devon

First published in the USA 1978 by
Harper & Row Publishers Inc
Barnes & Noble Import Division

Published in Canada
by Douglas David & Charles Limited
1875 Welch Street   North Vancouver   BC

Set in 11 on 13pt Garamond
and printed in Great Britain
by Latimer Trend & Company Ltd Plymouth

Contents

CONTENTS

Preface

This volume makes a fresh, topical approach to nineteenth- and early twentieth-century American literature. It is based on a study of American fiction, and draws on non-fictional sources only when fuller elucidation than the fiction itself can provide is called for. Each of the seven chapters of the book is structured around opposites – Dreams and Nightmares, for example, or Individual and Society – since American culture is best understood in terms of tensions if not paradoxes. Thus thematic insight rather than strict chronology is favoured – important writers are not neglected, but nor are they forced uncomfortably into periods. Substantial discussions of so wide-ranging and important a novel as *Huckleberry Finn*, for instance, appear in not one but several parts of the book. In addition, popular writing is discussed at some length, in the conviction that the novels of Gene Stratton-Porter, for example, though of small literary merit, usefully reflect (where greater works often dispute) widely held cultural beliefs.

It is the conviction of the authors that American literature differs from other literatures (including English) to the extent that and because it derives from a different culture. America has posed its writers many problems: how to write originally for and about a New World, for instance; and whether to put content before style in a passionate bid to preserve the ideals of the humanistic

American experiment. The themes of American fiction tell us a good deal about such dilemmas.

The American writer has rarely succeeded in reconciling the oppositions contained in his themes, except by way of statement. Robinson Jeffers' 'Shine, Perishing Republic' is a case in point; Walt Whitman's equation of body and soul another. The absence of neat answers is part of the puzzle of the literature, a literature shaped by, for instance, the asking of unanswerable questions – Ahab's 'Is it I, God, or who, that lifts this arm?' – and by that dualistic perception which leads to what might be termed the multiple choice ending.

Critics will vary in naming and sizing the pieces of the puzzle. Leslie Fiedler, for example, singles out love and death. The authors of this volume set out to indicate the framework of the puzzle, to give a sense of its complex and strangely assorted pieces: to help provide an understanding of the often contradictory forces which have shaped the national literature of the United States. To understand these is to start down the longer road toward a grasp of the national culture.

S.D. and A.M.

CHAPTER 1

The New World
and the Old World

Few literatures can compare with America's for sustained analysis of national character, and for regular discussion of alternative societies. Self-conscious comparison of what they had left with what they had found was characteristic of first-generation Americans; and through the phenomena of independence, republicanism and the melting-pot, the Old/New polarity became, and remains, a social and literary fixation. There was, of course, no single New World, no single Old: reactions and expectations varied from individual to individual, from one national to another. But the sense of a fresh start of gigantic potential and proportions, the chance to create the world over again, an Eden without a Fall, without an Eve, was common to everyone.

In one sense Americans were negative people, who came to get away. Nathaniel Hawthorne noted in *The Blithedale Romance* (1852):

> We were of all creeds and opinions, and generally tolerant of all, on every imaginable subject. Our bond, it seemed to me, was not affirmative but negative. We had individually found one thing or another to quarrel with in our past life, and were pretty well agreed as to the inexpediency of lumbering along with the old system any further.

9

But the process of leaving an old home involved seeking and finding a new one, and made for a positive unity. The early Americans were religious people, whose leaders expanded the covenant theory of Congregationalist theology into the notion of a special covenant between American man and God. To a world that was a new human experience – a nation born already mature and civilised; to a world that was a new geographical experience – in James Fenimore Cooper's words, a land 'where God has lavished his favors with an unsparing hand; where he has bestowed many climes with their several fruits . . . [where] the plains, teeming with verdure are spread over wide degrees; and yet where sweet valleys which a single heart can hold, are not wanting, – was added the concept of a world new in its special innocence, a virgin gift to the immigrants, their chance to retell the human story sinlessly. America was not just a Utopia, an El Dorado, an Elysium, an alternative; it was an Eden with pastoral, religious and anti-feminist connotations.

As the concept of the New and the Good took shape, so the concept of the Old and the Bad intensified. The Old stood for hierarchical injustice, institutional complexity and social decadence; the New for the equality of all men, the abolition of social distinction, for freedom, spontaneity, simplicity and vigour. The Old World was sophisticated and corrupt; America was simple and innocent. And although the ethnic groups who settled America, especially the Anglo-Saxon majority, retained many of the ways and moods of their homelands, American literature has tended to image the Old/New relationship as hostile not compatible. In Ezra Pound's eyes Americans were 'the best' who should not have given their lives in World War I,

> For an old bitch gone in the teeth
> For a botched civilization
> . . . .
> For two gross of broken statues
> For a few thousand battered books . . .

In Herman Melville's words:

> Escaped from the house of bondage, Israel of old did not follow
> after the ways of the Egyptians. To her was given an express
> dispensation; to her were given new things under the sun. And we
> Americans are the peculiar, chosen people – the Israel of our time;
> we bear the ark of the liberties of the world . . . God has pre-
> destinated, mankind expects, great things from our race; and great
> things we feel in our souls. The rest of the nations must soon be
> in our rear. We are the pioneers of the world; the advance guard,
> sent on through the wilderness of untried things, to break a new
> path in the New World that is ours. In our youth is our strength;
> in our inexperience, our wisdom . . . We cannot do a good to
> America but we give alms to the world . . .

The increasingly heterogeneous race which resulted from
America's free immigration policy made for a composite man, a
composite nation and a perpetual infusion of newness and
strength, physical and psychological, into America as it slowly
aged. The frontier process did the same thing; the questions
whither America and how to safeguard democracy were re-
debated as the population moved further west, with the admis-
sion of each new state to the Union. 'God is making the American,' cried a Jewish immigrant in Israel Zangwill's play *The
Melting-Pot* (1909). And through Scott Fitzgerald (*This Side of
Paradise*, 1920; *The Great Gatsby*, 1925), William Faulkner ('The
Bear', 1942), John Steinbeck (*East of Eden*, 1952) and Norman
Mailer (*Why Are We in Vietnam?*, 1969), the modern American
novelist has kept alive the concept of the New Adam which was
so prominent in earlier American literature.

The New Adam and the New Eden

The quintessential Adamic embodiment in American literature
and the earliest Adam-figure of any stature is Natty Bumppo,
whose creator, James Fenimore Cooper, owed something to the

historical novel technique of Sir Walter Scott, but who put that technique to his own, mythic use. Natty, though once tempted to marry, is an essential loner, whose companions, too, are self-sufficient: Chingachgook and Uncas, the last of the Mohicans, and Hard-heart, a Pawnee as stoical as Bumppo himself, and who adopts Bumppo as his (wifeless) father. Natty, whose 'ordinary expression . . . was that of simplicity, integrity and sincerity, blended in an air of self-reliance', is very near to complete innocence,

> . . . a sort of type of what Adam might have been supposed to be before the fall . . . It was said of the Pathfinder [Natty's nickname], by one accustomed to study his fellows, that he was a fair example of what a just-minded and pure man might be, while untempted by unruly or ambitious desires, and left to follow the bias of his feelings, amid the solitary grandeur and ennobling influences of a sublime nature; neither led aside by the inducements which influence all to do evil amid the incentives of civilization, nor forgetful of the Almighty Being, whose spirit pervades the wilderness.

But something militates against Natty's perfection: his Old World 'headstart', his relationship with a civilisation most of whose 'principles' and preconceptions are prejudiced. America must, then, rethink Old World premises. Cooper thinks its new morality will come about through a psychic miscegenation, a reconciliation and/or fusion of the best in each man, each race, each creed, symbolised by a psychic red/white amalgam. Objectivity is to replace subjective pride and prejudice. As Natty says:

> I am willing to own that my people have many ways, of which, as an honest man, I can't approve. It is one of their customs to write in books what they have done and seen, instead of telling them in their villages, where the lie can be given to the face of a cowardly boaster, and the brave soldier can call on his comrades to witness for the truth of his words.

Chingachgook and Uncas are converted to sparing rather than slaughtering enemies, 'abandoning their own previously expressed opinions with a liberality and candour, that, had they been the representatives of some great and civilized people, would have infallibly worked their political ruin, by destroying, for ever, their reputation for consistency'. Cooper gives many examples of indisputably universal truths; a white general's captive daughter can appeal to an Indian chief who has his own loved daughter; Indians mourning their dead 'understand' the rites of a white preacher. 'They listened like those who knew the meaning of the strange words and appeared as if they felt the mingled emotion of sorrow, hope and resignation they were intended to convey.'

Cooper is not always sanguine about his new man. In *The Pioneers* (1823), the middle-aged Natty has become a pathetic victim of the encroaching civilisation whose laws forbid him to hunt in what was once free land and is now private property. He is prosecuted and ends up in the stocks, asserting: 'I can live without venison; but I don't love to give up my lawful dues in a free country. Though for the matter of that, might often makes right here, as well as in the old country, for what I can see.' Change has been forced on Chingachgook, too:

> When John was young, eyesight was not straighter than his bullet. The Mingo squaws cried out at the sound of his rifle. The Mingo warriors were made squaws. When did he ever shoot twice! . . . 'But see,' he said, raising his voice from the low, mournful tones, in which he had spoken, to a pitch of keen excitement, and stretching forth both hands, 'they shake like a deer at the wolf's howl. Is John old? When was a Mohican a squaw, with seventy winters! No! the white man brings old age with him – rum is his tomahawk!'

But in *The Prairie* (1827), the book which describes Natty Bumppo's death, Cooper's optimism revives, and Natty, irritated beyond measure by a scientist discoursing on the achievement in art and architecture of the Egyptians, Chaldees, Greeks and

Romans, speaks up for the New World as Obed Bat maintains that

> '. . . many of the illustrious masters of antiquity have, by the aid of science and skill, even outdone the works of nature and exhibited a beauty and perfection in the human form that are difficult to be found in the rarest living specimens of any of the species, genus Homo.'

'Can your idols walk or speak, or have they the glorious gift of reason?' demanded the trapper with some indignation in his voice. 'Though but little given to run into the noise and chatter of the settlements, yet have I been into the town in my day to barter the peltry for lead and powder, and often have I seen your waxen dolls with their tawdry clothes and glass eyes – '

'*Waxen* dolls!' interrupted Obed. 'It is profanation in the view of the arts to liken the miserable handiwork of the dealers in wax to the pure models of antiquity!'

'It is profanation in the eyes of the Lord,' retorted the old man, 'to liken the works of his creatures to the power of his own hand.'

'Venerable venator,' resumed the naturalist, clearing his throat like one who was much in earnest, 'let us discuss understandingly and in amity. You speak of the dross of ignorance, whereas my memory dwells on those precious jewels which it was my happy fortune formerly to witness among the treasured glories of the Old World.'

'*Old* World!' retorted the trapper. 'That is the miserable cry of all the half-starved miscreants that have come into this blessed land since the days of my boyhood! They tell you of the *Old* World, as if the Lord had not the power and the will to create the universe in a day, or as if he had not bestowed his gifts with an equal hand, though not with an equal mind or equal wisdom have they been received and used. Were they to say a *worn-out*, and an *abused*, and a *sacrilegious* world, they might not be so far from the truth!'

Not that Natty holds himself up as an alternative. He has tried to be a new Adam in the American garden-wilderness but he has failed to curb animal instinct. 'The time has been when I have thought it possible to make a companion of a beast,' he recalls. 'Many are the cubs and many are the speckled fawns that I have reared with these old hands, until I have fancied them rational

14

and altered beings. But what did it amount to? The bear would bite and the deer would run . . .' He himself kills to survive with decreasing compunction. But Cooper has created such an impressively innocent man in Natty and such a splendidly egalitarian relationship between Natty and Chingachgook that the reader can, momentarily, glimpse the nucleus of a new human relationship, a new society, a New World.

Most American Adamic/Edenic writing manifests itself in three ways. Firstly, it takes the form of yearning for a perpetual nature idyll, and becomes part of the American version of pastoral. Secondly, it is integrated into that literature which celebrates and explores the concept of freedom. Thirdly, it manifests itself in the absence of flesh-and-blood women and adult, heterosexual love from the American novel. Woman is Eve, the temptress, an ancillary educator and child-bearer. Very few writers have dealt openly with the specifics of the Adamic/Edenic parallel. In the period up to 1920 there are two great exceptions, whose greatness allows them to avoid the predictable limitations of the parallel: Hawthorne and Mark Twain, masters of literary illusion and penetrating critics of historical illusion. Hawthorne sombrely, Twain humorously, make the point that in specific detail the parallel is untenable. They face and deny this particular aspect of New World mythology. Hawthorne, who was especially god- and devil-conscious, thought the whole parallel was yet another sin of pride stemming from the uneradicated, ineradicable original sin. A comment on the English suggests that, in any case, he was not in favour of a simple society.

They adhere closer to the original simplicity in which mankind was created, than we ourselves do: they love, quarrel, laugh, cry and turn their actual selves inside out, with greater freedom than any class of American would consider decorous . . . These Englishmen are certainly a franker and simpler people than ourselves, from peer to peasant: but . . . they owe these noble and manly qualities to a coarser grain in their nature, and . . . with a finer one in ours, we shall ultimately acquire a marble-polish of which they are unsusceptible.

In 'Rappacini's Daughter' (1844), adapted by Hawthorne 'from the writings of Aubepiné, which included "Le nouveau Père Adam et la nouvelle Mère Eve" ', he writes of a modern fall, of beauty ruined by a man, American style, of too much science and too much ingenuity. A student, Giovanni Guasconti, finds his lodging in Padua overlooks Rappacini's garden. The garden is strange, and so is its 'creator'.

> The man's demeanor was that of one walking among malignant influences, such as savage beasts, or deadly snakes, or evil spirits, which, should he allow them one moment of license, would wreak upon him some terrible fatality. It was strangely frightful to the young man's imagination to see this air of insecurity in a person cultivating a garden, that most simple and innocent of human toils, and which had been like the joy and labor of the unfallen parents of the race. Was this garden, then, the Eden of the present world? And this man, with such a perception of harm in what his own hands caused to grow – was he the new Adam?

Somehow Rappacini has created a garden in which the scent of the flowers emanates poison as does the breath of his daughter Beatrice. An abnormal species, human and vegetable, has been spawned; 'the production was no longer of God's making, but the monstrous offspring of man's depraved fancy'. Rappacini is appallingly pretentious, he is would-be god (creator) and would-be devil (who thinks he can tempt Giovanni into marrying Beatrice and perpetuating the Rappacini species). 'His bent form grew erect with conscious power; he spread out his hands over them in the attitude of a father imploring a blessing upon his children.' Beatrice is finally killed by an antidote to her father's poison, ministered by the loving but cautious Giovanni.

Twain, like his character Huckleberry Finn, found the prospect of being forever in a garden or on a river or in a state of nature or goodness or being solitary a boring and frightening prospect. He touches on the Adamic/Edenic theme in *Pudd'nhead Wilson* (1894), the story of a misfit, a lawyer without clients, the butt of his community, who, at the end of the novel, suddenly emerges as the only individual in that community with intelligence and integrity. The reader turns back with a new insight to the daily quotations from Wilson's Calendar – written by himself – which preface the chapters. They all attack the idea of a 'brave new world'.

> It was wonderful to find America, but it would have been more wonderful to miss it.
>
> Adam was but human – this explains it all. He did not want the apple for the apple's sake, he wanted it only because it was forbidden. The mistake was in not forbidding the serpent; then he would have eaten the serpent.
>
> Whoever has lived long enough to find out what life is, knows how deep a debt of gratitude we owe to Adam, the first great benefactor of our race. He brought death into the world.

But it is Twain's superb satirical story 'The Diary of Adam and Eve' which charmingly but drily deflates the standard notion of American specialness and describes an aspect of American difference that sociologists still comment on: the dominant role of the American woman, in fact if not in fiction. For Twain, America is an Eden with a vengeance of an Eve! She is the namer, the organiser, the *fons et origo* not, in this instance, of all humankind, but especially of Americans. As entries in the man's diary show she quickly corrupts and masters Adam.

> *Monday* This new creature with the long hair is . . . always hanging around and following me about.
>
> *Tuesday* Been examining the great waterfall. It is the finest thing on the estate, I think. The new creature calls it Niagara Falls – why, I am sure I do not know. Says it *looks* like Niagara Falls. That is not a reason, it is mere waywardness and imbecility. I get no chance to name anything myself. The new creature names everything that comes along, before I can get in a protest.

Wednesday Built me a shelter against the rain, but could not have it to myself in peace. The new creature intruded. When I tried to put it out it shed water out of the holes it looks with, and wiped it away with the back of its paws, and made a noise such as some of the other animals make when they are in distress. I wish it would not talk; it is always talking.

Friday The naming goes recklessly on, in spite of anything I can do. I had a very good name for the estate, and it was musical and pretty – GARDEN OF EDEN. Privately, I continue to call it that, but not any longer publicly. The new creature says it is all woods and rocks and scenery, and therefore has no resemblance to a garden. Says it *looks* like a park, and does not look like anything *but* a park. Consequently, without consulting me, it has been new-named – NIAGARA FALLS PARK. This is sufficiently high-handed, it seems to me. And already there is a sign up:

KEEP OFF
THE GRASS

My life is not as happy as it was.

Sunday Pulled through.

Tuesday She has taken up with a snake now. The other animals are glad, for she was always experimenting with them and bothering them; and I am glad because the snake talks, and this enables me to get a rest.

Friday She says the snake advises her to try the fruit of that tree, and says the result will be a great and fine and noble education. I told her there would be another result, too – it would introduce death into the world. That was a mistake – it had been better to keep the remark to myself; it only gave her an idea – she could save the sick buzzard, and furnish fresh meat to the despondent lions and tigers. I advised her to keep away from the tree. She said she wouldn't. I foresee trouble. Will emigrate.

But Eve chases him, the apple is eaten, and Adam is lost. Eve ties him to her with Cain and the mystery of childhood and fatherhood – though he knows neither term at first. Is 'it' a fish? No, it laughs and fish do not nor do they say 'goo goo'. Is it growing a tail? or fur? or a pouch? Whatever it is, it 'has learned to paddle around all by itself on its hind legs and says "poppa" and "momma". It is certainly a new species'. The American has been born and raised, old style, and Adam, whom, Eve had noted, now stands spread out like a derrick, is no different from any other man. He now thinks, 'It is better to live outside the Garden with her than inside it without her.' The last entry in his diary is made after her death, and reads: 'Wheresoever she was, *there* was Eden.' Eve too, is content, ominously so. In the section of her entry marked 'After the Fall' she writes: 'The Garden is lost, but I have found him, and am content . . . I love him . . . because he is mine and masculine. There is no other reason.'

Dissatisfaction

The American literary tradition of dissatisfaction with the New World, especially by the side of the Old, ranges from expressions of inferiority through anguished debate; from judgement reserved through partial rejection. Predictably, the nation's soul was more often assailed than soothed by its perfectionist, preaching writers. Early in American literature the writings of Washington Irving reflect an excessive, almost crippling consciousness of the English heritage and the English presence. Only a tiny proportion of his *œuvre* had America for its theme or setting; England, Spain, Mexico and Arabia were the primary scenes of his stories. But even in these territories Irving, as an American writer, felt insecure. He had to face substantial anti-American prejudice.

> It has been a matter of marvel, to my European readers, that a man from the wilds of America should express himself in tolerable English. I was looked upon as something new and strange in literature; a kind of demi-savage, with a feather in his hand, instead of on his head; and there was a curiosity to hear what such a being had to say about civilized society.

The process worked in reverse. To Irving, Europe itself seemed full of 'strange matter and interesting novelty'. In St Paul's

Cathedral and Westminster Abbey he felt like an ignorant child in grown-up clothing. But, unlike a child, Irving was able to articulate precisely what fascinated him about the Old World; and so was Melville, who had grown up with Europe in America beside his father's knee.

Of winter evenings in New York . . . he used to tell my brother and me . . . all about Havre, and Liverpool, and about going up into the ball of St Paul's in London. Indeed, during my early life, most of my thoughts . . . were connected . . . with fine old lands, full of mossy cathedrals and churches, and long, narrow, crooked streets without sidewalks, and lined with strange houses. And especially I tried hard to think how such places must look of rainy days and Saturday afternoons; and whether indeed they did have rainy days and Saturdays there, just as we did here; and whether the boys went to school there, and studied geography, and wore their shirt collars turned over, and tied with a black ribbon; and whether their papas allowed them to wear boots, instead of shoes, which I so much disliked, for boots looked so manly.

But Melville, visiting England in the 1840s, was the product of an aggressive, positive America, that euphoric period of Manifest Destiny sandwiched between President Andrew Jackson and the Civil War; Irving was more tentative, more respectful towards a Europe which 'held forth the charm of the storied and poetical' and an England which was 'a perpetual volume of reference'. He was fascinated by

. . . those peculiarities which distinguish an old country and an old state of society from a new one . . . Accustomed always to scenes where history was, in a manner, anticipation; where every thing in art was new and progressive, and pointed to the future rather than to the past; where, in short, the works of man gave no ideas but those of young existence, and prospective improvement; there was something inexpressibly touching in the sight of enormous piles of architecture, gray with antiquity.

The note was set for the expression in American literature of the irresistible lure of antiquity, the feeling that the new was neither as exciting nor as worthwhile as the old. For antiquity might mean decay – it also meant the existence of centuries of theory and practice in all the arts, including the art of living. Irving's *Bracebridge Hall* (1822), a series of sketches of English country life, institutions and types, embodied the author's subservient fascination with things Old World. When he did concern himself with the New, the tone is satirical. Who were the Pilgrims? Idealists? Utopians? No, says Irving; 'it is a facetious name meaning a people who are always seeking a better country than their own'. Who was the Yankee? A great pioneer of a great new race? No, 'the wandering Arab of America'.

His first thought, on coming to years of manhood, is to *settle* himself in the world – which means nothing more nor less than to begin his rambles . . . His whole family, household furniture, and farming utensils, are hoisted into a covered cart; his own and his wife's wardrobe packed up in a firkin – which done, he shoulders his axe, takes staff in hand, whistles 'Yankee doodle', and trudges off to the woods, as confident of the protection of Providence, and relying as cheerfully upon his own resources, as ever did a patriarch of yore, when he journeyed into a strange country of the Gentiles . . . A huge palace of pine boards immediately springs up in the midst of the wilderness, large enough for a parish church, and furnished with windows of all dimensions, but so rickety and flimsy withal, that every blast gives it a fit of the ague.

Having recreated a travesty of the trappings of the Old World culture, the Yankee moves on, in true frontier spirit, to be, for what it's worth, new again.

Like Irving, Edgar Allan Poe set very few stories in America, and went out of his way to change the American setting (the Hudson) of the true story which formed the basis for 'Murder in the Rue Morgue' to France. His 'The Domain of Arnheim' is, like Irving's *History of New York*, a debunking visit to Dutch New

England; an anti-Edenic story in that the architect–protagonist asserts that 'the original beauty is never so great as that which may be introduced'. Poe is always satirical in his rare incursions into Americana. In 'Some Words with a Mummy', the resuscitated Egyptian Mummy consistently betters her New World inquisitors; the Pyramids were structurally more complex than the Capitol in Washington, and railroads 'could not be compared, of course, with the vast, level, direct, iron-grooved causeways upon which the Egyptians conveyed entire temples and solid obelisks of a hundred and fifty feet in altitude'. The idea of New World achievement is sent up sky-high in the story's conclusion:

> The doctor, approaching the Mummy with great dignity, desired it to say candidly, upon its honor as a gentleman, if the Egyptians had comprehended, at *any* period, the manufacture of either Ponnonner's lozenges or Brandreth's pills.
>
> We looked with profound anxiety for an answer, but in vain. It was not forthcoming. The Egyptian blushed and hung down his head. Never was triumph more consummate; never was defeat borne with so ill a grace. Indeed, I could not endure the spectacle of the poor Mummy's mortification. I reached my hat, bowed to him stiffly and took leave.

Virtually all Cooper's writings are concerned with the social and political differences, actual and wished-for, between America and England. *The Pilot* (1823) and *The Two Admirals* (1842) are set largely in England, and both deal with the break-up of Anglo-American families as they took different sides during the American Revolution. The process of a new nationality in the making, 'that odd contrast between civilization and rude expedients which so frequently occurs on an American frontier, where persons educated in refinements often find themselves brought in close collision with savage life', fascinated Cooper. *Lionel Lincoln* (1825) deals with the return of some Anglo-Americans, after a few years in England, to revolutionary Boston of 1775, and their bewilderment with 'Americans' who see England as Satan, who maintain 'it was tea that tempted our common mother in Paradise'. In *Wyandotte* (1843) Sir Hugh Willoughby, living in frontier upper New York State, does not know whether to be Anglo or American when the war breaks out. His son fights for King George; his son-in-law for George Washington. In *Homeward Bound* (1838) the English-educated Eve Effingham is on ship returning to America, and there is great discussion as to whether she is going to be wasting herself.

> 'You have been taught music in general, by seven masters of as many different states, besides the touch of the guitar by a Spaniard; Greek by a German; the living tongues by the European powers; and philosophy by seeing the world; and now, with a brain full of learning, fingers full of touches, eyes full of tints, and a person full of grace, your father is taking you back to America, to "waste your sweetness on the desert air".'
>
> 'Poetically expressed, if not justly imagined, cousin Jack,' returned the laughing Eve; 'but you have forgot to add, "and a heart full of feeling for the land of my birth".'

Her father sees her as the founder of a new race, the new Eve, a mixture of the best of England and America. 'Independence of situation have induced independence of thought; study and investigation have rendered her original and just.' But Cooper cannot accede so easily to the Edenic myth; and he has other characters on board ship who are less sanguine about America. What about America's vaunted freedom, they ask? Has freedom its own arbitrary laws – is it 'excessively presuming in an American to pretend to be different from his fellow-citizens'? If one man is as good as another, why bother with elections? What about slaves and apprentices – where is their freedom? What does it mean to be an American? Eve's brother defines the term. It means 'just eighteen months. Antiquity is reached in five lustra, and the dark ages at the end of a human life . . . The whole country is in such a constant state of mutation that I can only liken it to the games of children.' On board along with these critics of America is a parody of American culture in the journalistic, entrepreneurial person of Mr Steadfast Dodge, editor of the *Active Inquirer* of Dodgetown, population eighteen, busy writing and reading aloud his ignorant, hostile commentary on Europe and his own puffs. He claims to be a Johnson in taste, a Chesterfield in style, a Scott in popularity!

In *Homeward Bound*'s sequel, *Home as Found* (1838), Eve arrives in America, and a contrast is immediately drawn with her early girlhood friend Grace Van Cortlandt. It is Grace who is snobbishly exclusive, a conspicuous consumer; Eve who is simple and egalitarian. She finds she has set foot in an already tainted New World, and that the Old World is the purer teacher.

'And why should not Mr Powis treat Sir George Templemore as one every way his equal, Grace?' she asked.

'Why, Eve, one is a baronet, and the other is but a simple gentleman.'

America did not contain two of the same sex, years, and social condition, less alike in their opinions . . . than the two cousins. Grace Van Cortlandt, of the best blood of her native land, had unconsciously imbibed in childhood the notions connected with hereditary rank, through the traditions of colonial manners, by means of novels, by hearing the vulgar reproached or condemned for their obtrusion and ignorance . . . Eve, so far from having become the dupe of the glitter of life, by living so long within its immediate influence . . . had learned to discriminate between the false and the real, and to perceive that which was truly respectable and useful, and to know it from that which was merely arbitrary and selfish. Eve actually fancied that the position of an American gentleman might readily become, nay, that it ought to be, the highest of human stations . . .

'A simple gentleman, Grace?' she repeated slowly after her cousin; 'and is not a simple gentleman, a simple American gentleman, the equal of any gentleman on earth – of a poor baronet in particular?'

Melville follows in Cooper's footsteps in the total ambivalence of his attitudes to the Old and New Worlds. At one moment he seems to subscribe to the most mystical of frontier theories.

West, West! Whitherward mankind and empires – flocks, cara-
vans, armies, navies, worlds, suns, and stars all wend! West, West!
Oh, boundless boundary! Eternal goal! Whitherward rush, in
thousand worlds, ten thousand thousand keels! Beacon, by which
the universe is steered! – Like the north-star, attracting all needles!
Unattainable for ever; but for ever leading to great things this
side thyself! Hive of all sunsets! Gabriel's pinions may not over-
take thee!

The next moment he looks back to the Old World, wishing that
'this world [were] an endless plain, and by sailing eastward we
could for ever reach new distances, and discover sights more
sweet and strange than any Cyclades or Islands of King Solomon'.
He fears that 'Columbus sailed over numberless unknown worlds
to discover one superficial Western one'.

What worries Melville about America is what worried Cooper –
the democratic shortfall which so signally failed to set the New
above the Old. His picture of Vivenza (America) in *Mardi* (1849)
demonstrates his poignant love/hate relationship with that
country. He loves its vigour and vitality, its egoistic, humanistic
self-confidence, as magnificent as Captain Ahab's: he loves a
'braggadocio nation . . . an army of spurred and crested roosters
. . . chanticleered at the resplendent rising of their sun . . . a fresh
start in the species'.

Vivenza was a noble land. Like a young tropic tree she stood, laden
down with greenness, myriad blossoms, and the ripened fruit
thick-hanging from one bough. She was promising as the morning.
Or Vivenza might be likened to St John, feeding on locusts and
wild honey, and with prophetic voice, crying to the nations from
the wilderness. Or, childlike, standing among the old robed kings
and emperors of the Archipelago, Vivenza seemed a young
Messiah, to whose discourse the bearded Rabbis bowed.

But in other respects Vivenza is appallingly Old World. It
seems as warlike as Dominora (England) from whose lion-like
loins it is unfortunately sprung. 'Though now in childhood she

anticipates her youth and lusts for empire like any Czar.' The inscription Melville and his Polynesian companions had deciphered on their arrival in Vivenza – 'In – this – re – publi – can – land – all – men – are – born – free – and – equal' – and its post-script: 'Except – the – tribe – of – Hamo' – which at the time they had taken to be waggish, is found to be horribly true. Momentarily the disappointed Melville sees slavery as a crime on a par with the crucifixion.

Under a burning sun, hundreds of collared men were toiling in trenches, filled with the taro plant, a root most flourishing in that soil. Standing grimly over these, were men unlike them; armed with long prongs, which descended upon the toilers and made wounds. Blood and sweat mixed; and in great drops fell.

Melville interprets the existence of slavery in America as indication that America is not a New World, its citizens no new race; indeed he interprets the presence of slavery even in America as an indication that there will never be a brave new world. A malignant world-fate exists, and is inescapable. The same fear that man is intrinsically unfree and that all the New World premises are false is one theme of *Moby-Dick* (1851), Melville's *chef-d'œuvre*, in which he showed himself as tightly bound to America as a whale by a harpoon rope; and tucked away in Chapter 114 of *Moby-Dick* lies Melville's comment on the origin of America, which he sees as a bastard, an orphan, not springing from the loins of God, or a second, Christ-like Adam, nor from some special founding fathers. 'Where is the foundling's father hidden? Our souls are like those orphans whose unwedded mothers die in bearing them; the secret of our paternity lies in their grave, and we must there to learn it.'

The humour that is present in nearly all Mark Twain's writings tends to mask the seriousness of his work. For all that he took indigenous American materials – frontiersmen, gold-rush millionaires, cracker-barrel philosophers; for all that he immortalised the California of his young manhood and the Missouri of his childhood, his nostalgia and his optimism were heavily qualified. He saw as clearly as Cooper that the democratic ideal of every individual ordering a splendid destiny for himself might lead to ethical laxity; he had no respect for the get-rich-quick ethic, which meant that 'to be a saloon keeper and kill a man was to be illustrious'. A comment on frontier justice in *Roughing It* (1872) showed just how little Twain thought of the common sense of the American man-in-the-street and his legislators. Why, Twain asks, were the men who murdered Virginia's original twenty-six cemetery occupants never punished? Because in the time of Alfred the Great, who invented trial by jury,

> . . . news could not travel fast, and hence he could easily find a jury of honest, intelligent men, who had not heard of the case they were to try – but in our day of telegraph and newspapers his plan compels us to swear in juries composed of fools and rascals, because this system rigidly excludes honest men and men of brains, ministers, doctors, superintendents – all read newspapers.

Twain's comparison is rarely as much in favour of the (hypothetical) Old World of Alfred if he had lived, but the New is often shown as no better than the Old. When the 'duke' and the 'king', travelling entertainers and tricksters, invade Huck's and Jim's raft the 'boys' rationalise their dislike of them by associating them with the Old World.

> '. . . I doan' hanker for no mo' un um, Huck. Dese is all I kin stan'.'
> 'It's the way I feel too, Jim. But we've got them on our hands, and we got to remember what they are, and make allowances.'

But that old head which sits on Huck's young shoulders reasserts itself; and he admits that the 'regular rapscallions' are symptomatic of the American condition, not just the Old World's.

'These warn't real Kings and dukes . . . [but] you couldn't tell them from the real kind . . . Sometimes I wish we could hear of a country that's out of kings.' The gullible reaction of the riverside communities as they fall for the numerous hypocrisies of the 'duke' and the 'king' lead Twain to doubt the common man. Southern white mobs cannot even organise a lynching (of a white man) properly. 'A mob without any MAN at the head of it, is beneath pitifulness.'

Like *A Connecticut Yankee in King Arthur's Court* (1889), *Innocents Abroad and The New Pilgrim's Progress* (1868) raise the question as to which society, if any, is or was the civilised society. On the one hand Twain's travels in Europe made him feel ashamed of gee-whiz American naïveté. On the other hand, in total contrast to Irving, Europe failed to come up to Twain's expectations. Everything he looked forward to was a disappointment. In Paris the *grisettes* were hideous, and the palatial barbershops unhygienic. 'New York had fifty wonders where Constantinople has one.' Athens by moonlight was beautiful, but it was the moonlight, not Athens, that appealed to him. For Twain what was old was known, tried and therefore dull; what was new was by definition if not good, at least better, and what life was about.

What is it that confers the noblest delight? What is that which swells a man's breast with pride above that which any other experience can bring to him? Discovery! To know that you are walking where none others have walked; that you are beholding what human eye has not seen before that you are breathing a virgin atmosphere . . . To be the *first* – that is the idea. To do something, say something, see something, before *any body* else – these are the things that confer a pleasure compared with which other pleasures are tame and commonplace, other ecstasies cheap and trivial. Morse, with his first message, brought by his servant, the lightning . . . Daguerre, when he commanded the sun, riding in the zenith, to print the landscape upon his insignificant silvered plate, and he obeyed; Columbus, in the Pinta's shrouds, when he swung his hat above a fabled sea and gazed abroad upon an unknown world! These are the men who have really *lived* – who have actually comprehended what pleasure is – who have crowded long lifetimes of ecstasy into a single moment.

Edith Wharton attacked the New World with the relish of an intermittent expatriate. Unlike James, she dealt almost exclusively with the pretensions of Americans in America, a country as corrupt as Europe, where 'beauty in the eyes of New York justified every success and excused a certain number of failings', where marriage, if honestly transacted, 'ought to have been transacted on the stock exchange'. *The Age of Innocence* (1920) is Mrs Wharton's bland, sarcastic title for a novel which explores a Gilded Age family, the Mingotts, and the immemorial way in which they and New York society deprive Countess Ellen Olenska, *née* Mingott, and Archer Newland, precariously engaged and precariously married to the matriarchal Mrs Mingott's granddaughter, May, of happiness. Although Archer and Ellen become lovers, Mrs Wharton casts them in the role of innocents, enjoying their love, not realising how every facet of their private relationship has been known to the family until they find themselves together at a farewell dinner for Ellen, given by May. As Archer's glance

. . . travelled from one placid well-fed face to another he saw all the harmless-looking people engaged upon May's canvas-backs as a band of dumb conspirators, and himself and the pale woman on his right as the centre of their conspiracy . . . He guessed himself to have been, for months, the centre of countless silently observing eyes and patiently listening ears, he understood that, by means as yet unknown to him, the separation between himself and the partner of his guilt had been achieved.

It was the old New York way of taking life 'without effusion of blood': the way of people who dreaded scandal more than disease, who placed decency above courage, and who considered that nothing was more ill-bred than 'scenes' except the behavior of those who gave rise to them.

Mrs Wharton allows no more brave new virtue to the slightly less wealthy, uncultivated American in *The Custom of the Country* (1913), which depicts the Spragge family, provincials made good and trying to get a foothold in New York society for their daughter Undine. Mr and Mrs Spragge at first seem painfully but refreshingly normal, a breath of fresh, if crude, western air. One day a visitor

> . . . with a smile, and echoes of *diverse et ondoyant* in his brain, had repeated her [Mrs Spragge's] daughter's name after her, saying: 'It's a wonderful find – how could you tell it would be such a fit?'
>
> 'Why, we called her after a hair-waver father put on the market the week she was born' – and then to explain, as he remained struck and silent. 'It's from *un*doolay, you know, the French for crimping; father . . . was quite a scholar.'

But it soon becomes clear that for Mrs Wharton such ignorance is symptomatic not of an unspoiled nature, but of a nature which is self-satisfied, narrow. All the Spragges care about is for Undine to do whatever she wants; and Undine at large is no Huckleberry Finn, to grow and mature with freedom. Her crudity knows no bounds as she uses a succession of men in an attempt to become as rich and powerful a woman as possible. A poor but aristocratic intellectual is discarded for a grander French marquis. Dissatisfied with the allowance he makes her she tries to sell his priceless family heirlooms to an American collector; and the marquis turns on her in an indictment in which she is made to represent the worst type of American who has nothing to offer the Old World or the New.

> 'You're all alike,' he exclaimed, 'every one of you. You come among us from a country we don't know and can't imagine, a country you care for so little that before you've been a day in ours you've forgotten the very house you were born in – if it wasn't torn down before you knew it! You come among us speaking our language and not knowing what we mean; wanting the things we want, and not knowing why we want them; aping our weaknesses,

exaggerating our follies, ignoring or ridiculing all we care about – you come from hotels as big as towns, and from towns as flimsy as paper, where the streets haven't had time to be named, and the buildings are demolished before they're dry, and the people are as proud of changing as we are of holding to what we have – and we're fools enough to imagine that because you copy our ways and pick up our slang you understand anything about the things that made life decent and honorable for us!'

This, admittedly at her blackest, was for Edith Wharton the custom-built American, Undine Spragge, who represented America at her nadir: inferior to the Old World.

The Affirmative Minority

The writers who contrast the Old and the New Worlds, and still affirm the New, constitute a distinguished minority, led by Nathaniel Hawthorne and William Dean Howells. Their experiences as American consuls in Liverpool and Venice respectively increased a chauvinism which was rooted in Puritanism. Hawthorne, whose New England roots stretched back to the Judge Hathorne who presided at the Salem witch trials, and Howells, who came from Ohio to Boston in 1865 and made New England his home, shared a fascination with that abrasive but clean society, which they tended to equate with America. At worst, it was merely better than any other society; at best, it had merit in its own right. Hester Prynne's life was not happy; but it was more fulfilling than Emma Bovary's.

Howells's fiction is distinguished by an absence of English settings and characters; and the comments on England which appear in his non-fiction are those of a slightly hostile, slightly defensive observer. 'Nothing in England seeks you out, except the damp,' he writes; 'one can never be certain just how the English take us, or whether they take us at all.' In Italy, which he preferred to England, he still applied a modernist's aggressive

American criteria. He disliked hearing about the ancient Pompeians, sophisticated degenerates, and preferred to hear the cries of the modern commercial Pompeians who pursued American gentlemen shouting, 'Buy it Poppa! Six for one franc. Oh, Poppa, buy it.' He loved Rome because it was the cleanest city in the world with the best hotels. In England he admired not so much the historic places to which he made the standard pilgrimages – Chester, York, Cambridge, Boston and London, but the battlefield of Marston Moor, where the Republicans defeated the Royalists, and the 'singularly noble presence' of the modern, industry-stained exterior of Liverpool's 'coal-smoked St George's Hall'.

Where Howells damned with faint praise, Hawthorne damned directly. *Our Old Home* (1863) pictures the English as an insensitive race, boorish, stolid, half-sagacious, 'invariably blind of one eye and often distorted of the other'. In his opinion it was the repulsion of 'this strange people' that compelled America to become a great nation in its own right; and so, in a curious way, he was deeply grateful for his English origins. Both he and Howells attributed to the English the undesirable characteristics James ascribed to such Americans as Mr Evans in 'Travelling Companions'. They pictured the English as loud-mouthed, complacent tourists, whose voices and comments betrayed 'a character of not much refinement'. They both defended the financial aristocracy of America: Howells in the character of Silas Lapham (*Silas Lapham*, 1885), a millionaire paint-manufacturer, superior in his crude simplicity to the still anglicised Bromfield Corey, head of one of Boston's first families; Hawthorne in *Our Old Home*, where he argues, somewhat unconvincingly, that there is no harm in the American version of rank because it is not hereditary, that is, although money can be inherited, the spiritual, rank-giving calibre of the fortune dies with the fortune-maker.

The excessively hostile picture Hawthorne draws of English women – 'It strikes me that an English lady of fifty is . . . a creature less refined and delicate . . . than anything that we

Western people class under the name of woman' – suggests, however, that he was more drawn to England than Howells, that he was trying to convince himself, as well as others, of the repulsion of England. In Italy it was Howells who was lured by antiquity. Remembering the Pisan *Duomo* he wondered he 'did not sit down before it and spend the rest of my life there'; when he sailed into New York harbour and compared it with the snow-topped Maritime Alps approach to Italy, 'I had to remember the Rocky Mountains, which I had never seen, and all the moral magnificence of our life before I could prevent the words of apology pressing to my lips.'

Morality is the key to Howells's ability to resist the old. At the impressionable age of twenty-four he was posted as American consul to Venice and came home a passionate American, admitting the beauty of St Mark's in the snow which 'lay lightly on the golden globes that tremble like peacock crests above the vast domes, and plumed them with softest white; it robed the saints in ermine: and it danced all over its work, as if exalting in its beauty', while believing that his response was 'a subtle, selfish yearning', and that to revel in such beauty was a selfish, escapist and therefore unrealistic act. The menace of the beautiful, sterile, unprogressive past is ever present to him. In *The Landlord at Lion's Head* (1897) Jeff Durgin, a country boy, is corrupted, first by what of Europe has been brought to Boston, and next by his own visits to Europe. The Lion's Head is changed from a simple inn with plain American fare to one of a chain of hotels of international indistinguishability. Significantly, one of Jeff's 'seducers', the socialite Boston girl Bessie Lynde, who forms and caters to Jeff's sophisticated tastes, is described in terms which make her sound Mediterranean. She had 'a dull thick complexion with liquid eyes, set wide apart and slanted upward slightly, and a nose that was deflected inward from the straight line; but her mouth was beautiful and vividly red like a crimson blossom'.

Hawthorne, too, warns against the seductiveness of Italy's

apparently 'brighter sky . . . softer turf . . . more picturesque arrangement of venerable trees'. In *The Marble Faun* (1860) the American sculptor Kenyon says to the Italian Count Donatello: 'You should go with me to my native country . . . In that fortunate land, each generation has only its own sins and sorrows to bear. Here, it seems as if all the weary and dreary Past were piled upon the back of the Present.'

Anti-expatriation was the logical corollary of affirmation; and in Howells's *Indian Summer* (1886) Colville, a journalist from Indiana, who sees no difference between the Ponte Vecchio spanning the Arno and the Main Street Bridge in Des Vaches, Indiana, voices Howells's disapproval of the effect of living out of America, particularly on a friend's child:

> His thoughts idled off to what Mrs Bowen's own untrammelled girlhood must have been in her Western city. For her daughter there were to be no buggy rides or concerts, or dances at the invitation of young men; no picnics free and unchaperoned as the casing air; no sitting on the steps at dusk with callers who never dreamed of asking for her mother; no lingering at the gate with her youthful escort home from the ball – nothing of that wild, sweet liberty which once made American girlhood a long rapture. But would she be any better for her privations, for referring not only every point of conduct, but every thought and feeling, to her mother?
>
> Colville contended for the old national ideal of girlish liberty as wide as the continent, as fast as the Mississippi.

For Howells the material for a heroine is the sweet, simple Clementina Cloxon of *Ragged Lady* (1899), a 'wonderful' American girl, untouched by her European experience except by an acquired taste for dancing. For Hawthorne the expatriate is the escapist.

> In such a case we are always deferring the reality of life till a future moment, and, by and by, we have deferred it till there are no future moments; or, if we do go back, we find that life has shifted

whatever of reality it had to the country where we deemed ourselves only living temporarily; and so between two stools we come to the ground, and make ourselves a part of one or the other country only by laying our bones in its soil.

Hawthorne's and Howells's affirmations are strengthened by the fact that neither is an out-and-out chauvinist. Hawthorne denies that the New World will ever reach perfection; Howells thinks that America is not half as morally good and socially democratic as it should be. But in the characters of Annie Kilburn (Howells) and Holgrave (Hawthorne), the two writers embody their ultimate identification with the New World as not only the best but as something very good. Holgrave, a man of many parts, is, when we meet him in Hawthorne's *The House of the Seven Gables* (1851), a daguerreotypist, an art form that Howells thought was perfectly American, perpetually contemporary in its snapshot practice. For Hawthorne, too, Holgrave was wonderfully American in 'his recklessness of whatever the ages had established in man's behalf'.

> The artist might fitly enough stand forth as the representative of many compeers in his native land . . . the representative of that beautiful spirit of youth . . . He could talk sagely about the world's old age, but never actually believed what he said; he was a young man still, and therefore looked upon the world . . . as a tender stripling, capable of being improved into all that it ought to be . . . He had that sense, or inward prophecy – which a young man had better never have been born than not to have, and a mature man had better die at once than utterly relinquish – that we are not doomed to creep on for ever in the old bad way, but that, this very now, there are the harbingers abroad of a golden era, to be accomplished in his own lifetime. It seemed to Holgrave, as doubtless it has seemed to the hopeful of every century since the epoch of Adam's grandchildren – that in this age, more than ever before, the moss-grown and rotten Past is to be torn down, and lifeless institutions to be thrust out of the way, and their dead corpses buried, and everything to begin anew.

As to the main point – may we never live to doubt it! – as to the better centuries that are coming, the artist was surely right. His error lay in supposing that this age, more than any past or future one, is destined to see the tattered garments of Antiquity exchanged for a new suit, instead of gradually renewing themselves by patchwork.

The patches would be made from New World cloth, woven by the versatile Holgrave, one of many who kept the New World ideals before him with an 'enthusiasm which would serve to keep his youth pure and make his aspirations high'.

The most affirmative of later American writers were those who had seen the immigrant make good or were themselves immigrants who had made good. Abraham Cahan, in *The Rise of David Levinsky* (1917), has the highly successful David recall his justified ecstasy at his first sight of New York.

Imagine a new-born babe in possession of a fully developed intellect. Would it ever forget its entry into the world? Neither does the immigrant ever forget his entry into a country which is, to him, a new world in the profoundest sense of the term . . . I conjure up the gorgeousness of the spectacle as it appeared to me on that clear June morning: the magnificent verdure . . . the tender blue of sky and sea, the . . . bustle . . . 'This, then, is America!' I exclaimed, mutely. The notion of something enchanted which the name had always evoked in me now seemed fully borne out.

In *O Pioneers!* (1913) and *My Antonia* (1918) Willa Cather celebrates with warmth and lyricism the Scandinavian and Bohemian families who, in the third and fourth generations, arrived at much prosperity in Nebraska and on the Great Plains. In old age some of the first generation of settlers think and wish 'they're in Norway, and keep asking to go to the water side and the fish quay'; but through optimism and hard work on reasonably good land, the immigrant girls who once worked in American kitchens come to manage 'big farms and fine families of their own; their children are better off than the children of the town women they used to serve . . . [Tradesmen compete] to sell provisions and farm machinery and automobiles to the rich farms where the first crop of stalwart Bohemian and Scandinavian girls are now the mistresses.' Unlike their parents and grandparents, but like Mark Twain's Eve, they fit in and take over: they 'like this kawntree'.

Henry James: Expatriate Extraordinary

Henry James's *Washington Square* (1881) was described by one critic as characteristic of 'Mr James's appalling contribution to the internal history of American domestic life'. James is often thought of as just such an extreme expatriate. His residence in England from 1877 to 1916 and the fact that in 1915 he became a British citizen suggest that he preferred, and was committed to, the Old World, especially England. A number of his novels deal almost exclusively with England and the English: *The Princess Casamassima* (1886), *The Tragic Muse* (1890), *The Spoils of Poynton* (1897), *What Maisie Knew* (1897), *The Awkward Age* (1899), *The Sacred Fount* (1901). Other important novels – *The American* (1877), *The Portrait of a Lady* (1881), *The Wings of the Dove* (1902), *The Golden Bowl* (1904) – describe Americans in a European setting. Only *The Europeans* (1878), which deals with Europeans in an American context, *The Bostonians* (1886) and *Watch and Ward* (1879) have a primarily American cast and setting. So English was James that he became an imperialist *manqué*, caring deeply for English greatness, wishing 'that England would do something – something striking and powerful . . . Can't she "take" something?' Unlike Hawthorne and Howells, he luxuriated in the poverty he saw in London.

> The most general appeal of the great city remains exactly what it is, the largest chapter of human accidents . . . The impression of suffering is a part of the general vibration; it is one of the things that mingle with all the others to make the sound that is supremely

37

dear to the consistent London-lover – the rumble of the tremendous human mill.

James admitted to loving the Old World with an almost indefinable, 'a rare emotion . . . in which the mind with a great passionate throb, achieves a magical synthesis of its impressions. You feel England; you feel Italy.' 'The light, the ineffable English light,' cries one of his characters getting a first glimpse of Herefordshire and Worcestershire from the Malvern Hills. 'Out of England it's but a garish world.' But although James produced good romantic, artistic reasons for preferring the varied, changeable light that streamed from the splendid English sky of 'combined and animated clouds' over the infinite beauty of the clear, solid American blue, he relished England in any light – even in the fog. 'In this inimitable island there was a certain mixture of fog and beer and soot which, however odd it might sound, was the national aroma, and was most agreeable to the nostril.' He took patina over polish, dirt over cleanliness, gloom over glare, variety over predictability. Sometimes his preference was justified. 'A twelvemonth ago the raw plank fences of a Boston suburb, inscribed with the virtues of healing drugs, bristled along my horizon: now I glance with idle eyes at a compacted antiquity in which a more learned sense may read portentous dates and signs – Servius, Aurelius, Honorius.' Sometimes it was not. The simple, beautiful white clapboard New England churches meant nothing to him once he had seen his first English village church. 'You must bury me here,' he cried. 'It is the first church I have seen in my life. How it makes a Sunday where it stands.'

But a close examination of James's fiction makes it clear that he was ambiguous in the extreme in his appreciation and depreciation of both Europe and America. His subjective preference for England and the English – 'the handsomest people in Europe', splendid travellers who were never irritated, never irritating, clashes splendidly with the English of *The Spoils of Poynton* – a race of dull, unpleasant philistines; and the loving portrait of

Lord Warburton in *The Portrait of a Lady* is challenged by the fairly thorough indictment of the English aristocracy in *What Maisie Knew*. All the English characters in the latter novel, including governesses, maids, soldiers and waiters, have their price; this, at the end of the novel is what Maisie knows. James might not care to endure the ambience of America himself; but the fiction of this extraordinary expatriate asserts that morally Americans led the world; that their capacity for innocence and improvement was unchallenged. Ultimately, James affirmed the New, though he liked and needed to live out of America. Like Isabel Archer in *The Portrait of a Lady*, he felt he was psychologically a non-American. Isabel's sister says of her, as William James might have said of Henry: 'Isabel's written in a foreign tongue. I can't make her [him] out.'

James contrasted what he enjoyed in Europe and disliked in America in *The Europeans*, where Felix and Eugenia Munster, Austrians visiting Boston and its environs, discover that 'to consider an event, crudely and boldly, in the light of the pleasure it might bring them, was an intellectual exercise with which . . . [their] young American cousins were almost wholly unacquainted'. Art as well as life was viewed strangely in this America, where Felix's uncle refused to have Felix paint his portrait because 'The Lord made it . . . I don't think it is for man to make it over again . . . My children have my daguerreotype. That is quite satisfactory.'

Understandably, the American artist whose ambition matched the size and scope of the New World – to sculpt an Adam and an Eve, like Roderick Hudson, or a Madonna of the Future, like Mr Theobald – felt that 'our crude and garish climate, our silent past, our deafening present . . . are . . . void of all that nourishes and prompts and inspires the artist'. So, too, for James, Europe was the home of the arts, though he never lost a residual attraction to America, which was clearly demonstrated in the descriptions in *Roderick Hudson* (1876) of the two-way transatlantic pull felt by the two halves of James's persona: Roderick, American artist and proud of it, and his patron Rowland Mallet, the travelled man who knew what Europe had to offer. Uniquely among American novelists, James was to respond strongly to European literary influences, especially those of Turgenev, Flaubert and George Eliot.

What differentiates James from other American authors who comment on the Old/New antithesis is the fact that he compares character as well as ambience. Although of the three dozen novels Howells wrote between 1871 and 1916 five were laid wholly or in large part in Italy, and fifteen made minor use of Italian background, these novels concentrate almost exclusively on an American family or colony; there are few Italian types, let alone characters. James, however, goes deeply and often into Italian character, notably in his fine short story 'The Last of the Valerii' and in *The Golden Bowl*. The story of 'The Last of the Valerii' is told by an elderly, chauvinistic American painter whose goddaughter, Martha, marries the handsome and urbane Conte Valerio. After some months of married life, Martha sponsors an archaeological excavation in the garden of their historic villa. A statue of Juno is discovered, and casts a kind of pagan spell over the beauty-loving, history-conscious count, who neglects his wife for Juno, revealing his true, Old World colours. 'I'm an old Italian and you must take me as you find me,' he tells the Americans.

> There have been things seen and done here which leave strange influences behind! They don't touch you, doubtless, who come of another race. But they touch me, often, in the whisper of the leaves and the odor of the moldy soil and the blank eyes of the old statues . . . I seem to see other strange eyes in the empty sockets, and I hardly know what they say to me.

The narrator sits in tragic triumph over Martha.

> 'I was a thousand times right,' I cried; 'an Italian count may be mighty fine, but he won't *wear*! Give us some wholesome young fellow of our own blood, who'll play us none of these dusky old-

world tricks . . .' What a heavy heritage it seemed to me, as I
reckoned up . . . the Count's interminable ancestry! Back to the
profligate revival of arts and vices . . . Such a record was in itself
a curse; and my poor girl had expected it to sit as lightly and grate-
fully on her consciousness as her feather on her hat!

But the poor girl proves to be one of James's formidable, decisive
American girls, who formulates and carries out a plan which re-
stores her husband to herself and the statue to the earth. The re-
burial, like the excavation, is symbolic. Martha sought the ethos
of the past; she found it alien. The Old and New Worlds are incompatible; when they meet the Old must go under. But, with
typical ambiguity, James has the reverse happen in *The Wings of
the Dove*. An American heiress, the gentle Milly Theale, bedridden
but apparently not mortally ill, is confronted with the fact that
the Englishman, Morton Densher, whom she loves, loves an
English girl, Kate Croy. Unlike Martha, Milly gives up. She wills
her money to the penniless Morton, thus making him eligible in
Kate's guardian's reasoning. Milly stops fighting her illness and dies.

How specifically, in *The Golden Bowl*, the Italian Prince Amerigo
is meant to represent the discoverers of the New World – Ves-
pucci and Columbus – or his father-in-law, Adam Verver, the
New World Adam, is difficult to say. In general terms they do
seem to embody their respective myths. They are diametrically
opposed and yet not unrelated. Amerigo says to his wife, Maggie
Verver: 'I'm like a chicken, at best, chopped up and smothered in
sauce; cooked down as a *crème de volaille*, with half the parts left
out. Your father is the natural fowl running about the *bassecour*.
His feathers, movements, his sounds – those are the parts that,
with me, are left out.' Adam compares himself and Maggie to a
rustic square and Amerigo to a Palladian church dropped down in
the square's centre. Adam is angular, while, he tells Amerigo,
'You're round, my boy . . . variously and inexhaustibly round . . .
you're a pure and perfect crystal.'

Amerigo *is* smooth, too smooth. He is made for leisure, not for life; for being himself, not for loyalty to others. But if he is different, an *objet d'art*, and thus represents a menace to the Americans, they too are capable of menace and deceit, imaged by the flawed, El Dorado–American golden bowl on sale in a London antique shop, and demonstrated by the uncompromising, outraged innocence of Adam and Maggie when they discover that Amerigo is having an affair. Amerigo feels this menace as Adam and Maggie skilfully separate him from Charlotte.

> He remembered to have read, as a boy, a wonderful tale by Allan Poe – which was a thing to show, by the way, what imagination Americans could have: the story of the shipwrecked Gordon Pym, who, drifting in a small boat further toward the North Pole – or was it the South – than anyone had ever done, found at a given moment before him a thickness of white air that was like a dazzling curtain of light, concealing as darkness conceals, yet of the color of milk or snow. There were moments when he felt his own boat move upon some such mystery. The state of mind of his new friends . . . had resemblances to a great white curtain.

Not for nothing does Adam Verver occupy himself as a collector for his great endowed museum in American City: he and Maggie are taking over the world for a relatively pure America. James writes that, like stout Cortés, Adam had stared at his Pacific – Europe – and had been enlightened. 'To rifle the Golden Isles had, on the spot, become the business of his future . . . he was equal, somehow, with the great seers.' He, not Amerigo, is now the discoverer.

While James found the Italians, for all their flamboyance and generosity, self-regarding and rarely flexible, he found the French much more difficult to assess. 'Madame de Mauves' suggests his contingent approval of promiscuity in aristocratic French circles. But when the French are confronted with an American who can be principled *and* flexible, James's preference is clear. Christopher Newman, the significantly named hero of *The American*, a fine specimen of humanity and a highly successful businessman with a rags-to-riches story, has reached a crisis in his life when the novel opens. A sudden disgust with the neo-corruption of much of Wall Street trading comes over him. Instead of clinching a deal he drives into the country.

> I spent the morning looking at the first green leaves on Long Island; I was sick of business; I wanted to throw it all up and break short . . . I seemed to feel a new man inside my old skin, and I longed for a new world . . . As soon as I could get out of the country I sailed for Europe.

And so, ironically, at the outset of the novel, the New and Old seem reversed. Newman is looking for a purer way of life in Europe.

He enjoys the first feeling of change and liberation, and gets much pleasure out of the European art world; but the rest of his European experience is not what he expected. Rather, it is an agonising baptism into self-knowledge through his relationships firstly with the Tristram family, American expatriates, and secondly with the Bellegarde family, *ancien régime* Catholics. Mr Tristram's anti-Americanness reinforces Newman's dormant patriotism. Mrs Tristram is responsible for introducing Newman to the woman who embodies her idea of the perfect wife for him: Claire de Cintré, *née* Bellegarde, quiet and sincere, with whom Newman falls in love. Her family loathe him, as Newman admits when he proposes.

> Your brother told me that my antecedents and occupations were against me; that your family stands, somehow, on a higher level than I do. That is an idea which of course I don't understand and don't accept . . . You will decide for yourself whether you like me or not. What there is you see before you. I honestly believe I have no hidden vices or nasty tricks. I am kind, kind, kind! Everything that a man can give a woman I will give you.

Newman's great wealth makes him acceptable to the Bellegardes; his humanity endears him to Claire; the couple become engaged. But it is hard for the family to accept the match, not just because they strongly react against a non-aristocrat tainted with commerce, but, primarily, because this relatively and perhaps absolutely good man is too large for their narrow system. Perhaps the Bellegardes have noticed how even the French servants respond to Newman with a kind of dignified equality. 'The [serving] man's dull face brightened as he perceived our hero, for Newman, for indefinable reasons, enjoyed the confidence of the liveried gentry.' James was being ironic. The reasons were not indefinable; they lay in Newman's New World goodness and simplicity. When James writes 'there was something lugubriously comical in the way Newman's thoroughly contemporaneous optimism was confronted with this dusky old-world expedient' (the Bellegardes have put the weak-willed Claire in a convent), he is using 'dusky' as a term of opprobrium. Now America seems old (civilised) and new (egalitarian and honest) in the best senses of the words; France seems new (youthfully barbaric) and old (morally corrupted) in the worst senses. 'In America, Newman reflected, lads of twenty-five and thirty have old heads and young hearts, or at least young morals; here they have young heads and very aged hearts, morals the most grizzled and wrinkled.'

It is not necessarily good to go to Europe, James admits, although Lambert Strether of *The Ambassadors* (1903), as well as Newman, benefit from the experience. Was it good for Milly, for Roderick, or for Isabel Archer, whose downfall is hastened by the actions of five variously corrupted expatriates? Mr Touchett, Sr, who had left Vermont decades earlier for an English country mansion, fools himself in thinking that he can take what he wants from England and leave what he does not want. He had had 'no intention of disamericanizing, nor had he a desire to teach his only son [Ralph] such subtle art'. But Ralph and his father undertake an enterprise of un-American freedom in connection with Isabel, Mrs Touchett's niece, who is persuaded by her aunt to come to

Europe. As he dies Daniel Touchett accedes to Ralph's request to make Isabel an heiress. 'I should like to put wind in her sails ... see her going before the breeze,' thinks he, in marked contrast to the father in *The American* who 'whenever he looked at his son felt extreme compunction at having made a fortune'.

Her inheritance makes Isabel prey to two American expatriates, Serena Merle and her ex-lover Gilbert Osmond, both of whom want comfort and beauty to excess. Alarmingly for Isabel, who marries him, Osmond knows just how sterile a dilettante he has become. He is comfortable in the sophisticated expression and acknowledgement of that sterility – so comfortable that reform or change are out of the question.

> Italy ... had spoiled a great many people; he was even fatuous enough to believe at times that he himself might have been a better man if he had spent less of his life there. It made one idle and dilettantish and second-rate; it had no discipline for the character ... 'We're sweetly provincial,' said Mr Osmond.

Osmond uses the word 'provincial' tongue-in-cheek; he is a connoisseur of much distinction. Yet for James the word is appropriate – there is no more limited, anomalous class than the expatriate. Ralph admits it. 'If we're not good Americans we're certainly poor Europeans; we're mere parasites crawling over the surface; we haven't our feet in the soil.'

It is the Christopher Newmans, the Basil Ransoms, the Caspar Goodwoods of America, straight and true physically and mentally, who are James's ultimate heroes: quintessential Americans who exist in thousands. Other races are more fascinating, but are they as good? In *The Portrait of a Lady* James uses a conversation between Lord Warburton, 'his temperament fertilized by a high civilization', and Henrietta Stackpole, an American journalist who 'shimmered in fresh dove-colored draperies ... as crisp and new and comprehensive as a first issue before the folding', to make the distinction.

'Why don't you give it up . . . ?' Miss Stackpole inquired.

'Give up – a – ?' asked Lord Warburton, meeting her harsh inflexion with a very mellow one.

'Give up being a lord.'

'Oh, I'm so little of one! One would really forget all about it if you wretched Americans were not constantly reminding us. However, I do think of giving it up, the little there is left of it, one of these days.'

'I should like to see you do it!' Henrietta exclaimed rather grimly.

'I'll invite you to the ceremony; we'll have a supper and a dance.'

Lord Warburton's sisters and James's other dull but worthy Englishwomen are not on a par with 'the American girl'. It is this girl, the supposed butt of James's satire, whom he treats with most consistent tenderness. She is always recognisable by her great elegance, often, like Daisy Miller, distinguished by a frankness which can look like indelicacy and by 'an extraordinary mixture of innocence and crudity'. The American girl 'carried within herself a great fund of life, and her deepest enjoyment was to feel the continuity between the movements of her own soul and the agitations of the world'. Susie Pocock, Verena Tarrant, Milly, Henrietta, Maggie, Daisy and Isabel, independants all, express James's own attitude to life: it is only meaningful in terms of one's own responses and reverberations. James himself needed Europe in order to become a reverberator. He spoke of himself when he wrote of Isabel Archer's unshaken preference for Europe: 'To live in such a place was, for Isabel, to hold to her ear all day a shell of the sea of the past. This vague eternal rumor kept her imagination awake.'

CHAPTER 2

City and Country

Two Versions of Pastoral

Since the nomadic hunter first learned to cultivate the earth, men have worshipped the land. Gods and goddesses of fertility inhabit every mythical Olympus; prayers supplicate their aid, invocations seek their beneficence. Roman literature – particularly the *Eclogues* of Virgil – transformed this earth-worship into a sophisticated literary form, the pastoral. Since then, schoolboys throughout Europe have laboured to compose Virgilian imitations, replete with poetic shepherds hymning their love of and affinity with the land. But this has never been a prevalent practice in American schools, and for the best of reasons: in America, the pastoral ideal has been regarded not as a literary convention but as a perfectly reasonable goal.

While the worship of nature, in other words, has become primarily a 'poetica' idea in Europe, in America it remains a dead serious matter. To the first English settlers gazing on the lush greenery of Jamestown island or the sterner coasts of Massachusetts Bay, America *was* nature, as yet undespoiled, a place where myth seemed fact. They said so, and were believed. As a consequence, the United States is the only nation where pastoral is taken seriously, rather than as an exercise in Latin composition.

Pastoralism exerts a powerful pull on the American mind, but it is important to distinguish between two kinds. The first, less an expression of thought than of emotion, romanticises the natural world as an alternative to the urban life still so cordially despised in most American popular culture. The nation's mass culture provides ongoing evidence of the persistence of this sentimental version of pastoral: the romantic western *Bonanza* leads all television programmes in popularity, and tremendous crowds pay homage to Andrew Wyeth's representational paintings of rural life, while, on a lower level of excellence, Norman Rockwell's magazine-cover paintings of homely scenes proclaim the simple virtues of bygone days on the farm. These complementary themes – the superiority of the simple pastoral life and the lamentation for a golden age that existed somewhere in the vague past – recur constantly in popular American writing as well. The garden is always lost, and the sentimentalist bemoans its passing.

Serious American writers, on the other hand, exhibit a different sort of pastoralism. Though motivated by much the same nostalgic drive, they perceive the snakes in the garden (urbanism and technology), are aware of the tension between the ideal and reality, and attempt to resolve that tension through a variety of responses – with bitterness as in the case of Mark Twain, with irony as in the case of Stephen Crane. A century earlier, in the classical statements of American pastoral by Hector St John de Crèvecoeur and Thomas Jefferson, there was no room for either irony or bitterness. But neither were these eighteenth-century gentlemen, devoted to rationalism as they were, fully susceptible to blind sentimentalism.

The Middle Landscape

Crèvecoeur lived in the colonies for more than twenty years before returning to France to write his *Letters from an American Farmer* (1892). In those letters, which affect a spurious simplicity,

Crèvecoeur attempted to isolate the qualities which made American life and the American people distinctive. (Half a century later another Frenchman – the remarkably prophetic Alexis de Tocqueville – undertook a similar task in his *Democracy in America*.) What, Crèvecoeur asked, was this new man, the American? He was, first of all, a transplanted European, but remarkably changed in the transplantation. A 'western pilgrim' carrying the culture of the Old World to the New, he was motivated to work out of self-interest, and did not labour as in Europe for the betterment of his masters. The American was, in short, the European regenerated by contact with 'new laws, a new mode of living, a new social system'.

In an extended metaphor, Crèvecoeur outlined the theory of organic determinism which runs through American pastoral thought in curious counterpoint to repeated defences of the doctrine of free will. Almost by definition, Americans are supposed to be singularly free, and yet they are shaped willy-nilly by their environment. Here for example is Crèvecoeur's famous expression of determinism:

> Men are like plants; the goodness and flavor of the fruit proceed from the peculiar soil and exposition in which they grow. We are nothing but what we derive from the air we breathe, the climate we inhabit, the government we obey, the system of religion we profess, and the nature of our employment.

Though according to this passage institutions as well as natural surroundings can determine a man's personality and behaviour, the dominant metaphor (man as plant, growing out of the earth) is the operative one, for in America there were so few established institutions that emphasis fell on the relationship between man and his physical environment.

For Crèvecoeur as for most American pastoralists, the ideal was not the primitive and remote wilderness which bred discord and foul reptiles, nor the great city where art and artifice corrupted the settler who would do better to till his own land. As Leo Marx has demonstrated, 'the middle landscape' constituted the pastoral ideal as early as Virgil, and in America, with the mysterious terrors of the vast wilderness set against the sinister evils of city life, it was on the farm, the land brought under cultivation, where men might prosper and grow in health and wisdom as well. As Richard Price, another eighteenth-century colonial observer, put it, 'The happiest state of man is the middle state between the *savage* and the *refined* or between the wild and the luxurious state.'

This concept of the middle landscape predominates in literary evocations of the pastoral ideal. In his *Arthur Mervyn* (1800), for example, the nation's first practising novelist, Charles Brockden Brown, explored the hackneyed literary situation (conventional in the English novel from *Tom Jones* onwards) of the young man who leaves the country to seek his fortune in the city. Young Arthur comes to Philadelphia, encounters a crooked mentor and remains to survive a terrifying and vividly described epidemic of yellow fever. (Brown had observed such an epidemic himself.) He is aided in his urban tribulations by a reservoir of physical strength and moral probity gained during his youth on the farm, but is nearly undone by an attack from another quarter – the wilds of the New Jersey pine forests, whence came his stepmother Betty. Arthur feels superior to Betty, a former servant, who is loud, dresses in poor taste and is afflicted with 'numerous kindred', but she quickly separates Arthur from the inheritance he had anticipated from his father.

The contrast between the wilderness and civilisation inherent in Brown's novel runs through the Leatherstocking Tales of Cooper. On the surface, it may seem that Cooper celebrates the primitive, and certainly he invokes the beauty of nature undefiled, as for example that of Lake Glimmerglass in *The Deerslayer* (1841). To Natty Bumppo, the hero of the five Leatherstocking novels, nature represents both a temple of God and his true love. Thus he rejects the attractive if headstrong Judith Hutter at least partly because he is in love with the natural world around him and not with mere mortals. Furthermore, Natty and his Indian companion Chingachgook (pronounced 'Chicago', Mark Twain insisted in derogation of Cooper) have learned the secrets that the forest has to teach them, knowledge far more useful than that 'of one who has look'd into so many books, that his eyes are not able to tell a moose from a wild-cat!' Yet Natty is by no means solely a creature of the wilderness; he has been educated by the Moravians, and has somewhere acquired a strong sense of social position, so that he knows himself superior to Judith Hutter but inferior to, say, Oliver Effingham and Elizabeth Temple of *The Pioneers*.

As one might expect of a man who cultivated acquaintances among the British and French aristocracy, Cooper consistently came down on the side of civilisation in contrast to the wilds. Cities, to be sure, might inculcate false values, but at least the law controlled behaviour there. Without the rule of law to guide them, however, such Cooper characters as Thomas Hutter and Hurry Harry in *The Deerslayer*, or Ishmael Bush in *The Prairie*, go morally awry. Hutter and Hurry Harry adopt the code of the bad Indians (there are both good and bad Indians in Cooper's fiction) and pursue redskin scalps for the bounty they will bring. Bush is a squatter, a man who has settled on land without first obtaining legal title to it, and, to make it clear how much this practice offends him, Cooper implies that Bush has murdered an officer of the law back in Kentucky when the lawman tried to evict a group of squatters.

The great tale of communion with nature in American literature is, of course, Henry David Thoreau's *Walden* (1854). Subtitled *Life in the Woods*, *Walden* relates Thoreau's attempt to 'front the essential facts of life' while living in a cabin at Walden Pond near Concord, Massachusetts, for more than two years (in the book, the time is telescoped into one twelvemonth). Simplify, simplify, Thoreau preached; live without possessions, he taught, for they will burden you; get into harmony with nature, he insisted, and you will be born anew each morning. 'There are two worlds,' he wrote, 'the post-office and nature: I know them both.' The post-office world of laws and institutions and restraints he emphatically rejected in his prose, for in that world, he felt sure, 'the mass of men lead lives of quiet desperation'.

Besides, he felt temperamentally more at home in the open than in the drawing-room of his benefactor, fellow Transcendentalist and Concord resident, Ralph Waldo Emerson. The 'captain of the huckleberry party', Emerson called him, and other townspeople put the case against the eccentric jack-of-all-trades with still less charity. It may be, as Leon Edel has recently maintained, that Thoreau went to the Pond in order to escape the ire of other Concord residents who knew he had been responsible for starting a fire which destroyed three hundred acres of woodland. Whatever the reason for Thoreau's exile, however, his sojourn at Walden was not a full-scale retreat from the post-office world. His cabin was heated and plastered. He was within daily commuting distance of his mother's cookie jar. He occasionally dined at the homes of his Transcendental friends. A good many visitors came to call on him as well. In short, he talked 'as if he lived in the wilderness but he lived in the suburbs'. Still, he talked superbly. He advised his readers (perhaps no book has ever attempted so passionately to persuade them) to escape to the world of nature, to take to the woods, and as in most Transcendental writing he stated his case with reckless hyperbole.

Nature Sweet and Pure?

D. H. Lawrence understood as well as anyone the American's tendency to sentimentalise the untracked wilderness while maintaining his abode securely in the lap of civilisation. No one has been more guilty of this kind of literary double-think than Crèvecoeur himself, who announced at the end of his *Letters from an American Farmer* that he was headed, any time now, back to the wilderness where he would live in peace and harmony with those children of nature, the Indians. Of course he did no such thing; as Lawrence put it, 'Crèvecoeur was off to France in high-heeled shoes and embroidered waistcoat' while we 'must perforce follow him into the backwoods'. But Crèvecoeur could commit such a literary falsehood only because he was 'absolutely determined' that nature was sweet and pure and all men were angels. 'Therefore,' according to Lawrence, 'he wisely kept away from any too close contact with Nature.'

But on occasion Crèvecoeur became too good an artist to romanticise nature. He liked the buzz of the hornets who nested in his home and appreciated that they kept the house free of flies, but he also observed:

> I am astonished to see that nothing exists but what has its enemy, one species pursue and live upon another: unfortunately our king-birds are the destroyers of those industrious insects [the bees]; but on the other hand, these birds preserve our fields from the depredations of the crows, which they pursue on the wing with great vigilance and astonishing dexterity.

Pursuit and capture and destruction: if there is an economy in nature, as Crèvecoeur, like Jefferson and Franklin, would have insisted (Jefferson spoke of the beneficial effects of yellow fever in reducing over-population in the cities), it was an extraordinarily cruel economy.

If anything, Emerson took a more favourable view of the economy of nature than did Crèvecoeur. But Melville, whose experience of the salt sea was more extensive than Emerson's, made bitter sport of the Transcendentalist's cosmic optimism in *The Confidence-Man* (1857), and in other novels, stories and poems depicted a far more foreboding physical universe than any the Concord Transcendentalist (whose views were of course in basic harmony with those of English Romanticism) was willing to conceive. In *Moby-Dick* the White Whale indifferently snuffs out the lives of his pursuers, while other Melvillian monsters of the deep seem still more actively malign. (See below, Chapter 3, pp 110–12.) Consider, for example, the pale Maldive shark and the 'sleek little pilot-fish' which guide him to prey as they 'liquidly glide on his ghastly flank'. Commenting on the work of his friend Hawthorne, Melville called admiring attention to the 'blackness ten times black' that seemed to pervade his tales. For these men, nature possessed depths that were better not explored.

These two views – the Transcendental nature-worship of Emerson and Thoreau and the nature-terror of Hawthorne and Melville – combined in Mark Twain's curiously ambivalent attitude towards the world about him. Growing up on the Mississippi, Twain developed a feeling for the beauty of the great river at an early age, but as an apprentice pilot he also learned of the dangers lurking, half-hidden, beneath the surface. Perhaps the point is best illustrated by this account of dawn on the river:

Two or three days and nights went by; I reckon I might say they swum by, they slid along so quiet and smooth and lovely. Here is the way we put in the time. It was a monstrous big river down there – sometimes a mile and a half wide; we run nights, and laid up and hid daytimes; soon as night was most gone we stopped navigating and tied up – nearly always in the dead water under a towhead; and then cut young cottonwoods and willows and hid the raft with them. Then we set out the lines. Next we slid into the river and had a swim, so as to freshen up and cool off; then we set down on the sandy bottom where the water was about knee-deep, and watched the daylight come. Not a sound anywheres – perfectly still – just like the whole world was asleep, only sometimes the bullfrogs a-cluttering, maybe. The first thing to see, looking away over the water, was a kind of dull line – that was the woods on t'other side; you couldn't make nothing else out; then a pale place in the sky; then more paleness spreading around; then the river softened up away off, and warn't black any more, but gray; you could see little dark spots drifting along ever so far away – trading-scows, and such things; and long black streaks – rafts; sometimes you could hear a sweep screaking; or jumbled-up

voices, it was so still, and sounds come so far; and by and by you
could see a streak on the water which you know by the look of the
streak that there's a snag there in a swift current which breaks on
it and makes the streak look that way; and you see the mist curl up
off of the water, and the east reddens up, and the river, and you
make out a log cabin in the edge of the woods, away on the bank
on t'other side of the river, being a wood-yard, likely, and piled
by them cheats so you can throw a dog through it anywheres; then
the nice breeze springs up, and comes fanning you from over
there, so cool and fresh and sweet to smell on account of the
woods and the flowers; but sometimes not that way, because
they've left dead fish laying around, gars and such, and they do
get pretty rank: and next you've got the full day, and everything
smiling in the sun, and the song-birds just going it!

In this passage from *The Adventure of Huckleberry Finn* (1884),
Huck uses the vernacular to suggest the glory of the dawn, but is
realist enough to see the snag in the water, smell the decaying
fish, and even denigrate the commercial ethics of lumber dealers.
Huck has no preconceived notions about nature sweet and pure;
he simply reports, with sensitivity and verisimilitude, how it feels
to watch dawn spread over the river, and no one will challenge
his account. The passage is of course a brilliant piece of writing,
full of approximations ('nearly always', 'sometimes', 'maybe',
'likely') which give it believability, and moving almost imper-
ceptibly from the past tense (the time went by) through the condi-
tional (you could see, could hear) to the vividness and immediacy
of the present, with the red sky smiling and the song-birds in
morning choir. But perhaps Twain's achievement was not so
much in technique as in wisdom, for only infrequently have
American writers – and almost never have American historians or
public philosophers – been capable of reconciling dark and light,
Heaven and Hell, nature sweet-and-pure and nature malignant.

Instead, the tendency among the nation's serious writers in the
last hundred years has been to treat beatific visions of the natural
world with irony. Stephen Crane, who possessed a natural bent

toward irony, frequently satirised romantic views of nature. Both in 'The Open Boat' (1897) and 'The Blue Hotel' (1899), for example, he depicted human beings in unequal struggle with violent storms at sea and on land. (To Emerson, the snowstorm was merely a 'fierce artificer' rearranging the scenery, and for William Cullen Bryant, whose romantic poetry predated Emerson's, even the destructive hurricane provided cause to glory in the majesty of what God had wrought.) When trapped in a snowstorm, Crane writes, 'One viewed the existence of man . . . as a marvel, and conceded a glamor of wonder to these lice which were caused to cling to a whirling, fire-smote, ice-locked, disease-stricken, space-lost bulb.'

In his most famous work, *The Red Badge of Courage* (1895), Crane played similarly ironical variations on the sweetness of nature. Henry Fleming, a Youth (he is so called, with the capital letter, for much of the novel), goes off to fight in the Civil War, but breaks and runs when confronted by the enemy. Alone and frightened in his exile, he takes heart from his surroundings, believing like most Americans that he could take refuge 'in the vast expanses of untouched and innocent nature away from the ills and limitations of human society'. The Transcendentalists even thought that through nature man could 'become a transparent eyeball', and commune directly with God. Armed with these preconceptions, Henry Fleming finds real assurance in the forest, where a natural 'religion of peace' seems to prevail. Borrowing from the doctrine of correspondence, he finds justification for his own cowardice in the flight of a squirrel. But finally, his foolish rationalising from nature's example is confounded by a decomposing corpse, a feeding-place for ants, which stands – an 1895 *Lord of the Flies* – at the very centre of the forest cathedral. Nature does not symbolise, has nothing to do with spirit. Under the circumstances, it is no wonder that critics have divided on the tone of the book's apparently optimistic ending, when Henry – who has returned to fight with brave success –

feels he has rid himself of the 'red sickness of battle' and turns 'with a lover's thirst to images of tranquil skies, fresh meadows, cool brooks – an existence of soft and eternal peace'.

Down on the Farm

Even if nature was not inherently benevolent, however, the farm maintained its image in American mythology as the *locus* of health and virtue. The classical statement of the beneficial effects of agrarian life came from the nation's secular near-saint, Thomas Jefferson, in his *Notes on the State of Virginia* (1784). In words that have become a cliché to intellectual historians, he spelt out his faith:

> Those who labor in the earth are the chosen people of God, if ever He had a chosen people, whose breasts He has made His peculiar deposit for substantial and genuine virtue. It is the focus in which he keeps alive that sacred fire, which otherwise might escape from the face of the earth. Corruption of morals in the mass of cultivators is a phenomenon of which no age nor nation has furnished an example. It is the mark set on those, who, not looking up to heaven, to their own soil and industry, as does the husbandman, for their subsistence, depend for it on casualties and caprice of customers. Dependence begets subservience and venality . . .

The yeoman farmer, Jefferson's ideal citizen, tilled his acres and derived virtue along with the independent living he wrested from the earth. Convinced that the 'proportion which the aggregate of the other classes of citizens bears in any State to that of its husbandmen, is the proportion of its unsound to its healthy parts', Jefferson urged against importation of factory workers. 'While we have land to labor then, let us never wish to see our citizens occupied at a work-bench, or twirling a distaff.' Let Europe keep the workshops, for otherwise skilled workers would settle in American cities to become 'panders of vice, and the instruments by which the liberties of a country are generally overturned'. The mobs of cities, he was certain, 'add just so much to the support of pure government, as sores do to the strength of the human body'.

Jefferson was of course an amazingly talented man (John Kennedy, having invited many of the nation's leading artists, writers, musicians, architects and statesmen to the White House, remarked that he had assembled the greatest array of talent since Thomas Jefferson dined there – alone), but perhaps his greatest talent was as a maker of myths, so that although not one American in a thousand could identify the author of *Notes on the State of Virginia*, a substantial majority would still agree with the Jeffersonian sentiment that life on the farm is indeed healthier and more likely to inculcate virtuous behaviour than urban existence. It was an idea in almost universal circulation during Jefferson's time, so that even the city-dwelling printer, tradesman, scientist and statesman Benjamin Franklin identified virtue with agricultural pursuits. Nations, he observed, could become wealthy in one of three ways: by war, which amounted to plundering or robbery; by commerce, which was usually cheating, or by agriculture, 'the only *honest way*, wherein man receives a real increase of the seed thrown into the ground, in a kind of continual miracle'. With Jefferson, he thought that as long as most Americans laboured as cultivators of the earth, reinvigorated and restored to moral probity by their affinity with the virgin land, so long would America prosper.

If man worked on the land, Emerson was also persuaded, he stayed close to nature and his God, the first cause. Furthermore, though he might not like hard work, 'every man has an exceptional respect for tillage, and a feeling that this is the original calling of his race'. Children might have still other reasons to celebrate country at the expense of city, for as Henry Adams testifies about his youth, 'Town [Boston] was restraint, law, unity. Country [suburban Quincy], only seven miles away, was liberty, diversity, outlawry, the endless delight of mere sense impressions given by nature for nothing, and breathed by boys without knowing it.' But *The Education of Henry Adams* (1907) described a learning process available only to the élite, and most popular literature laid its emphasis on the country not as the site of irresponsible escape but as the seat of true virtue.

One of the most striking examples of sentimentalising rural life was Gene Stratton-Porter's *The Harvester* (1911). A Midwesterner whose name is preserved for posterity at a rest stop on the Indiana turnpike, Mrs Porter was a sensationally successful writer during the first two decades of this century; her two best-known books, *The Girl of the Limberlost* (1909) and *Laddie* (1913), sold in the hundreds of thousands. As the titles suggest, Porter's work consistently stressed the superiority of homely country life. The point is made with her usual heavy hand in *The Harvester*, a book 'offered in the [forlorn] hope that in cleanliness, poetic temperament and mental force, a likeness will be seen to Henry David Thoreau', wherein the title character, a rustic herb-gatherer, engages in conversation with his faithful dog Bel on the question of their residence: ' "Well then," said the man, "which shall it be? Do I leave home for the noise and grime of the city, open an office and enter the money-making scramble?" ' There is no response from Bel. ' "Or do I remain at home to harvest the golden seal, mullein, and ginseng, not to mention an occasional hour with the black bass or tramps for partridge and cottontail?" ' The dog leaps up and licks the face of his master.

> 'Good old Bell!' he cried exultantly. 'Six years you have decided for me, and right – every time! We are of the woods, Bel, born and reared here as our fathers before us. What would we of the camp fire, the long trail, the earthy search, we harvesters of herbs the famous chemists require, what would we do in a city? . . . If ever you sentence us to life in the city, you'll finish both of us, that's what you'll do!'

But the harvester's life is too wild and remote, too brutally self-sufficient, too much to the pattern that Thoreau coldbloodedly recommended, and so Porter introduces a girl-friend to appeal to the audience and tidy up the unkempt wilderness.

Like the farm, the country village remained almost sacrosanct sentimental territory, populated by just plain, kindly, homely folks. Up until 1920, Mark Schorer maintains, popular American fiction 'had been picturing village life as sweet and good, the middle class as kindly when not noble, the provinces as aglow with an innocence in sharp contrast to the cruelty and corruption of the cities'.

Once again, however, serious American fiction followed a different path from that of the popular novel, and began to undermine the prevailing imagery of a pure and simple rural countryside. Specifically, the iconoclastic E. W. Howe took a dark look at Midwestern life in *The Story of a Country Town* (1883), and Hamlin Garland in *Main-Travelled Roads* (1891) sketched out the harsh and barren existence led by farmers and their families. It remained for H. L. Mencken, forever a puncturer of pomposities, however, to deal most violently with the lingering Jeffersonian concept of 'the husbandman' in *Prejudices, 4th Series* (1924):

The farmer is praised by all who mention him at all, from archbishops to zoologists, day in and day out. He is praised for his industry, his frugality, his patriotism, his altruistic passion. He is praised for staying on the farm, for laboriously wringing our bread and meat from the reluctant soil, for renouncing Babylon to guard the horned cattle on the hills. He is praised for his patient fidelity to the oldest of learned professions, and the most honorable, and the most necessary to all of us. He takes on, in political speeches and newspaper editorials, a sort of mystical character. He is no longer a mundane laborer, scratching for the dollar, full of staphylococci, smelling heavily of sweat and dung; he is a high priest in a rustic temple, pouring out his heart's blood upon the altar of Ceres. To murmur against him becomes a sort of sacrilege, like murmuring against the Constitution, Human Freedom, the Cause of Democracy . . . Nevertheless, being already doomed, I herewith and hereby presume to do it. More, my murmur is scored in the manner of Berlioz, for ten thousand trombones *fortissimo* . . . Let the farmer, so far as I am concerned, be damned forevermore! To hell with him, and bad luck to him! He is, unless I err, no hero at all, and no priest, and no altruist, but simply a tedious fraud and ignoramus, a cheap rogue and hypocrite . . . He deserves all he suffers under our economic system, and more . . . No more grasping, selfish and dishonest mammal, indeed, is known to students of the Antheopoidea. When the going is good for him he robs the rest of us up to the extreme limit of our endurance; when the going is bad he comes bawling for help out of the public till.

But the reaction of Mencken, an eternal iconoclast, no more represented that of the general populace than did his extravagant and learned rhetoric.

The major literary debunking of the early twentieth century, in fact, centred not on the farm but on the small communities which had grown up as marketing centres to serve rural areas. In 'The Sculptor's Funeral', for example, the talented Willa Cather expressed her scorn for the small-minded materialism of Sand Creek, Kansas. In his satiric and widely read *Main Street* (1920) Sinclair Lewis laid bare the pretentiousness and hypocrisy of Gopher Prairie, Minnesota. But the best example of this artistic 'revolt from the village' was Sherwood Anderson's *Winesburg, Ohio* (1919).

Anderson, who wrote the twenty-three sketches which make up the book while living in a Chicago rooming-house, held traditional feelings towards both city and country. Thus in *Marching Men* (1917) he described the city at twilight with cordial detestation:

The people of Chicago go home from their work at evening – drifting they go in droves, hurrying along . . . The people have bad mouths . . . Their mouths are like the shoes they wear. The shoes have become run down at the corners from too much pounding on the hard pavements and the mouths have become crooked from too much weariness of soul . . . Everyone has dirty ears. The stench in the street cars is horrible . . . Everything is cheap. When the people get home to their houses they sit on cheap chairs before cheap tables and eat cheap food. They have given their lives for cheap things.

By contrast, Anderson evokes the healthy cycle of growing things:

> And back of Chicago lie the long corn fields that are not dis-
> orderly. There is hope in the corn. Spring comes and the corn is
> green. It shoots up out of the black land and stands up in orderly
> rows . . . Fruition comes to the corn and it is cut down and dis-
> appears. Barns are filled to bursting with the yellow fruit of the
> corn.

But, alas, 'Chicago has forgotten the lesson of the corn. All men
have forgotten.'

All, that is, except Sherwood Anderson himself, who left a
successful business career in middle life in order to write fiction.
His Winesburg is a small town surrounded by cornfields, not
unlike Clyde, Ohio, where he had been raised. One might expect
an idyllic, nostalgic portrait of this middle western village, but
instead Anderson presents a gallery of 'grotesques' twisted by
experience into loneliness and eccentricity. George Willard, a
young man growing up in Winesburg, gradually uncovers the
stories behind the town's 'grotesques', and goes off to college at
the end of the book understanding more of them – and of himself.
But though something has gone terribly wrong in the lives of his
characters, Anderson is hardly disposed to place the blame on
rural life. Indeed, the very first of his 'grotesques', Wing Biddlebaum, movingly invokes the agrarian idyll: 'Out of the dream
Wing Biddlebaum made a picture for George Willard. In the
picture men lived again in a kind of pastoral golden age. Across a
green open country came clean-limbed young men, some afoot,
some mounted upon horses.' In Biddlebaum's dream the young
men gather at the feet of an old man who talks to them 'beneath
a tree in a tiny garden', clearly Wing's idealisation of his days as a
teacher, before his habit of laying a friendly hand upon his young
male students robbed him of an occupation. But it is noteworthy
that Biddlebaum locates his dream in 'a pastoral golden age', as
does Anderson himself. In another of the book's sketches, the
author rather clumsily intrudes to comment that

It will perhaps be somewhat difficult for the men and women of a later day to understand Jesse Bentley. In the last fifty years a vast change has taken place in the lives of our people . . . the coming of industrialism, attended by all the roar and rattle of affairs, the shrill cries of millions of new voices . . . In our day a farmer standing by the stove in the store in his village has his mind filled to overflowing with the words of other men. The newspapers and the magazines have pumped him full. Much of the old brutal ignorance that had in it also a kind of beautiful childlike innocence is gone forever. The farmer by the stove is brother to the men of the cities, and if you listen you will find him talking as glibly and as senselessly as the best city man of us all.

Anderson's lament is for a time long past, before the twin devils of industrialism and urbanism altered America's occupation from agriculture to business and moved its home from the farm to the city. He would gladly accept the old brutal ignorance if it would bring back the 'beautiful childlike innocence', but that is lost forever. Nor will going back to the small town of one's youth, as the 'grotesques' in their desperate loneliness know, bring back the past. Once a man throws in his lot with progress and follows his opportunity to the city, it is too late to reverse directions. In Howells's *A Hazard of New Fortunes* (1890) the rustic newly rich Dryfoos family move to New York after oil is discovered on their land, but they have trouble adjusting to city ways and Mrs Dryfoos soon begins to talk about going back to the farm. Her husband knows better.

'There's no farm any more to go back to. The fields is full of gas-wells and oil-wells and hell-holes, generally; the house is tore down, and the barn's goin' – '
'The *barn!*' gasped the old woman.

Her violent response echoed that of American citizens generally. The city remained a sink of corruption, and the country a well-spring of virtue, but there was not much future on the land and, to get ahead, young people moved to Chicago or New York or St Louis. Even Thomas Jefferson, in a letter to a Philadelphia physician a century earlier, had been forced to acknowledge the superior opportunities of city life. Writing on behalf of his grandson, Jefferson issued his rather milder-than-customary diatribe against 'placing men in populous cities, because they acquire there habits and partialities which do not contribute to the happiness of their after life', but then explained that he was sending young Randolph to Philadelphia anyway, for 'there are particular branches of science (botany, natural history, anatomy), which are not so advantageously taught anywhere else in the U.S. as in Philadelphia'. Whether for educational purposes, or – as in most cases – economic opportunities, young people left the farm and migrated to the city. In 1908 President Theodore Roosevelt convened the Country Life Commission to see what could be done to reverse the flow of population. They concluded that there was not much hope of doing so. As time went on, even the journey to the city became less arduous; it was only necessary to buy a one-way ticket and climb aboard a railroad car.

The Machine in the Garden

Walden Pond was no refuge from the railroad, *the* machine in the American garden during the latter half of the nineteenth century. The Fitchburg line touched the Pond about a hundred yards from Thoreau's shack, and the whistle of the locomotive penetrated the woods at all seasons, 'sounding like the scream of a hawk'. When he saw the string of cars moving off 'like a comet' trailing clouds of steam, or when he heard the iron horse snort like thunder while breathing fire and smoke, it seemed 'as if the earth had got a race now worthy to inhabit it'. But, Thoreau promptly added, 'If all were as it seems, and men made the elements their servants for noble ends!' Instead, the railroad served as the instrument of shoddy trade: 'Up comes the cotton, down goes the woven cloth;

64

up comes the silk, down goes the woolen; up come the books, but down goes the wit that writes them.' No, he concluded, we do not ride on the railroad; it rides upon us. 'We have constructed a fate, an *Atropos*, that never turns aside . . . Every path but your own is the path of fate. Keep on your own track, then.' Otherwise, men will become the tools of their tools.

Emerson, more specifically, saw what the coming of the railroad meant to agriculture. Not only did it eliminate one of the farmer's principal occupations, that of driving his crops or his livestock to market (on the Fitchburg Thoreau observed a 'carload of drovers' among the calves and sheep, 'on a level with their droves now, their vocation gone, but still clinging to their useless sticks as their badge of office'), but provided easy jobs as an alternative to laboriously tilling the soil. 'Ellery [Channing] declares,' Emerson remarked in his journals,

> . . . that the Railroad has proved too strong for all our farmers and has corrupted them like a war, or the incursion of another race – has made them all amateurs, given the young men an air their fathers never had; they look as if they might be railroad agents any day.

Theirs was not a congenial point of view in mid-nineteenth-century America, when the frantic laying of railway track was widely hailed as a great service in linking hamlet to city, opening new paths of trade and proving the national genius for technological progress. Hearing the bombastic rhetoric of the time, Hawthorne was moved to compose 'The Celestial Railroad' (1843), in which he demonstrates in effect that you cannot get to heaven in a railway car.

Even in the standard rhetorical paeans to the railroad, however, an undertone of fear ran beneath the current of praise. Here, for example, is Benjamin R. C. Low's 'The Little Boy to the Locomotive':

Big iron horse with lifted head,
Panting beneath the station shed,
You are my dearest dream come true;
I love my dad, I worship you!

Your noble heart is filled with fire,
For all your toil you never tire,
And though you're saddled-up in steel,
Somewhere, inside, I *know* you feel.

All night in dreams when you pass by,
You breathe out stars that fill the sky,
And now, when all my dreams come true,
I hardly dare come close to you.

This bit of sentimental doggerel tries to have it both ways. The iron horse is both inhuman, tireless, made of steel, unapproachable, an object of awe rather than love; and at the same time the little boy invests it with human qualities: it pants, it feels, it has both head and heart. In children's literature especially, the emphasis falls on the second of these contradictory reactions – the gameness and never-say-die spirit of the redundant engine which still 'thinks it can', so that it is clear that one way of accommodating the terror that technological wonders awake is to treat the wonders themselves as if they had human or at least animal characteristics. (The American space programme seems to have hit on an ideal compromise by naming its missions after pagan gods, supermen like Apollo who command respect if not worship.)

Still another way of reducing uneasiness is to make sport of technological monsters, or of those who disbelieve in them, like the yokel who insisted of the locomotive that 'they'll never get it going' and when they did was equally certain that 'they'll never get it stopped'. Emily Dickinson's poem, 'I Like to See it Lap the Miles' (c1862), is usually regarded as a humorous approach to the coming of the railroad to Amherst, Massachusetts, where her father, like other leading citizens, was a booster for the Amherst and Belchertown Railroad. (A town without a railroad, it was generally assumed, could not survive in competition with nearby communities served by rail.) But the poem deserves a closer reading.

> I like to see it lap the Miles –
> And lick the Valleys up –
> And stop to feed itself at Tanks –
> And then – prodigious step
>
> Around a Pile of Mountains –
> And supercilious peer
> In Shanties – by the sides of Roads –
> And then a Quarry pare
>
> To fit its Ribs
> And crawl between
> Complaining all the while
> In horrid – hooting stanza –
> Then chase itself down Hill –
>
> And neigh like Boanerges –
> Then – punctual as a Star
> Stop – docile and omnipotent
> At its own stable door –

The voice here, critics have generally felt, 'sparkles with pleasure' or shows 'silly playfulness', but the tone is ironic and the first five words are not to be taken literally.

Though depicted as an animal, the iron horse is given no sex. This neuter creature gluttonously laps and licks and feeds on the Connecticut valley. Then it takes on airs, mincing around mountains and invading the privacy of the workmen, living in insubstantial wooden shanties, who have built the railway. Stuffed, the locomotive squeezes painfully through a narrow gap in the rock, making 'horrid-hooting' noises. This sexless, prodigious, supercilious, complaining monster chases itself downhill and comes to rest 'docile and omnipotent/ At its own stable door'. But the two adjectives are paradoxical, and though the sons of thunder

(Boanerges) enthusiastically declaim the technological and economic virtues of this machine in the garden, Emily Dickinson mistrusts its docility and fears its power. This thing is in the saddle, ready to ride mankind.

One great danger, of course, was that technological progress might despoil the natural countryside. Thus Mark Twain late in life writes of Huck and Tom, fifty years after, returning to Hannibal, Missouri, and searching for the Cold Spring: 'they can't find it – all railway tracks. No levee & no steamboats.' Similarly, Hank Morgan, in *A Connecticut Yankee in King Arthur's Court*, puts the pragmatic skills learned at the Colt Arms factory to work in sixth-century England, but is really a 'perfect ignoramus' and ends by using his technological know-how to blow up the Arthurian world. (Hank, an ingenious Yankee mechanic knocked out in a nineteenth-century fight, has woken up in Camelot, AD 528.) Human nature, as well as physical nature, stood to suffer. from the effects of too much technological progress, a point Herman Melville had made thirty years earlier in 'The Tartarus of Maids' (1855). That story describes a paper-factory in the Woedolor Mountains, where 'at rows of blank-looking counters sat rows of blank-looking girls, with blank, white folders in their blank hands, all blankly folding blank paper'. A huge, piston-like machine stamps the corner of each sheet of rose-hued notepaper with a wreath of roses. The visitor, struck by the contrast, looks from the rosy paper to the pallid cheek, but says nothing.

In *A Hazard of New Fortunes*, the best among dozens of novels written by Howells, the twin demons of industrialisation and urbanisation merge, for in this novel the railroad – specifically, the Elevated Railroad (the El, as it was called) – comes to symbolise New York City itself. The book specifically contrasts that incredibly populous, turbulent city with the more settled and socially homogeneous Boston which the book's protagonists, Basil and Isabel March, leave in order to come to New York. One of the things that distinguishes the two cities is poverty; in New

York it is inescapable, so that one of the first things the Marches see in New York is an indigent foraging for scraps of food in garbage cans, right on Third Avenue. Basil gives him a coin, and that, for the moment, seems to absolve his social responsibilities. Howells himself views the question of social reform from several angles, however, and even March's attitude gradually changes to one of genuine concern under the influence of the idealists and socialists whom Howells introduces.

None the less, the Marches remain primarily spectators in *A Hazard of New Fortunes*, and the spectacle that interests them most is the Elevated Railroad, especially the East Side El that runs down Third Avenue providing an 'incomparable perspective' on the various 'nationalities, conditions, and characters' of the great city: 'The small eyes, the high cheeks, the broad noses, the puff lips, the bare, cue-filleted skulls, of Russians, Poles, Czechs, Chinese; the furtive glitter of Italians; the blond dullness of Germans; the cold quiet of Scandinavians.' Here, surely, was the melting-pot of Israel Zangwill's 1909 play. For Isabel March, riding the Elevated becomes 'the most ideal way of getting about the world'. Like Thoreau who remarked that he had travelled widely in rustic Concord, the Marches 'first and last . . . did a good deal of travel on the Elevated roads'.

But the Elevated functions as more than a theatre seat for what must have been, in 1890, the world's fastest-growing city. Simply as a gigantic mechanism, the Elevated fascinates the Marches; it's the most beautiful thing in New York, Basil remarks, and his wife agrees, yes, yes, but instinctively draws back in terror as the train approaches. With subtle skill, Howells equates the El with the Marches' perception of the city as a Darwinian universe where the play of energies is 'as free and planless as those that force the forest from the soil to the sky; and then the fierce struggle for survival, with the stronger life persisting over the deformity, the mutilation, the destruction, the decay of the weaker'. This constitutes the naturalistic view of the city as 'lawless, godless' where forces were operating far beyond the power of mere man to control. Thus, Henry Adams contrasted twentieth-century America with twelfth-century Europe by positing two kingdoms of force – one the force of the Virgin, which was still felt at Lourdes, and the other the force of a dynamo capable of doing the work of a twenty-million-horsepower society. In Philadelpha, Adams stood before the massive dynamo, despite himself struck dumb with awe and the realisation that Americans worshipped the Dynamo, not the Virgin.

Like the Elevated itself, New York City was at once fascinating and terrifying, but always full of vitality. Even Isabel March, who laments the loss of Boston's intellectual refinement, finds the New England city curiously deathlike by way of contrast. After a brief visit there, she is glad to return to Basil 'in the immense friendly homelessness of New York'. To others less well placed financially or socially than Isabel March, New York would come to seem immense and homeless, but hardly friendly.

Maggie, Carrie and the Streets of the City

William Dean Howells's middle name was prophetic, for by the end of the century he had taken over the role of cultural leader or dean occupied by Emerson in 1850. Thus, when he expressed the credo of American realism in *Criticism and Fiction* (1891), Howells spoke almost *ex cathedra*. In large part this treatise reiterates the principles of French naturalism which had been illustrated in novels like Émile Zola's *Germinal*. In a famous passage, for example, Howells called for emphasis on the real rather than a pale imitation:

> I see that you are looking at a grasshopper there which you have found in the grass, and I suppose you intend to describe it. Now don't waste your time and sin against culture in that way. I've got a grasshopper here, which has been evolved at considerable pains and expense out of the grasshopper in general; in fact, it's a type.

It's made up of wire and card-board, very prettily painted in a conventional tint, and it's perfectly indestructible. It isn't very much like a real grasshopper, but it's a great deal nicer . . . You may say it's artificial. Well, it is artificial; but then it's ideal too, and what you want to do is cultivate the ideal . . .

Then, dropping the tone of irony (directed against Victorian euphemisms and such American writers as Henry Wadsworth Longfellow, who liked to seclude himself in his private, ideal, dream world), Howells went straight to the point:

. . . the people who have been brought up on the ideal grasshopper, the heroic grasshopper, the impassioned grasshopper, the self-devoted, adventureful, good old romantic cardboard grasshopper, must die out before the simple, honest, and natural grasshopper can have a fair field.

But though the basic artistic principles were the same as in France, Howells clearly distinguished American subject matter from that of continental naturalists. In the United States, he maintained, life deserved a more optimistic treatment. 'Our novelists . . . concern themselves with the more smiling aspects of life, which are the more American.' People die and fall ill in America, to be sure, 'but this is tragedy that comes in the very nature of things, and is not peculiarly American, as the large, cheerful average of health and success and happy life is'. Furthermore, Howells did not approve of the obsession with sexual matters which, he thought, characterised the French.

If the novel were written for men and for married women alone, as in continental Europe, it might be altogether different. But the simple fact it is that is not written for them alone among us, and it is a question of writing under cover of our universal acceptance, things for young girls to read which you would be put out-of-doors for saying to them.

Given this preconception, it is hard to understand the enthusiasm with which Howells greeted the publication of Stephen

Crane's *Maggie*, subtitled *A Girl of the Streets*, only two years later (1893). For Maggie Johnson succumbs to the wiles of a seducer, and following her fall from respectability plunges to a suicidal death in New York's East River. Crane himself, only twenty-one, probably knew he was treading on dangerous ground: he published his novel under the pseudonym of 'Johnston Smith'. Yet Howells greeted *Maggie* at once for its 'quality of fatal necessity which dominates Greek tragedy', and continued to prefer it even to Crane's subsequent masterpiece, *The Red Badge of Courage*. On what grounds did he so overrate *Maggie*?

For one thing, the novel displayed a fascination with New York's slums that Howells, like his character Basil March, also shared. Crane had not, in fact, lived in the Bowery where his novel is set; it is there that Maggie 'blossoms in a mud-puddle' to be later deflowered and wilt away. But he had walked Bowery streets much as Howells did those of another ghetto in his 'An East-Side Ramble' (1890), and Crane's novel paints an impressionistic portrait.

Perhaps more important, *Maggie* earned a certain acceptance by almost, but not quite, falling within the compass of a recognised genre, the melodrama of the innocent youth corrupted by the city. Before the Civil War, the subject of prostitution lay beyond the pale. Following 1865 certain novels broached the topic, but hardly with the verisimilitude of, say, Zola's *Nana*. The fallen woman of these unrealistic books was usually a poor country girl, lured to the city, then driven by poverty to undertake a life of vice. Usually, the young innocent, boy or girl, could – and did – find redemption by returning to a home in the country, but Maggie Johnson as a city girl born and bred had no such alternative.

In commenting on his own book, Crane paid his obeisance to the basic tenets of naturalism: that it should portray low subject matter, that it should not shrink from depicting violence in an animalistic universe, that it should take a dispassionate clinical approach, and that it should reflect a deterministic world-view. In

Maggie, Crane meets the first two of these standards, but his sympathy for Maggie denies the book a place among naturalistic case studies, and on the issue of determinism he failed to achieve the goals he had set for himself.

'Preaching,' Crane proclaimed, 'is fatal to art and literature. I try to give to readers a slice out of life; and, if there is any moral lesson in it, I do not try to point it out.' Elsewhere, however, he remarked that *Maggie* was meant 'to show that environment is a tremendous thing in this world, and often shapes lives regardlessly'. To the extent that Crane conceived of the Bowery environment as a singularly combative one – the novel begins with a gang fight, and goes on to describe a series of blows suffered and inflicted by members of the Johnson family – indeed as a warlike one (upon seeing a serene sketch of a great white cruiser at anchor against the line of city towers, Crane at once gave it a title: 'The Sense of a City is War'), he may be said to succeed.

But *Maggie*, despite its bows toward determinism, remains a book with strong moral underpinnings. One should not forget that Stephen Crane's father was an itinerant and devout Methodist minister and his mother a former president of a branch of the Women's Christian Temperance Union in Port Jervis, New York. Like many another 'preacher's kid', Crane throughout his short life did exactly what he should not have done, ending with marriage to the former proprietress of the Hotel de Dream, a whorehouse in Jacksonville, Florida. None the less, he never cast off the powerful moral code he had inherited, and in *Maggie* it expresses itself in the savage irony with which he attacks the norms of cultural respectability, norms which are ludicrously and tragically out of place in a city whose residents coexist in the uneasy state of undeclared war.

This irony saves the book from being just another sentimental city melodrama, but at the same time is so obtrusive as to inhibit the novel's effectiveness. Crane's wrath is vented on Jimmie who, after discovering that his friend Pete has seduced his sister Maggie, wonders 'vaguely for an instant if some of the women of his acquaintance had brothers'. It is explicitly directed at Ma Johnson, a drunken harridan who brutalises her children and reacts to Maggie's fall with hypocritical piety:

'May Heaven forgive dat girl' was her continual cry. To attentive ears she recited the whole length and breadth of her woes. 'I bringed 'er up deh way a daughter oughta be bringed up, an' dis is how she served me! She went teh deh devil deh first chance she got! May Heaven forgive her.'

The most vicious irony of all is reserved for the plump clergyman whom Maggie, seeking a word of Christian solace, approaches in her despair. As the girl 'timidly accosted him he made a convulsive movement and saved his respectability by a vigorous side-step. He did not risk it to save a soul. For how was he to know that there was a soul before him that needed saving?'

The morality behind this bitter irony does not resemble that of the muckrakers, who in the last decade of the century were gearing up their magazine campaigns for legislative reform. Crane was scornful of such reformers and of their faith in the healing effects of rural life. If, he wrote a friend, 'you will have Mr Rockefeller give me a hundred street cars and some money I will load all the babes off to some pink world where cows can lick their noses and they will never see their families any more'. Crane does not hope to reform institutions; like all satirists, he aims instead to show human beings in all their hypocrisies and ugliness. But not everyone in the Bowery is cruel and self-seeking. Maggie herself disproves any theory of environmental determinism, for she resolutely refuses to toughen her heart against others.

In 1893, when *Maggie* was published, Theodore Dreiser, like Crane born in 1871 but destined to live much longer, was writing earthy local colour stories for newspapers in Chicago and St Louis. (Crane had a similar job in New York.) That same year, Daniel Burnham and others erected the great plaster White City of Chicago's Columbian Exposition, its classical buildings no-where more representative of American Utopias than in the false fronts they presented to fairgoers. But it was a fascinating show for all – Hamlin Garland wrote to his parents back in North Dakota to 'sell the cook-stove if necessary and come' – and so was Chicago itself, a boom-town rising out of the prairie.

Dreiser had come to the city six years before, a fifteen-year-old small-town boy from Indiana, and was immediately captured by its excitement and stimulation. Frank Lloyd Wright, arriving from Wisconsin that same year, found much to appall and little to enchant; to him, Chicago spelt nightmare:

Chicago. Wells Street Station: Six o'clock in late spring, 1887. Drizzling. Sputtering white arc-lights in the station and in the streets, dazzling and ugly. I had never seen electric lights before. Crowds. Impersonal. Intent on seeing nothing . . . Followed the crowd . . . Shivering. Hungry . . . The flood of hard lights made the unseeing faces of the crowd in the drizzle, livid – ghastly . . . There were glaring signs on the glass shop-fronts against the lights inside, sharp signs in the glare of the sputtering arc-lamps outside. Hurrah signs, Stop signs, Come-on-in signs . . . Chicago! Immense gridiron of noisy streets. Dirty . . . Heavy traffic crossing both ways at once, managing somehow, torrential noise . . . cross-currents of horses, trucks, streetcars grinding on hard rails mingling with streams of human beings in seeming confusion and clamor . . . Dreary – dim – smoked. Smoked dim and smoking. A wide, desolate, vacant strip ran along the waterfront over which the Illinois Central trains puffed, shrieked and ground incessantly, cutting the city off from the lake. Terrible, this grinding and piling up of blind forces. If there was logic here who could grasp it. To stop and think in the midst of this would be to give way to terror. The gray, soiled river with its mist of steam and smoke was the only beauty. And that smelled to heaven.

Wright's reactions bespeak the extraordinary sensitivity to sur-roundings one might expect in a great architect, but Dreiser's sense of stimulation was more typical and entirely understandable, for Chicago of all American cities most aptly symbolised the massive movement of young people from middle western farm to middle western metropolis. Appropriately, Dreiser's image for the city in *Sister Carrie* was a giant magnet.

It was in 1900 that *Sister Carrie*, Dreiser's first novel, was published, if it could be called a publication. Largely on the recommendation of Frank Norris, the author of America's first truly naturalistic novel, *McTeague* (1899), Doubleday, Page & Company decided to publish Dreiser's book, despite the fact that it presented seduction, adultery, bigamy and theft as almost inevitable actions for which no one need necessarily be punished. But Mrs Frank Doubleday read the novel in proof and was horrified at its vulgarity and immorality; on reflection her hus band agreed, and the firm tried to back out of its agreement with Dreiser. Dreiser angrily refused and so, late in 1900, *Sister Carrie* appeared in a thin printing of about 1,000 copies and without any promotion whatever. Since the novel was difficult to obtain, it soon vanished into oblivion, to be rescued some years later by Dreiser's own efforts to interest other houses in printing editions from the plates, which he himself secured.

What was it about *Sister Carrie* that so offended Mrs Doubleday? The subject matter of seduction, after all, had been a commonplace in the novel since Samuel Richardson's *Pamela* 160 years before. But the standard novel of seduction observed certain conventions which Dreiser simply ignored. His seducers are not punished. Carrie's first lover, Drouet, is better-off at the end than at the beginning of the book. Hurstwood, who steals Carrie from Drouet and then leaves family and job to take her to New York, does degenerate into poverty and suicide, but his sorry end is less a consequence of his sins than of his attempt to make a new life in a new city at too advanced an age. Nor, worst of all, does Carrie suffer for her moral lapses. She can, all too easily, be had for a steak dinner and 'two soft, green, handsome ten-dollar bills', and Dreiser's insistence that 'Carrie was certainly better than this man [Hurstwood], as she was superior, mentally, to Drouet' is no more convincing than his explanation of why this is so:

> She came fresh from the air of the village, the light of the country still in her eye. Here was neither guile nor rapacity . . . She was too full of wonder and desire to be greedy. She still looked about her upon the great maze of the city without understanding. Hurstwood felt the bloom and the youth. He picked her as he would the fresh fruit of a tree.

In any case, her country upbringing provides no defence against seduction; she *'brings no reservoir of virtue'* from Columbia City to Chicago!

The title 'sister' nicely suits Caroline Meeber, since her experience rather closely parallels that of one of Dreiser's own sisters. (Another sister's fall from virtue is depicted in his novel *Jennie Gerhardt* (1911).) Perhaps this accounts for the author's obvious sympathy with a young woman who, according to the prevailing mores of the time, deserved to suffer the tortures of the damned for so casually succumbing to seduction. But it is still more likely that Dreiser simply attempted in this novel to be faithful to the facts. Far more than Crane, he functions as a reporter, putting down in sometimes excruciating detail and without a trace of moral indignation his account of what has happened. Dreiser was better-equipped for his reporting job than Crane, since he was going over familiar territory. While Crane was scribbling the first draft of *Maggie* in a Syracuse University fraternity house, Dreiser was learning what it was like to come to the city without money or prospects and to need a helping hand. A single sentence describing Maggie's mother, F. O. Matthiessen believes, effectively shows the difference between the two writers: 'With lurid face and tossing hair she cursed and destroyed furniture all Friday afternoon.' But this rampant destruction of furniture overlooks a fact that Dreiser 'would not have forgotten, that there would be no money to replace it'.

Dreiser, in short, wrote a naturalistic novel, with Carrie – and all other characters – presumably acting under the influence of uncontrollable forces. She is, Dreiser insists, ruled by her emotions and not by reason, though her behaviour in Chicago is that of a girl who knows what will make her comfortable and, after she moves to New York, what will best adorn her person. These emotions, presumably, render her powerless to resist her seducers, 'a waif amid forces' as a chapter heading has it, 'a harp in the wind' who falls victim to 'the city's hypnotic influence'. At the very beginning of his novel, when Carrie has just arrived in Chicago, Dreiser outlines the alternatives that face her, as a country girl, in the metropolis:

> When a girl leaves her home at eighteen, she does one of two things. Either she falls into saving hands and becomes better, or she rapidly assumes the cosmopolitan standard of virtue and becomes worse. Of an intermediate balance, under the circumstances, there is no possibility. The city has its cunning wiles, no less than the infinitely smaller and more human tempter. There are large forces which allure with all the soulfulness of expression possible in the most cultured human. The gleam of a thousand lights is often as effective as the persuasive light in a wooing and fascinating eye.

Yet Chicago, for all its alluring wiles, retains a certain country atmosphere which is sadly missing in New York. Carrie is eventually attracted by New York's glitter, the fine clothes, the food at Sherry's, but her first reaction is one of distress that unlike Chicago there are no lawns. For Hurstwood, her companion, New York is a 'walled city'. Attempting to start anew after his embezzlement, he changes his name and opens a restaurant. But he encounters

> ... nothing like the class or patronage which he had enjoyed in Chicago ... These people hurried in and out without seeking the pleasures of friendship. It was no gathering or lounging place. Whole days and weeks passed without one such hearty greeting as he had been wont to enjoy every day in Chicago.

Desperately lonely, unable to keep pace with Carrie's success as an actress, Hurstwood travels down the road to ruin, standing in queues for the free noon lunch at the Sisters of Mercy, the midnight loaf at Fleishman's bakery, but making no friends along the way. A basic difference between *Maggie* and *Sister Carrie* is that in the latter novel it is the seducer who commits suicide, while the woman he has wronged faces the future with no more punishment than to sit 'still waiting for that halcyon day when she should be led forth among dreams made real'.

The trouble with Carrie lies in her cultivation of illusions that can never be satisfied. Thus the novel concludes with Dreiser intruding his version of Carrie's future: 'Know, then, that for you is neither surfeit nor content. In your rocking-chair, by your window dreaming, shall you long, alone. In your rocking-chair, by your window, shall you dream such happiness as you may never feel.' But the rocking-chair was too comfortable and the punishment hardly extreme enough to satisfy Mrs Frank Doubleday.

The trouble with Crane's Maggie, who works in a sweatshop, becomes Pete's mistress, turns to prostitution and ends in a watery grave within the space of four pages (Dreiser employs a hundred pages to chronicle Hurstwood's fall) is remarkably similar: she has an excess of imagination, a willingness to accept the illusory blandishments of her Unreal City. The structure of *Maggie* is that of a play within a play. The initial street fight is viewed by a curious but passive audience; in the same spirit the neighbours listen in on the Johnson family quarrels; and to underline this quality of theatrical unreality, three scenes are set in a beer-hall that presents plays 'in which the dazzling heroine was rescued from the palatial home of her treacherous guardian by the hero with the beautiful sentiments'. The audience at the beer-hall identifies with the wronged innocent: 'Unmistakably bad men evinced an apparently sincere admiration for virtue.' In a similar spirit of theatricality, Ma Johnson plays the role of the mistreated mother for the benefit of her neighbours, and so will not forgive her daughter until she has taken her life. Ma Johnson and the 'bad men' pretend to abide by certain standards of respectability, but are inherently corrupt. They know it is all sham, they have no dreams, and they survive. Maggie, the dreamer, does not.

Furthermore, the dreams which the city imposes on these two young women are singularly shallow. Carrie (like other Dreiser characters) is always yearning after some amorphous and superlative beauty, but she readily enough identifies beauty with outward display, with the clothes money can buy. She fatally confuses the spiritual with the material realm, so that beauty and wealth are inextricably linked in her mind. The city spawned not only unworthy ideals, but unattainable ones. The approach to a great city at night, Dreiser wrote, was a wonderful thing; a thrill ran abroad then, and 'old illusions of hope' were forever repeated. There the worker's soul spoke to him of freedom: 'I shall be in the ways and the hosts of the merry. The streets, the lamps, the lighted chamber set for dining, are for me. The theater, the halls, the parties, the ways of rest and the paths of song – these are mine in the night.' But the thrill was momentary and the hope forlorn. In books which prepared the way for the American city novel of the twentieth century, for the work of John Dos Passos and James T. Farrell and Nelson Algren and Saul Bellow, Crane and Dreiser both condemned the city for fostering but not delivering on its false promises. But neither were they willing to endorse the agrarian myth, the pastoral ideal. In *The Titan* (1914) Dreiser articulated the dilemma of the doubting mind: 'Woe to him who places his faith in illusion – and woe to him who does not. In one way lies disillusion with its pain, in the other way regret.'

CHAPTER 3

Dreams and Nightmares

The 'American Dream' concept – the possibility of a good and great life for everyone – permeates much American literature. More often than not it is presented in juxtaposition to its opposite – the nightmare which was anything less than the dreams of individual success and national excellence come true. Possibilities involved responsibilities; and any failure to live up to the physical and moral promise of the variety and space of an awesome, abundant, clearly God-given America had its effect on the themes and images of major and minor writers alike. They were the sanguine prophets, the sometime Jeremiahs, the perpetual custodians and the sharers of the dreams of a chosen people.

Many of those who emigrated to America were idealistic dreamers when they set out; others became so when they arrived and saw that America was relatively good, free, different and vast; at very least, all had come with the dream of a better life in a better land. Whether they settled in the early nineteenth century on grim Plymouth Rock, with hostile Indians nearby or, in the late nineteenth century, in grimmer Chicago, where machines displaced men, they clung to the dream, and even magnified it for compensation and consolation. The dream could and did become an escape from reality instead of the brave new reality of a dream come true, from Washington Irving, who incessantly worked in and over a world of faery and fantasy, through the anti-hero of Kurt Vonnegut's *Slaughterhouse-Five* (1969), Billy Pilgrim, who finds mid-twentieth-century life tolerable only when he succeeds in dreaming up a personalised, outer-space Paradise.

American fiction not only mirrored the dream in all its individual variations and national phases; it used dreams and nightmares as central structural and stylistic devices. Emotionally the devices allowed the writers to give neat expression to their recognition that the dream could be wonderful, or fantastic, or illusory. Technically the devices helped to give the writer artistic distance from what might otherwise have become a socio-political tract. Additionally, whether in a specifically American context or not, the dream-variations were regularly used in fictional explorations of the nature of the mind and of reality.

At no stage in American history or fiction did the dream die, as theme or technique. Continuous immigration replenished it; and every time the population moved farther west and broke new land, great hopes were replanted and recultivated. In each decade and each region the dream was so clearly unfulfilled, so clearly threatened, that it never passed into the realms of disuse or forgotten achievements. Writers steeped in the Puritan tradition, like Hawthorne and Melville; maverick, marginal writers like Poe, born in Boston and brought up in early-nineteenth-century Virginia; writers from Ohio (Howells) and Missouri (Twain); writers who frequently went to the South of France (Fitzgerald); writers at work before, during and after a Civil War that saw half a million killed for a unity and emancipation that existed only on paper: all lived and worked in a highly charged, dream–nightmare ambience, where the dream lurked in the shadows, and increasingly different dreams clashed by day and by night. The individualist clashed with the collectivist; the country with the city; the North with the South; the East with the West; the Protestant with the Catholic; the intellectual with the Middle American. One American's dream proved another's nightmare.

Yet the dream persisted and persists, through Nathanael West's *The Dream Life of Balso Snell* (1931) and Edward Albee's *The American Dream* (1961). Arthur Miller's comment on his partial American archetype, Willy Loman, in *Death of a Salesman* (1949) – 'A Salesman is got to dream, boy. It comes with the territory' – is profoundably applicable to the American writer. He wanted his art to be larger than life; and when the American imagination outran the resources of the phenomenal country – a more extraordinary reality than any dream – the result was likely to be weird. The American writer had to think and write wildly, to exaggerate and to fantasise in order to seem creative or original. The gothic trappings of sensationalism and supernatural horrors found in the early novels of Susanna Rowson, Isaac Mitchell and Charles Brockden Brown were clearly derived from the English writers Samuel Richardson, Hugh Walpole, 'Monk' Lewis and Mrs Radcliffe; but soon American writers began to put their own stamp on European forms.

The Time–Space Traveller

Washington Irving was one of the earliest American writers to take liberties with time and space. His *History of New York, From the Beginnings of the World to the End of the Dutch Dynasty, by Diedrich Knickerbocker* (1809) is as much a work of imagination as of history. The chronology is nonsensical: for example, Thomas Jefferson, third President of the United States (1801–9), appears in the person of a seventeenth-century Dutch American. In one sense the book is a light, burlesque dream history, with everything delightfully topsy-turvy; in another, something of the nightmare is present when Irving indicates his reservations about the theory of American exceptionalism – reservations which were especially serious because they were formulated so early in the American experience.

Who can seriously believe, that Noah and his immediate descendants, knew less than we do, and that the builder and pilot of the greatest ship that ever was, a ship which was formed to traverse an unbounded ocean, and had so many shoals and quicksands to guard against, could be ignorant of, or should not have communicated to his descendants the art of sailing on the ocean? Therefore, they did sail on the ocean . . . they sailed to America – therefore America was discovered by Noah.

Irving rarely attacks the dream directly, but keeps his distance through a variety of pseudonyms – 'Knickerbocker', 'Geoffrey Crayon' and 'Lancelot Langstaff' – and a hundred and one Arabian *personae* in *Salmagundi* (1808); through the comparatively impersonal description of types – 'the stout gentleman', 'the widow', 'the son' – instead of characters, and by using macabre Old World legends to indicate that such phenomena as fear, the supernatural, the incalculable might be relevant to America. 'The Spectre Bridegroom', 'Dolph Heyligher' and 'The Storm Ship' (about a kind of *Flying Dutchman*) involve fantastic, sometimes terrifying adventures in haunted houses and ghost ships. On land and at sea, as Hawthorne and Melville were to make plain, the American path was by no means straight, America's destiny by no means straightforward. Irving strongly suggests in his dream–nightmare stories that reality is indefinable, opposed, threatening; that he distrusts appearances; that a fine house and an Edenic landscape may be equally deceptive.

In 'The Legend of Sleepy Hollow' (1820), 'found among the papers of the late Diedrich Knickerbocker', Irving equates the Hollow with original America. 'However wide awake . . . people may have been before they entered that sleepy region, they are sure, in a little time, to inhale the witching influence of the air, and begin to grow imaginative – to dream dreams and see apparitions.' The story is not a specific allegory. The Headless Horseman who is rumoured to appear in the Hollow has no precise counterpart. But although America is a place to dream, and people dream there, their dreams are no more likely to materialise than is a real headless horseman. The schoolmaster–protagonist Ichabod Crane, who loves Katrina but is frightened by his rival, Brom Bones, disguised as the Horseman, is a fittingly grotesque figure – for to Irving, dreamers are grotesquely optimistic.

> The cognomen of Crane was not inapplicable to his person. He was tall, but exceedingly lank, with narrow shoulders, long arms and legs, hands that dangled a mile out of his sleeves, feet that might have served for shovels, and his whole frame most loosely hung together. His head was small, and flat at top, with huge ears, large green glassy eyes and a long snipe nose, so that it looked like a weathercock, perched upon his spindle neck, to tell which way the wind blew. To see him striding along the profile of a hill on a windy day, with his clothes bagging and fluttering about him, one might have mistaken him for the genius of famine descending upon the earth, or some scarecrow eloped from a corn-field.

In his best-known story, 'Rip Van Winkle' (1820), Irving again upsets time to express his disbelief in American exceptionalism. In pre-Revolutionary days Rip, a much nagged husband, goes hunting in the Catskills and meets some strange, goblin-like men. He drinks some liquor they offer him and falls asleep for ten years, during which the Revolutionary War and the winning of American Independence takes place. He wakes an old man, and returns to his village, where George Washington has replaced King George, even on the inn sign. The story of his phenomenal survival is slowly unravelled; he does not recant his royalism but lives happily now, for his shrewish wife is dead, and he moves in with a loving daughter. What makes the difference is neither old nor new America, merely the temperament of his household. And, significantly, Rip's happiness is not a dream realised. He had never been so foolish as to dream; his was the accidental reward of a long, dreamless sleep.

Irving demonstrates the special dilemma and the special qualities of the self-conscious, dream-conscious American writer who found it very difficult to draw the line between fiction and fact, past, present and future. His 'stories' are so slight in characterisation, so vague in outline, so marked by his own intrusion as a character-narrator, that they can barely be distinguished from his essays. Paradoxically, his historical writings, which included *A History of the Life and Voyages of Christopher Columbus* (1828), and were based on years of painstaking scholarly research in Europe, were decked out with a lot of deliberately misleading fiction. The first edition of his *Chronicle of the Conquest of Granada* (1829) carried an introduction explaining that he got his material from the venerable Fray Antonios Agapida, whose identity and integrity Irving was at great pains to establish. The revised edition (1850) admitted that the monk was an imaginary personage, a mere personification of the monkish zealots 'who hovered about the sovereigns in their campaigns'. Cooper and Melville, too, regularly fabricated detailed introductions to their novels: how they had heard a story from such-and-such a stranger, who had been in such-and-such a place at such-and-such a time. The fabrications served no good literary purpose; but they did demonstrate that the American writer was semi-organically, almost hypnotically disposed to think and write in a mysterious strain.

Falling asleep and waking up decades or centuries earlier or later, introducing visitors from other worlds, visiting fantasy countries; these dream devices have recommended themselves to the span of American novelists from Irving to Science Fictionists. At the bottom of the artistic scale, politicians and reformers have turned to such fiction to embody their hopes and fears. In *Looking Backward* (1888) the socialist author Edward Bellamy had his hero Julian West, significantly named after the imperial Old World and the symbol of the New, wake up in the year 2000 in an America of blissful pacificism and equality. He had been presumed dead in the capitalistic, hierarchical year of 1887, though he had merely been in a hypnotic trance. A miraculous deep-freeze preserved him. In *Caesar's Column* (1891) the populist Ignatius Donnelly described America in 1988, reft by bloody class conflict, its liberals exiled in Africa. The poet Joaquin Miller in *The Building of the City Beautiful* (1907) looked centuries ahead in prose to a millennial, pastoral California; the poet Vachel Lindsay in his novel *The Golden Book of Springfield* (1920) wrote about American society in the year 2020, tolerant, ecumenical, responding to the civilising influences of an environment derived from Frank Lloyd Wright's designs. But positing a Utopia has been a central concern of America's major writers, too. As America became an older and more complex society, and the original dream receded, so writer after writer embodied his disappointment, and his dream, in novels which reflected their desire to see something simple, primitive and beautiful replace the status quo.

In *The Monikins* (1835) James Fenimore Cooper makes a critical allegorical journey to islands representing France, England and America; but he pointedly introduces a dream race, the Monikins, and their dream country, more like a fulfilment of the best American ideals than the United States in 1835. In *Mardi* Melville did much the same thing, when he described an imaginary voyage to a group of Polynesian islands (which represented all known political systems) and to the dream country of Mardi itself, again favourably contrasted with the United States. Melville embodied his dream in the beautiful, evasive maiden Yillah. She and Taji (Melville) made love a few times but she disappeared; the dream materialised and then vanished. Hawthorne's search for an idealised America, *The Blithedale Romance*, was based on an actual experiment in community living at Brook Farm, Massachusetts; but, ironically, this temporary enactment of an ideal turned him away from what seemed to him the unreal, timeless and therefore anachronistic perfection of a dream come true.

> I was beginning to lose the sense of what kind of a world it was, among innumerable schemes of what it might or ought to be . . . Our great globe floated in the atmosphere of infinite space like an unsubstantial bubble. No sagacious man will long retain his

sagacity, if he live exclusively among reformers and progressive people, without periodically returning into the settled system of things, to correct himself by a new observation from the old standpoint.

It was now time for me, therefore, to go and hold a little talk with the conservatives, the writers of the *North American Review*, the merchants, the politicians, the Cambridge men, and all those respectable old blockheads who still, in this intangibility and mustiness of affairs, kept a death-grip on one or two ideas which had not come into vogue since yesterday morning.

It is from Hawthorne that we get one of the classic statements of the dream–nightmare theme. In 'The Celestial Railroad' he imagines himself making a pilgrimage over Bunyan's Everyman's exact path. Since this is the New World man making the pilgrimage in a new, unpolluted world, everything has been made over, rebuilt, cleaned out. Or has it? How thoroughly have things changed, in fact, and have they changed for the better, asks Pilgrim Hawthorne?

'Is that,' inquired I, 'the very door in the hillside which the shepherds assured Christian was a byway to hell?'

'That was a joke on the part of the shepherds,' said Mr Smooth-it-away, with a smile. 'It is neither more nor less than the door of a cavern which they use as a smoke house for the preparation of mutton hams.'

And then did my excellent friend Mr Smooth-it-away laugh outright, in the midst of which cachinnation a smoke-wreath issued from his mouth and nostrils, while a twinkle of lurid flame darted out of either eye, proving indubitably that his heart was all of a red blaze. The impudent fiend! To deny the existence of Tophet, when he felt its fiery tortures raging within his breast.

Thank heaven it was a Dream!

Mark Twain, too, was a dreamer and, like Hawthorne, on occasion a doubter and a cynic. In *A Connecticut Yankee in King Arthur's*

Court he seems at first to be satirising Arthurian England. Hank Morgan rises to power in Arthurian Britain by applying his nineteenth-century knowledge of gunpowder, electricity and so on. But in the end, Hank and his five hundred knights on bicycles whom he has trained in nineteenth-century skills and sharp business practices seem less desirable than the simple, dignified, sixth-century Britons whom they deceive. At the end of the book Merlin puts Hank to sleep until the nineteenth century; and Twain leaves us wondering which of the societies he is setting up as the dream, and which as the nightmare.

Perhaps it is a mark of the greater writers that their perception of the complexities of the dream–nightmare prevents their definitive response. A talented though lesser writer like Howells takes on a tinge of the didact in *A Traveller from Altruria* (1894). Mr Homos comes to America from imaginary Altruria, which was doing everything idealists might expect America to be doing and what Brook Farm tried to do. Everyone worked three hours a day at manual tasks in return for food and other goods supplied from government sources. Property was communally owned, family life was subordinate to civic life, and all questions from dress to architecture were democratically decided. The socialistic Jack London also saw issues in black-and-white extremes. *The Iron Heel* (1907) imagines a great battle between the fascist American government and the working class in the years 1912–16. It is nightmare more than dream; the forces are unequal, the slaughter of the workers dreadful, and the workers themselves so far downtrodden that their triumph, which London, footnoting the book an imaginary 700 years later, describes as a golden age of collectivism, seems something to dread. But for London, all that was temporarily wrong with a temporarily brutish people was that they had lost the power to dream; they lived in an age when, however many generations and centuries ahead they looked, they could imagine no improvement in their lot; an age which disliked the adjective *Utopian*. The mere utterance of it could damn any

89

scheme no matter how sanely conceived, of economic ameliora-
tion or regeneration.' Irving was reversed: *not* to dream was an
effective nightmare.

Horror Stories

The most tormented and Kafkaesque imagination in American
literature belongs to Edgar Allan Poe. An orphaned childhood,
an unhappy upbringing as a foster-child, a drop-out experience as
a student, a marriage possibly consummated with his mother-in-
law rather than his wife, a drift into gambling and debauchery
and an all-too-intimate acquaintance with the horrors of alco-
holism: Poe's own life was a horror story. His was a talented,
erratic, morbidly sensitive mind which ranged from extreme
depression to extreme exaltation, and which, in both states of
mind, believed in dreams not merely as a literary device but as
keys to the essential meaning of existence. 'The realities of the
world affected me as visions, and as visions only, while the wild
ideas of the land of dreams became, in turn, not the material of
my everyday existence, but in very deed that existence utterly and
solely in itself.' Poe personified this philosophy in 'The Angel of
the Odd', whom he ironically pictured as a solid, heavily Ger-
manic Angel, who had for a head 'one of those Hessian canteens
which resemble a large snuff-box with a hole in the middle of the
lid', and whose mouth was deceptively that of a very precise old
maid. The Angel persecutes Poe until he answers affirmative to
the question: 'You pelief, ten, in te possibility of te odd?'

Unlike Irving and Hawthorne, who would admit that appearance *could* be deceptive, Poe argued that anyone who did not
assume that appearances and happenings were deceptive by definition, that is, were 'appearances' and 'happenings' in a supernatural sense, was a fool. To Poe ghosts, freaks and hallucinations
represented the very substance of life, not its insubstantial dimension. But even he had to admit that he could neither fully know

nor predict nor control events in this real other world; he, too, was subject to terror, and the force of his best stories stems from the fact that the author–narrator, as well as the reader–victim, is in a state of terrified doubt. Poe is like Roderick Usher in 'The Fall of the House of Usher', who becomes governed by 'the grim phantasm fear' and whose crazy imaginings in some way bring about his death, his twin sister Madeleine's death, and the disappearance of the House in a tarn. Fatally, Roderick could not stop dreaming of the unknowable.

If life is deceptive, so is Poe. Hoax manuscripts in bottles, hoax trips to the moon by Mr Hans Pfall; enigmas, conundrums, hieroglyphs, murder apparently committed by an orang-outang, premature burials: Poe's *Tales of the Grotesque and Arabesque* (1840) and *Tales of Adventure, Mystery and Imagination* (1852) mock and question reality. Like the wife of a Maryland congressman, live people can really seem dead, and be buried. In her instance,

> . . . a careful investigation rendered it evident that she had revived within two days after her entombment; that her struggles within the coffin had caused it to fall from a ledge, or shelf, to the floor, where it was so broken as to permit her escape . . . On the uppermost of the steps which led down into the dread chamber was a large fragment of the coffin, with which, it seemed, that she had endeavoured to arrest attention by striking the iron door. While thus occupied, she probably swooned, or possibly died, through sheer terror; and in falling, her shroud became entangled in some ironwork which projected interiorly. Thus she remained, and thus she rotted, erect.

But Poe is never prepared merely to narrate other people's horrors. Masochistically, he has to transmit the horror into his imaginary personal experience, and it is, he insists, experience, 'no dream and no nightmare'. One of his 'experiences' was that 'someone had buried me – nailed me up in some common coffin – and thrust [me] deep, deep, and forever, into some grave'.

Yet, paradoxically, to dream is to die: this is a theme taken up in 'The Pit and the Pendulum', where Poe dreams he is in prison, caught between an ever-descending scythe-like pendulum which will cut him to death and the alternative death of leaping into a bottomless pit. When the moment of choice arrives he faints (going into one unknown to escape another). When he wakes up out of prison, and in his own bed, he is left with 'the madness of memory which busies itself among forbidden things'.

The contemplation of women drove Poe to a kind of madness. On the one hand he thought female beauty the greatest beauty, but his admiration was tinged with the morbid qualification that the death of a beautiful woman was the most beautiful fact and concept of all (the morbidly strange beauty that so influenced Baudelaire and Dostoyevsky); on the other his own sexual life was far from being satisfying or satisfactory. And so, in Poe's fiction, women become potential vampires, evil Eves, to be destroyed at all costs. In 'Berenice' his beautiful cousin of that name becomes ill – probably because Poe has been psychically, unconsciously sucking life from her – and he turns from Berenice, also his prospective wife, repulsed by her thin

> . . . and shrunken lips. They parted; and in a smile of peculiar meaning, *the teeth* of the changed Berenice disclosed themselves slowly to view. [When she had left the room] I saw them *now* even more unequivocally than I beheld them *then*. The teeth! – the teeth! – they were here, and there, and everywhere, and visibly and palpably before me; long, narrow, and excessively white, with the pale lips writhing about them, as in the very moment of their first terrible development. Then came the full fury of my *monomania*, and I struggled in vain against its strange and irresistible influence. In the multiplied objects of the external world I had no thoughts but for teeth. For these I longed with a frenzied desire. And the evening closed it upon me thus – and then the darkness came . . .

Some time later Poe is informed of Berenice's death. He attends the funeral. And then:

> I found myself sitting in the library, and again sitting there alone. It seemed to me that I had newly awakened from a confused and

exciting dream . . . There came a light tap at the library door – and, pale as the tenant of a tomb, a menial entered upon tiptoe . . . He pointed to my garments; they were muddy and clotted with gore. I spoke not, and he took me gently by the hand: it was indented with the impress of human nails. He directed my attention to some object against the wall. I looked at it for some minutes; it was a spade. With a shriek I bounded to the table, and grasped the box that lay upon it. But I could not force it open; and, in my tremor, it slipped from my hands, and fell heavily, and burst into pieces; and from it, with a rattling sound, there rolled out some instruments of dental surgery, intermingled with thirty-two small, white, and ivory-looking substances that were scattered to and fro about the floor.

And what, Poe asked himself, was the cause of all these horrors? His will to dream, all day and every day.

This monomania, if I must so term it, consisted in a morbid irritability of those properties of the mind in metaphysical science termed the *attentive*. It is more than probable that I am not understood; but I fear, indeed, that it is in no manner possible to convey to the mind of the merely general reader, an adequate idea of that nervous *intensity of interest* with which, in my case, the powers of meditation (not to speak technically) busied and buried themselves in the contemplation of even the most ordinary objects of the universe . . . In the strange anomaly of my existence, feelings with me, *had never been of the heart*, and my passions *always* were of the mind.

'The Narrative of Arthur Gordon Pym' is Poe's most sophisticated horror story, in which he sustains a gripping, novella-length narrative which becomes incredible only in its latter stages, but which from the outset prepares the reader for the dénouement of Poe's view of reality. The introductory note sets up the fictional persona of Pym with seemingly factual background, citing Pym's natural reluctance, overcome only by a Mr Poe of the *Southern Literary Messenger*, to tell such a true but fantastic tale.

The incidents to be narrated were of a nature so positively marvelous that, unsupported as my assertions must necessarily be (except by the evidence of a single individual, and he a half-breed Indian), I could only hope for belief among my family, and those of my friends who have had reason, through life, to put faith in my veracity – the probability being that the public at large would regard what I should put forth as merely an impudent and ingenious fiction.

Poe had deliberately concealed the fact that the story *was* based on real life – Benjamin Morelle's *Narrative of Four Voyages to the South Seas and Pacific* (1832). For, internal evidence to the contrary, Poe was not concerned with the scientific facts of adventure and discovery, however extraordinary they might be; he was concerned to use the existence of strange and unknown countries, tribes and customs to underline his own nihilistic philosophy. Nothing is knowable, nothing is what it seems.

Seemingly Pym's story is one of highly credible human interest. He stows away with a friend on a boat; the friend, the captain's son, is above decks, and for some reason is late in releasing Pym, who is left in a stuffy, exitless hold so long that

I fell, in spite of every exertion to the contrary, into a state of profound sleep, or rather stupor. My dreams were of the most terrific description. . . . Serpents held me in their embrace, and looked earnestly in my face with their fearfully shining eyes. Then deserts, limitless, and of the most forlorn and awe-inspiring character spread themselves out before me. Immensely tall trunks of trees, gray and leafless, rose up in endless succession as far as the eye could reach. Their roots were concealed in wide-spreading morasses, whose dreary water lay intensely black, still, and altogether terrible, beneath . . . The scene changed; and I stood, naked and alone, amid the burning sand-plains of Zahara. At my feet lay crouched a fierce lion of the tropics . . . Stifling in a paroxysm of terror, I at last found myself partially awake. My dream, then, was not all a dream. Now, at least, I was in possession of my senses. The paws of some huge and real monster were pressing heavily upon my bosom – his hot breath was in my ear – and his white and ghastly fangs were gleaming upon me through the gloom.

Reality seems to dispel the dream. The monster is his New-foundland dog, Tiger, a fellow stowaway. Pym's friend finally contacts him with the news of mutiny on board, and the death of the captain. Pym survives an eventful voyage to be shipwrecked on an island among hostile tribes, whom he keeps at bay from a geologically unique set of white fissures and chasms with strange hieroglyphics scrawled over them. The ominous symbolism of apparent purity, echoed in the White Whale and in the powdered white arms and ballooning white dress of Daisy Fay, had entered American literature, suggesting the menace of the unknown and of the Virgin Land of America. It is at this point that the reality which Pym describes becomes more terrible than the dreams he had in the hold, more terrifying than the slaughter and canni-balism on the boat. Having set up a series of horrific–credible incidents, Poe finishes with an incredible horror which he sees as real – thereby casting doubt on the sanity of the narrator, but, more crucially, on the judgement of the reader, who, until the dénouement, never doubts the narrator. Was any part of the story true? If so, the reader wonders which part, as Poe–Pym describes his 'escape' from the white menace under the 'protection' of a volcano, as the sea carries them towards

. . . a limitless cataract, rolling silently into the sea, from some immense and far-distant rampart in the heaven. The gigantic curtain ranged along the whole extent of the southern horizon. It emitted no sound . . . The darkness had materially increased, re-lieved only by the glare of the water thrown back from the white curtain before us. Many gigantic and pallidly white birds flew continuously now from beyond the veil . . . And now we rushed into the embraces of the cataract, where a chasm threw itself open to receive us. But there arose in our pathway a shrouded human figure, very far larger in its proportions than any dweller among men. And the hue of the skin of the figure was of the perfect whiteness of the snow.

The artistic success of this tense story is vitiated by an appendix stating that Pym is dead and that the publishers are pleased to offer a translation of the hieroglyphics, which amounts to a series of statements about the terror of whiteness. But philosophically, the appendix rounds off the story to perfection. The confusion of truth and falsehood, reality and unreality was complete in the scholarly interpretation of a made-up language.

Ambrose Bierce, who described a ghost as 'the outward and visible sign of an inward fear', is often thought of as Poe's psychological and stylistic heir, and the similarities are certainly striking. After Poe only Bierce made a speciality of the horror genre and all the Poesque devices – mysteriously lost and discovered manuscripts, haunted houses, mothers risen from the dead. He is fascinated by parricide and fratricide and all unnatural relationships. 'The Damned Thing' deals with a shape 'so white it can't be seen'; and 'The Man with the Snake' takes further Poe's 'The Sphinx'. In Poe's story a man almost dies at the apparent approach of a black, shaggy monster with two pairs of wings, each a hundred yards in length, a monster which proves to be an insect reflected in part of his spectacles' lens; in Bierce's a man takes for real a stuffed snake in his bedroom, and, in panic, suffers a fatal heart attack.

But, unlike Poe, Bierce uses the grotesque to grope towards the expression of the dark side of American life. Many of his stories in *Tales of Soldiers and Civilians* (1891) and *Can Such Things Be?* (1893) are set in the context of the American Civil War, that worst of all types of war, which is itself a metaphor of horror, involving gothic ironies and coincidences. In Poe the grotesque, the surprise ending, morbidity, were expressions of an individual belief in a universal blackness; in Bierce the same phenomena are grounded in the American nightmare, and images of dreams which prove to be nightmares characterise his work. In 'An Occurrence at Owl Creek Bridge' he describes how Peyton Farquhar, an Alabaman, is hanged by Northern troops at the bridge side. As the rope tightens Peyton fights against it, manages to fall in the river, fights to release the rope, does so, surfaces, is fired on, and eventually swims out of rifle range to the shore. 'His neck was in pain and lifting his hand to it he found it horribly swollen. He knew that it had a circle of black where the rope had brushed it. His eyes felt congested; he could no longer close them. His tongue was swollen with thirst.' Still he manages to make his way home, and at last sees his wife on the veranda of their house.

Ah, how beautiful she is! He springs forward with extended arms. As he is about to clasp her, he feels a stunning blow upon the back of the neck; a blinding white light blazes all about him with a sound like the shock of a cannon – then all is darkness and silence. Peyton Farquhar was dead; his body, with a broken neck, swings gently from side to side beneath the timbers of Owl Creek Bridge.

What for Poe were imaginary horrors were real ones for Bierce. The Civil War did see faces with jaws torn away, and family situations more horrific than the life and death of the Usher twins occurred. One sunny afternoon, a six-year-old boy strayed into the woods near Chickamagua. He was caught up in the periphery of battle, and enjoyed seeing the retreat of a column of maimed men.

He moved among them freely, going from one to another and peering into their faces with childish curiosity. All their faces were singularly white and many were streaked and gouted with red. Something in this – something too, perhaps, in their grotesque attitudes and movements reminded him of the painted clown whom he had seen last summer in the circus, and he laughed as he watched them . . . To him it was a merry spectacle. He had seen his father's Negroes creep upon their hands and knees for his amusement – had ridden them so, 'making believe' they were his horses. He now approached one of these crawling figures from behind and with an agile movement mounted it astride.

His games finally took him in a direction which seemed familiar.

G   97

> He recognized the blazing building as his own home! For a
> moment he stood stupefied by the power of the revelation, then
> ran with stumbling feet, making a half-circuit of the ruin. There,
> conspicuous in the light of the conflagration, lay the dead body
> of a woman – the white face turned upward, the hands thrown out
> and clutched full of grass, the clothing deranged, the long dark
> hair in tangles and full of clotted blood. The greater part of the
> forehead was torn away, and from the jagged hole the brain pro-
> truded, overflowing the temple, a frothy mass of gray, crowned
> with clusters of crimson bubbles – the work of a shell.

He just recognises his mother. But he cannot cry; he is a deaf-
mute.

Excepting his rib-tickling tall stories, which might concern a
man sold 3,201ft of lightning-conductors, detectives trying to
find a stolen white elephant or a jumping-frogs contest, Mark
Twain's short stories deal largely with the grotesque and the
mysterious. In 'A Curious Dream' the narrator meets a macabre
group of graveyard corpses who do not like being dead – and
wakes up soberly wondering how he will like death. 'Cannibalism
in the Cars' describes how one railroad passenger tells another
how he was snowbound in a train with twenty-three others for
weeks on end, and how they were reduced to cannibalism. The
'cannibal' tells this story not with shame, but with succulent relish. Morgan of Alabama was juicy, he remembered. Messick was
highly flavoured. Was the narrator, as the trainman said, a madman, or, as the madman indicated in his appreciative comments on
Twain's solid torso, still a cannibal?

Twain's last work, *The Mysterious Stranger* (1916), published
posthumously, is more cynical than anything written by Poe. Poe
was a maverick American writer – highly self-centred, not particularly concerned with the fate of his nation. But Twain, who
lived through seventy-five years of American history, was optimistic or pessimistic as he watched the national barometer. The
lower it fell, the grimmer became his fiction, and he ended his life
in an America which was oppressively imperialistic, where one-

eighth of the people owned seven-eighths of the wealth. Could there then be a God? or good? or reason? Or was there simply a valueless, irrational universe? Twain answered yes to the last question in his story, set in medieval times, of a stranger who professes to be Satan, who visits the Austrian home of Theodor Fischer. Satan suggests driving everyone crazy who is not already mad, because, he says, God is evil, and earthly happiness is restricted to the mad. His visit proves to be a dream, but Theodor feels he now understands that if there is a so-called God, He is as crazy and malicious as Satan. How else could He allow terrible things to happen to humanity and expect humanity to worship Him? For Twain as for Poe, waking up does not end the dream; its influence lingers on.

Even as subtle, sophisticated and expatriate an American as Henry James was fascinated by the inexplicably horrific. 'The Jolly Corner' used precisely the same macabre device as Poe's 'William Wilson' – the physical existence of the good and bad identities of a schizophrenic – two William Wilsons and two Spencer Brysons. The characters in James's 'The Friends of Friends' are grotesquely visited by the dead; and in 'The Third Person' two spinsters inherit a house and a smuggler ghost. James's vampire story *The Sacred Fount* (1901) is appallingly macabre, and shows how sophisticated the horror genre could be. In the setting of a weekend party at a stately, aristocratic English home, James looks at the way youth feeds on age, and stupidity on intelligence. Brissenden, a young man, marries a middle-aged woman. She absorbs his youth, and when he reaches the age she was on their wedding-day, she has gone back to his age on that day. The witty May Server becomes dull and silly while her lover, the once boring Gilbert Long, now shines with an all-consuming intelligence. James writes:

> I saw as I have never seen before what consuming passion can make of the marked mortal on whom, with filed beak and claws, it has settled as on a prey. She [May] reminded me of a sponge

wrung dry, and with fine pores agape. Voided and scraped of everything, her shell was merely crushable . . . Poor Briss had succumbed to inexorable time, and Mrs Server given way under a cerebral lesion . . . Gilbert Long's victim had reached the point of final simplification and Grace Brissenden's the limit of age recorded of any man.

James brings the same sense of physical and psychological menace to *The Turn of the Screw* (1898), where a dead valet and governess appear to their former charges, Miles and Flora, drawing them into an indefinable circle of evil. This story beautifully combines an evocation of a traditional haunted house with the kind of indescribable Poesque, Melvillesque terror that ultimately makes Miles die of fright. It also questions the reality of that horror. Was it possible that Peter Quint and Miss Jessel were figments of the overcharged imagination of the children's new governess? Was she responsible for Miles's death? How, when, where and why did a dream become a nightmare?

The Dream/Reality Antithesis

Hawthorne once apologised to his readers for the kind of fiction an American writer was forced to produce. In the introduction to *The Blithedale Romance* he wrote:

In the old countries, with which fiction has long been conversant, a certain conventional privilege seems to be awarded to the romancer; his work is not put exactly side by side with nature; and he is allowed a license with regard to every-day probability, in view of the improved effect which he is bound to produce thereby. Among ourselves, on the contrary, there is as yet no such Faery Land, so like the real world, that, in a suitable remoteness, one cannot well tell the difference, but with an atmosphere of strange enchantment, beheld through which the inhabitants have a propriety of their own. This atmosphere is what the American romancer needs. In its absence, the beings of imagination are compelled to show themselves in the same category as actually living mortals; a necessity that generally renders the paint and pasteboard of their composition but too painfully discernible.

His apology was unnecessary; for in such a novel as *The House of the Seven Gables* (1851), with plenty of Old World faery-cursed wells, pictures which come to life, a house with a malignant personality – the strength of the work lies in just that aspect which Hawthorne so delicately disclaimed: the marvellous quality of the inner life of the individual and the interplay of inner lives. Hawthorne makes the real mystery of every individual's heart and soul more romantic, more dream-like, than any conventional supernatural phenomena; and the characters themselves find the inner life more real than the outer. Clifford Pyncheon, a falsely accused murderer, recently released, finds the outside world intolerable, a train journey more nightmarish and fantastic than any prison experience, and can only approach reality through romance.

> He read Phoebe [his rosy country niece] as he would a sweet and simple story; he listened to her as if she were a verse of household poetry, which God, in requital of his bleak and dismal lot, had permitted some angel, that most pitied him, to warble through the house. She was not an actual fact for him, but the interpretation of all that he had lacked on earth brought warmly home to his conception; so that this mere symbol, or life-like picture, had almost the comfort of reality.

Phoebe's lover, Holgrave, ends up 'discerning that man's best directed effort accomplishes a kind of dream, while God is the sole worker of realities', while Clifford's sister, Hepzibah, a genteel New Englander fallen on hard times, could only come to terms with opening a cent shop by ignoring reality and substituting a dream.

> She appeared to be walking in a dream; or, more truly, the vivid life and reality assumed by her emotions made all outward occur-

rences unsubstantial, like the teasing phantasm of a half-conscious slumber. She still responded, mechanically, to the frequent summons of the shop bell, and, at the demand of her customers, went prying with vague eyes about the shop, proffering them one article after another, and thrusting aside – perversely as most of them supposed – the identical thing they asked for. There is sad confusion indeed, when the spirit thus flits away into the past or into the more awful future, or, in any manner, steps across the spaceless boundary betwixt its own region and the actual world; where the body remains to guide itself as best it may, with little more than the mechanisms of animal life.

Hawthorne's masterpiece, *The Scarlet Letter* (1850), is a work of such subtlety and complexity, and as such comparable with Stendhal's *Charterhouse of Parma* (1832), that to define its themes and its symbols would be foolhardy. Who can decide between the symbolism of the beneficent red rose which blooms against the black flower of New England society, the prison, in Chapter I, and the lurid, blood-red imagery which develops in subsequent chapters? The relative merits of natural or man-made law, of truth and deception; the possibility of fulfilled love in Puritan New England; the effect of guilt, the need to be truthful, the capacity for mental independence – these are but a few of the issues raised. But it can be said that a common cause of the many tragedies in the book lies in the failure to face reality. Old Roger Chillingworth has unsuitably married a young, beautiful wife; she has accepted the unnatural relationship of decay and budding youth. Hester Prynne and Arthur Dimmesdale have dreamed of a sexual relationship between a married woman and a bachelor clergyman, impossible in their society. Two of the most important scenes in the book are painted in terms of this kind of unreality. First, the private midnight vigil of Dimmesdale on the scaffold where he confesses that he was the father of Hester's child – an unpublic confession which he vainly expects will bring relief; secondly, Arthur's and Hester's meeting in the wood.

'Hester! Hester Prynne!' said he. 'Is it thou? Art thou in life?'
'Even so!' she answered. 'In such life as has been mine these seven
years past! And thou, Arthur Dimmesdale dost thou yet live?'

It was no wonder that they thus questioned one another's actual
and bodily existence, and even doubted of their own. So strangely
did they meet, in the dim wood, that it was like the first encounter,
in the world beyond the grave, of two spirits who had been inti-
mately connected in mutual dreams, as not yet familiar with their
state, nor wonted to the companionship of disembodied beings.
Each a ghost, and awe-stricken at the other ghost!

The novel's gothic devices reinforce an uncertain reality. Since
the adulterous Dimmesdale is a clergyman, the yawning graves
and lurid skies which he conjures or attracts, the fact that his
daughter Pearl is a kind of witch-baby, serve to suggest either a
disapproving deity or, since on balance the signs are somewhat
contradictory, the impossibility of putting a definitive interpretation on the universe and the absence of discernible logical
laws. Man's vision of the world, his reality, has no determinable
validity.

Much of Hawthorne's fiction concerns the dream/reality antithesis. Sailing on the Concord in 1846, he noted:

The slumbering river has a dream picture in its bosom. Which,
after all, was the most real – the picture, or the original? – the
objects palpable to our grosser senses, or their apothesis in the
stream beneath. Surely the disembodied images stand in closer
relation to the soul.

Yet a tragic note characterises the stories he wrote soon after this
river trip, stories where those who are not content with reality
bring harm and destruction on themselves and others. In 'The
Birthmark' Aylmer becomes fixated by a tiny mole on his exquisite
wife's cheek; she overhears him in a dream saying, 'It is in her
heart now; we must have it out.' She takes his dream seriously,
urges him to experiment with removing it – and he kills her in the
process. 'Young Goodman Brown' enters the realms of anti-

reality when he allows a stranger, who looks like an older version of himself (a hint here that Brown was indulging in wishful thinking), to take him to a black-magic rite in the forest. He believes he sees his wife, Faith, there, convenanting with the devil. Could he have fallen asleep and dreamed? To Hawthorne, it made no difference. To the reader who wants to think it is a dream he says: 'Be it so, if you will; but alas! it was a dream of evil omen for Young Goodman Brown. A stern, a sad, a darkly meditative, a distrustful, if not a desperate man did he become from the night of that fearful dream.'

Hawthorne, then, uses the dream juxtaposed with reality as a technique for exploring the human psyche, the human soul, of whatever nationality; but in 'The Hall of Fantasy', when his imagination takes him to visit 'the contemporary Rialto of dreamers', he homes into the American base, satirising his fellow countrymen much as Dickens was to do in *Martin Chuzzlewit*. American dreamers outdreamt the world; who else would believe they could make a machine for the condensation of morning mist into square blocks of granite?

> There was a character of detail and matter of fact in their talk which concealed the extravagance of its purport, in so much that the wildest schemes had the aspect of everyday realities. Thus the listener was not startled at the idea of cities to be built, as if by magic, in the heart of pathless forests; and of streets to be laid out where now the sea was tossing; and of mighty rivers to be stayed in their courses in order to turn the machinery of a cotton mill. It was only by an effort, and scarcely then, that the mind convinced itself that such speculations were as much matter of fantasy as the old dream of Eldorado, or as Mammon's Cave, or any other vision of gold ever conjured up by the imagination of needy poet or romantic adventurer.
>
> 'Upon my word,' said I, 'it is dangerous to listen to such dreamers as these. Their madness is contagious.'
>
> 'Yes,' said my friend, 'because they mistake the Hall of Fantasy for actual brick and mortar, and its purple atmosphere for unsophisticated sunshine.'

Melville's *Pierre* (1852) is a subtle, sobering exploration of the capacity to consistently detect, or prefer, reality to unreality. Pierre Glendinning lives with his youthful, widowed mother – sister Mary as she likes him to call her – in an atmosphere of wealth, taste and good works. He is conscious of his privileged position, and adores the dead father who gave him that position. Externally, Pierre, 'the complete polished steel of the gentleman, girded with Religion's silken sash', made perfect sense. Only one thing mars his happiness, the haunting dream of a girl's dark, passionate, beautiful, tragic face. But it transpires that Pierre has been lying to himself, and to his fiancée Lucy Tartan, when he calls this a dream face – it is in fact the face of Isabel, a servant girl recently arrived in the village. Pierre has been pretending that reality is a dream in order to get rid of a reality which he suspects is troublesome, and which proves so when the girl writes to him that she wants to meet him, and reveals that she is his father's illegitimate daughter.

Pierre is bewildered. He cannot bear to tarnish his father's name; he knows his proud mother will never accept the truth, nor can he accept it – openly; so he decides to flee to New York and set up house with Isabel. As a perverse guarantee of respectability, Isabel will pose as his wife. A nucleus of wrong dreams is exposed, which itensify the situation – and which, more than the situation itself, doom the characters: the false dream of an untarnished husband and father; Mrs Glendinning's dream of Pierre as she wants him, not as he is; and Isabel's dreams – she has little evidence of her past, and neither she nor Pierre are quite sure that they are related. 'Scarcely know I at any time whether I tell you real things, or the unrealist dreams. Always in me, the solidest things melt into dreams and dreams to solidities,' she says. And what of Pierre's dreams for himself? Had they always been more sexual than the fair, frail, ingenuous Lucy could cope with? Mrs Glendinning had brought forward the date of Pierre's marriage because she thought he was suffering from unfulfilled dreams. Pierre, looking at himself in the mirror and seeing there the last male Glendinning, found 'this thought was not wholly sad to him. Nay, sometimes it mounted into an exultant swell. For in the ruddiness, and flushfulness, and vain gloriousness of his youthful soul, he fondly hoped to have a monopoly in capping the fair column, whose tall shaft had been erected by his noble sires.' How would Pierre have faced the reality of Isabel if she had been ugly? What, 'If accosted in some squalid lane, a humped and crippled, hideous girl, should have snatched his garment's hem, with "O Save me, Pierre – love me, own me, brother: I am thy sister"?' What motivated Pierre? Is the real Pierre selfish, or altruistic? At the very moment that he tells Isabel of his plan for a pure, unconsummated, fictitious marriage, he finds himself other than he intended.

> The girl moved not; was done with all her trembling; leaned closer to him, with an inexpressible strangeness of an intense love, new and inexplicable. Over the face of Pierre there shot a terrible self-revelation; he imprinted repeated burning kisses upon her; pressed hard her hand; would not let go her sweet and awful passiveness.
>
> Then they changed; they coiled together, and entangledly stood mute.

Pierre fights the impending incest; Isabel tells him it is a dream, and that in a dream sin is impossible. Pierre's eventual acceptance of her rationale leads to nightmarish and incredible happenings. Lucy comes to live with them in a macabre threesome: she eventually dies of grief; Pierre kills a cousin who has secured the Glendinning inheritance, and he and Isabel commit suicide in his prison cell. The subtitle of *Pierre* is *The Ambiguities*, and the book is Melville's most sophisticated treatment of the question of identity and reality, which he summed up thus:

> The wisest man were rash, positively to assign the precise and incipient origination of his final thoughts and acts. For as we

blind moles can see, man's life seems but an acting upon mysterious hints; it is somehow hinted to us, to do thus or thus. For surely no mere mortal who has at all gone down into himself will ever pretend that his slightest thought or act solely originates in his own defined identity.

A mother who pretended to be a sister conditioned Pierre for a sister who wanted to be a wife.

The later Melville was even more disillusioned; and in *The Confidence-Man* (1857), he assembled a ship of fools on the Mississippi steamboat *Fidèle*, a vessel of falsehoods. The goings-on demonstrate all too clearly that the author cannot believe in humanity, largely because humanity, wilfully, stupidly, cannot and will not distinguish fact from fantasy. Passengers are prepared to believe that a pathetic legless Negro beggar is 'some white operator, twisted and painted up for a decoy'. Fraudulent sellers of the useless Omni-Balsam Reinvigorator and the Samaritan Pain Dissuader, 'Thrice blessed, Warranted to remove the acutest pain within less than ten minutes', canvassers for the nonexistent Seminole Widows and Orphans Society, meet guillible victims; and the biggest confidence-man of all is the only passenger professing confidence in men – 'Frank Goodman, Philanthropist and Citizen of the World': the American Everyman.

In *The Gilded Age* (1873), Twain elaborates the character of a confidence-man's perfect victim, the arch dreamer Colonel Beriah Sellers, a Dickensian eccentric. Colonel Sellers not only regularly invests all he has in crooked ventures; he dreams against the odds. If he has only turnips to eat, he will try to convince others and will definitely prove to himself that turnips are the most nutritious and pleasing source of energy and brain power; that olive oil can be extracted from them. His dreams pervert daily reality to an extent that makes not a virtue but a vice of necessity. His clock, for instance, 'a clock which never came within fifteen strikes of striking the right time, and whose hands always latched together at twenty-two minutes past anything and travelled in company the rest of the way home'. Twain uses Sellers's clock to poke serious fun at a dreamer who did not know when to stop.

'Remarkable clock!' said Sellers, and got up and wound it. 'I've been offered – well, I wouldn't expect you to believe what I've been offered for that clock. Old Governor Heager never sees me but he says, "Come, now, Colonel, name your price – I MUST have that clock!" But my goodness I'd as soon think of selling my wife. As I was saying to – silence in the court, now, she's begun to strike – You can't talk against her – you just have to be patient and hold up till she's had her say . . . Ah – well as I was saying, when – she's beginning again! Nineteen, twenty, twenty-one, twenty-two, twen— ah, that's all. Yes, as I was saying to old Judge – go to it, old girl, don't mind me – Now how is that? isn't that a good, spirited tone? She can wake the dead! Sleep? Why you might as well try to sleep in a thunder-factory. Now just listen to that. She'll strike a hundred and fifty, now, without stopping – you'll see. There ain't another clock like that in Christendom.'

When there was silence, Mrs Sellers [as would Mrs Micawber] lifted . . . a face that beamed with a childlike pride, and said:

'It belonged to his grandmother.'

Twain's boy heroes, dreamers all, have the best grip on reality of any of his characters. Edward Tudor, the Prince of *The Prince and the Pauper* (1882), comes to grips with the realities of life in his kingdom through the nightmare experiences of accidentally changing place with the Pauper urchin Tom Canty, who in his turn had deliberately used dreams as a safety-valve. He 'soon forgot his aches and pains in delicious picturings to himself of the charmed life of a petted prince in a regal palace', a life of hunger and beatings was thus made tolerable.

Tom Sawyer and Huck Finn, superstitious though they are, confront dreams and realities as they occur. One day, in *Tom Sawyer* (1876), they discover treasure and some formidable thieves, and in bed that night, Tom wonders if he had dreamt it, and submits his doubt to a variety of pragmatic tests. There was one very strong argument in favour of reality:

> Namely, that the quantity of coin he had seen was too vast to be real . . . He had never had supposed for a moment that so large a sum as a hundred dollars was to be found in actual money in any one's possession. If his notions of hidden treasure had been analyzed, they would have been found to consist of a handful of real dimes, and a bushel of vague, splendid, ungraspable ones.

Second, next day he taps Huck's knowledge.

> Huck was sitting on the gunwale of a flat boat, listlessly dangling his feet in the water, and looking very melancholy. Tom concluded to let Huck lead up to the subject. If he did not do it, then the adventure would be proved to have been only a dream.
> 'Hallo, Huck!'
> 'Hallo, yourself.'
> Silence of a minute.
> 'Tom, if we'd a left the blame tools at the dead tree we'd a got the money. Oh, ain't it awful!'
> ' 'Tain't a dream, then. 'Tain't a dream! Somehow I most wish it was. Dog'd if I don't.'
> 'What ain't a dream?'
> 'Oh, that thing yesterday. I ben half thinking it was.'
> 'Dream! If them stairs hadn't broke down you'd a seen how much dream it was! I've had dreams enough all night, with that patch-eyed Spanish devil going for me all through em, rot him!'

In the same way, in *The Adventures of Huckleberry Finn*, the two boys make a clear distinction between dream and reality as they create a fantasy situation around Jim, a black they want to help escape from slavery. They supply him with ropes in pies, notes in blood and every trapping of the means and signs of a dramatic escape, when all they had to do was let him out through the hole they had bored into his hut. Jim, too, consciously partakes of the fantasy, though quite why Twain fails to make clear; the end of the book is altogether obscure. But in spite of being as superstitious as the boys in inessentials – perhaps it is because he too is childish that Twain credits him with the boys' residual clear sight – Jim too can and does distinguish between reality and romance. At one point in their journey down the Mississippi, Huck, in the canoe, is separated from Jim, on the raft, by currents and fog. When Huck finds the raft, Jim is asleep, and when he wakes the boy tells Jim, who has been deeply anxious for Huck, that his anxiety, and his loss of Huck, are figments of his imagination; Huck had never been separated from Jim and the raft. Jim accepts Huck's word, and begins to psychoanalyse his 'dream'. But a glimpse of the battered, befoliaged canoe tells him the truth, and he spells out for Huck the truth about substituting fiction for fact, about pretending reality is a dream, 'Dat truck is TRASH; en trash is what people is dat puts dirt on de head er dey frens en makes em ashamed.' This is the incident that begins to form a moral being out of Huck; this ability to see and admit what is real and what is fabricated is, for Twain, the virtue of virtues.

Of all nineteenth-century American novels, Melville's *Moby-Dick* gives epic expression to the search for reality. Is that White Whale, which reaped away Ahab's leg as a mower a blade of grass, malignant or indifferent, independent, or an agent of fate? At moments Ahab thinks he knows.

> The White Whale swam before him as the monomanic incarnation of all those malicious agencies which some men feel eating in them, till they are left living on with half an ear and half a lung . . . All that most maddens and torments; all that stirs up the lees of things; all truth with malice in it; all that cracks the sinews and cakes the brain; all the subtle demonisms of life and thought; all evils, to crazy Ahab were visibly personified, and made practically assailable in Moby-Dick. He piled upon the whale's white hump the sum of all the general rage and hate felt by his whole race from Adam down; and then, as if his chest had been a mortar, he burst his hot heart's shell upon it.

But if he suggests he can pierce the pasteboard masks of visible objects and is more real than any dream – 'Reality outran apprehension. Captain Ahab stood upon his quarter deck' – the book creates counter-concepts which, cumulatively and with great sophistication, suggest the greater reality of the dream world. In a novel which is nailed to the facts of life on a whaling ship as strongly as Ahab nailed to the *Pequod*'s mast a dubloon for the first man to sight the White Whale, the ultimate message is the mystery of man and the unfathomed marvel of the universe. The narrator, Ishmael, is terrified of Moby-Dick and what he symbolises. 'The whiteness of the whale . . . above all things appalled me – mystic sign of nameless things. Though in many of its aspects this visible world seems formed in love, the invisible spheres were formed in fright.' Yet he joins in the crew's promise to hunt the whale to the death.

> I, Ishmael, was one of that crew; my shouts had gone up with the rest; my oath had been welded with theirs; and stronger I shouted, and more did I hammer and clinch my oath, because of the dread in my soul. A wild, mystical, sympathetical feeling was in me; Ahab's quenchless feud seemed mine. With greedy ear I learned the history of that murderous monster against whom I and all the others had taken our oaths of violence and revenge.

It was not merely Ahab's charisma that conquered Ishmael; even more fundamentally it was the fact that man, however down-to-earth he may be, is an instinctive dreamer, with 'doubts of all things earthly, and intuitions of some things heavenly'. To launch into life – to go to sea – is because 'meditation and water are forever wedded'; because man wants to grasp 'the ungraspable phantom of life', imaged by the White Whale. 'The great floodgates of the wonder-world swing open, and in the wild conceits that swayed me to my purpose, two and two there floated into my inmost soul, endless procession of the whale, and, midmost of them all, one grand, hooded, like a snowhill in the air.'

Ishmael–Melville conducts his search realistically. He studies every theory, picture and skeleton of the whale, only to conclude: 'Dissect him how I may then, I go but skin deep, I know him not, and never shall.' All he can affirm, and he affirms it strongly, is his belief that everything real hides something mysterious. 'Some certain significance lurks in all things, else all things are little worth, and the round world itself but an empty cipher except to sell by the cartload, as they do hills about Boston, to fill up some morass in the Milky Way.'

If Ahab is the greatest dreamer in nineteenth-century American fiction, Fitzgerald's Jay Gatsby, in *The Great Gatsby*, is the greatest twentieth-century dreamer of them all. A poor boy who has made phenomenally good, Gatsby has arrived at the fringes of the exclusive society where Mrs Tom Buchanan, Daisy Fay as she was in St Louis when she and Gatsby, her social inferior, had struck sparks off each other, now reigns. Gatsby tells Nick Carraway, Daisy's cousin, of his dream.

> He wanted nothing less of Daisy than that she should go to Tom and say 'I never loved you'. After she had obliterated four years with that sentence they could decide upon the more practical measures to be taken . . .
> 'I wouldn't ask too much of her,' I ventured. 'You can't repeat the past.'
> 'Can't repeat the past?' he cried incredulously. 'Why of course you can . . .'

As Yillah to Melville–Taji, so Daisy to Fitzgerald–Gatsby. The unattainable Daisy represented the specific, identifiable thing that Gatsby had wanted most in his life; she represented too his quintessential American belief that he could achieve the impossible, achieve any dream, define, create his own reality.

And yet even Gatsby's great capacity to dream is not fulfilling; for when the dream approaches realisation it ceases to be a dream, it loses its magic. In St Louis 'he knew when he kissed this girl, and forever wed his unutterable visions to her perishable breath, his mind would never romp again like the mind of God'. And when Nick reintroduced Daisy and Jay, he saw

> . . . that the expression of bewilderment had come back into Gatsby's face, as though a faint doubt had occurred to him as to the quality of his present happiness. Almost five years! There must have been moments even that afternoon when Daisy tumbled short of his dreams – not through her own fault, but because of the colossal vitality of his illusion. It had gone beyond her, beyond everything. He had thrown himself into it with a creative passion, adding to it all the time, decking it out with every bright feather that drifted his way. No amount of fire or freshness can challenge what a man can store up in his ghostly heart.

Once again the dream dreamed, not the dream materialised becomes the best reality, not only for Jay, but for an America which set itself impossible ideals. In the last paragraph of the book Nick fathoms this dream – its historicity, its impossibility, its sad magnificence, as he thinks of

> . . . the old island here [Manhattan] that flowered once for Dutch sailors' eyes – a fresh green breast of the new world. Its vanished trees, the trees that had made way for Gatsby's house, had once pandered in whispers to the last and greatest of all human dreams; for a transitory enchanted moment man must have held his breath in the presence of this continent, compelled into an esthetic contemplation he neither understood nor desired, face to face for the last time in history with something commensurate to his capacity for wonder.
>
> And as I sat there brooding on the old, unknown world, I thought of Gatsby's wonder when he first picked out the green light at the end of Daisy's dock. He had come a long way to this blue lawn, and his dream must have seemed so close that he could hardly fail to grasp it. He did not know that it was already behind him, somewhere back in that vast obscurity beyond the city, where the dark fields of the republic rolled on under the night.

The Pollyanna–Western Syndrome

Very few American authors have been sanguine dreamers. In an astounding irony, up to 1920, the major novelists of a still outrageously promising New World were pessimists. A bevy of largely undistinguished, immensely popular women like Louisa M. Alcott, Eleanor Porter, Gene Stratton-Porter and Kate Douglas Wiggin represent a good half of these sanguine dreamers. The message of their books is unanimous: the reality of an honest life is wonderful, nothing more so; the reality of an honest face is beautiful, nothing more so. Stratton-Porter called her nature stories 'Tales You Won't Believe'; a defiant proclamation of her belief that if only man will be his simple, unconscious, good self, the good life will follow, whether it is lived in city or country, in poverty or in luxurious ease. 'The way to be happy is to be good, Little Sister,' says Stratton-Porter's Laddie. Stratton-Porter avoided calling her characters by their Christian names – to her they were types which could be mass-produced in the right conditions: Harvester, Angel, Bird-Woman, Naturalist, Princess, Man of Affairs ('brusque of manner but big of heart'). The Harvester – Mrs Porter does prefer the rural setting – puts his creator's point of view.

> 'That's the bedrock of all the trouble on the earth,' interrupted the Harvester. 'We are a nation and a part of a world that spends our time on "seeming". Our whole outer crust is "seeming". When we get beneath the surface and strike the *being*, then we live as we are privileged by the Almighty. I don't think I give a tinker how anything *seems*. What concerns me is how *it is*.'

In Chapter 5 of Stratton-Porter's *Freckles* (1914), 'Where an Angel Materializes and a Man Worships', Freckles, the one-armed, unassuming, shabby Irish labouring boy, is totally unpretentious, and for that reason his reward comes, in the shape of a sweet and pretty rich girl.

But not only the pretty little rich girl is dream-woman material. In Louisa M. Alcott's *Little Women and Good Wives* (1869) the physical equivalent of the Angel, pretty blonde Amy, is, in character, the least attractive of Mrs March's four daughters, though becoming a mother helps soften her; and it is plain old Jo, full of fun and sensitivity, who is the heroine of the March family saga. Not for her a traditional knight in shining armour – but the burly, balding, middle-aged, golden-hearted Dr Fritz Bhaer. Kate Wiggin's *Rebecca of Sunnybrook Farm* (1903) is carotty-haired and gawky, *Pollyanna* (1913) is little better looking; but the charm of that impetuosity which leads them into scrapes (being, not seeming) ultimately gives Rebecca the power to bring unprecedented happiness to her conventional aunts Jane and Matilda, who, until Rebecca came to live with them, had been heaven-bent on the preservation of appearances. And it is Rebecca who will ultimately marry the local magnate and acme of all natural virtues, Mr Adam Ladd. Pollyanna too converts her aunt and a whole small town to natural happiness. The girl has a philosophy of life that holds good for all the women authors: real goodness and real beauty are not artificial dream-states; they are wonderfully here around us; we merely fail to perceive them. Their moral is: adopt the Pollyanna philosophy.

It's a game Miss Pollyanna's father learned her ter play. She got a pair of crutches once in a missionary barrel when she was wantin' a doll; an' she cried, of course, like any child would. It seems 'twas then her father told her that there wasn't ever anythin' but what there was somethin' about it that you could be glad about; an' that she could be glad about them crutches . . . he told her she *could* be glad – 'cause she didn't need 'em . . . And after that she said he made a regular game of it – findin' somethin' in everythin' to be glad about. An' she said ye would do it too, and that ye didn't seem ter mind not havin' the doll so much, cause ye was so glad ye *didn't* need the crutches. An' they called it the 'jest bein' Glad Game' . . . She's played it ever since.

Incongruously rubbing shoulders with Freckles and Co as symbols of the fantastically good life here and now was the cowboy. The Western came into its own as a genre with the dime pamphlet-novels of 1860 onwards (shipped by the car-load to American troops in the Civil War); *Deadwood Dick* and *Calamity Jane*, for example. For anyone convinced that life on earth could be as good as the wildest dreams, the primitive frontier was the most satisfactory proving-ground, for the male at any rate. Here natural man could be observed. The dime novels tended to be all blood and guts; but in 1912 Owen Wister's *The Virginian* appeared, a semi-autobiographical novel carefully and skilfully constructed to put over Wister's claim that the cowboy, imperfect though he was, did show a kind of quality that people might believe was dead, or still-born, or merely a fleeting dream. Describing his first trip West, Wister wrote:

> There was scarce a face among them that had not in it something very likeable . . . City saloons rose into my vision, and I instantly preferred this Rocky Mountain place . . . Even where baseness was visible, baseness was not uppermost. Daring, laughter, endurance – these were what I saw upon the countenances of the cow-boys. And this very first day of my knowledge of them marks a date with me. For something about them, and the idea of them, smote my American heart, and I have never forgotten it, nor ever shall, as long as I live. In their flesh our natural passions ran tumultuous; but often in their spirit sat hidden a true nobility, and often beneath its unexpected shining their figures took a heroic stature.

The Virginian himself proves his natural aristocracy by upstaging the sophisticated Easterners; first the young man (Wister) whom he has come to meet off the train, who found

> This handsome, ungrammatical son of the soil had set between us the bar of his cold and perfect civility. No polished person could have done it better . . . If he had tried familiarity with me the first two minutes of our acquaintance, I should have resented it; by what right, then, had I tried it with him? It smacked of patroniz-

ing: on this occasion he had come off the better gentleman of the two. Here in flesh and blood was a truth which I had long believed in words, but never met before. The creature we call a *gentleman* lies deep in the hearts of thousands that are born without chance to master the outward graces of the type.

The second person over whom the Virginian has the advantage is Molly Wood, the schoolteacher from Bennington, Vermont, with whom he has fallen in love.

> 'All men are born equal,' he now remarked slowly.
> 'Yes,' she quickly answered, with a combative flash. 'Well?' . . .
> 'Do yu' tell the kids so?'
> 'Of course I teach them what I believe!'
> But when she grades her students, he has his comeback. 'Well, it *is* mighty confusin'. George Taylor, he's your best scholar, and poor Bob, he's your worst, and there's a lot in the middle – and you tell me we're all born equal!'

The Virginian has the capacity, equalled by very few of the glut of Westerns that continue to follow it, to suggest convincingly that the cowboy often did have natural dignity and wit; that he lived fully in every direction and dimension, and unmaliciously: a hero without wings. Wister suggests that his passing was as tragic for America as Gatsby's: 'The cowboy is now gone to worlds invisible. The wind has blown away the white ashes of his camp-fires; but the empty sardine box lies rusting over the race of the Western earth.'

One hesitates before classifying Sinclair Lewis as one of America's few optimistic dreamers. With the tendency of American critics as well as writers to affirm criticism of their society, *Babbitt* (1922) and *Main Street* (1920) have been hailed as indictments of Middle America. Lewis stated otherwise, and if we look to see whether the initial rosy dreams of Babbitt and Carol Kennicott are validated or invalidated by the end of each book, it is clear that not only does Lewis *not* allow their dreams to come true, but that he argues that in spite of this, maybe because of this, they were very happy.

George Babbitt, a realtor from Floral Heights, Zenith, regularly dreams a magic dream. He enters a midnight garden where

> . . . for years the fairy child had come to him. When others saw but George Babbitt, she discerned gallant youth. She waited for him, in the darkness beyond mysterious groves . . . he darted to her. His wife . . . sought to follow, but he escaped, the girl fleet beside him, and they crouched together on a shadowy hillside. She was so slim so white so eager. She cried that he was gay and valiant that she would wait for him. They would sail . . .

And then George wakes to the sight of his wife

> . . . Myra Babbitt – Mrs George F. Babbitt – [who] was defiantly mature. She had creases from the corners of her mouth to the bottom of her chin, and her plump neck bagged. But the thing that marked her as having passed the line was that she no longer had reticences before her husband, and no longer worried about not having reticences. She was in a petticoat now, and corsets which bulged, and unaware of being seen in bulgy corsets. She had become so dully habituated to married life that in her full matronliness she was as sexless as an anemic nun. She was a good woman, a kind woman, a diligent woman, but no one, save perhaps Tinka, her ten-year-old, was at all interested in her or entirely aware that she was alive.

And yet, George's attempt to drop out with socialists and fast women who flatter him – Lewis described neither group sympathetically – fails; he comes back to Myra willingly and with renewed love when she develops severe appendicitis. 'In muttered incoherencies they found each other.' Babbitt had done the right thing. As a life-long proposition the alternative society could not be compared with the satisfaction of a regular home and business. By putting an end to Babbitt's dream, Lewis affirmed his own belief in the dreamy here and now.

In *Main Street* Carol Milford, a graduate of Blodgett College, Minnesota, marries Dr Will Kennicott of Main Street, Gopher Prairie, Minnesota, USA. She determines to make the hick community over into a beautiful Georgian or Colonial American city, and an Athens of culture. But not a citizen in Gopher Prairie is really discontented; and Carol bitterly resents the lack of sympathy even Will shows for her schemes.

> A thousand dreams governed by the fiction she had read, drawn from the pictures she had envied, absorbed her drowsy lake afternoons [they were at their marginally attractive summer cottage] but always in the midst of them Kennicott came out from town, drew on khaki trousers which were plastered with dry fish-scales, asked 'enjoying yourself?' and did not listen to her answer.

Yet Carol's bitterness dies. By the end of the book after two children and a liberated year alone in Washington, she knows what she likes best in life's alternatives – Main Street, Gopher Prairie. She returns, and accedes to the town's standards.

> 'Let's all go to the movies to-morrow night. Awfully exciting film,' said Ethel Clark.
> 'Well, I was going to read a new book but – All right, let's go,' said Carol.

Be average, be natural; accept Main Street with its two-storey brick shops and its storey-and-a-half wooden residences; its huddle of Fords, its broad, unenticing gashes of streets, its unsparing, unapologetic ugliness, its planlessness. Accept the great good reality offered in that small, typical town in the symbolic heartland of America: the real, and therefore the Ideal America. There is no better dream.

CHAPTER 4

Individual and Society

Puritanism and Its Discontents

Individualism, according to Webster's dictionary, can be defined as, first, a doctrine that the interests of the individual are or ought to be ethically paramount (also conduct guided by such a doctrine); or, second, the conception that all values, rights and duties originate in individuals; or, third, a theory maintaining the political and economic independence of the individual and stressing individual initiative, action and interests (also conduct or practice guided by such a theory).

Doctrine, conception, theory.

As in most such definitions, the original abstraction breaks down into further abstractions, and the philosopher's dictum, 'Define your terms', sounds like an impossible imperative. Still, *doctrine* has religious and moral connotations, while *conception* suggests the intellectual and *theory* the scientific realm. At least these terms communicate what is broadly true, the pervasive influence of individualism in all areas of American thought; this point is still more powerfully made in those parenthetical parts of the definition: 'also conduct guided' by such a theory, such a doctrine. For it is the *conduct* shaped by individualism – political, economic and social behaviour – that has formed one of the persistent and fascinating themes in American literature.

Perhaps a more useful way of defining the term is through the technique of opposites – not what individualism is, but what it most conspicuously is not. In the United States, no one demands and receives more respect (sometimes adoration) than the self-made, self-sufficient man. The Declaration of Independence reflects and sanctifies the prevailing faith in the importance of the individual and his right to freedom and equality, goals which are often incorrectly assumed to be similar or at least complementary. The American hero is he who sets off on his own, makes his own way: Roger Williams, Daniel Boone, Andrew Jackson, Abraham Lincoln, Charles Lindbergh. Admirable though these men may have been, it remains arguable whether the free and unfettered individual (who has never, in ideal form, existed) actually constitutes a particularly welcome or admirable figure in any culture. Almost always he expresses himself in sharp opposition to certain established institutions: so Jackson, for example, fought the Seminoles and the Second Bank of the United States with equal fervour and with equal lack of regard for contractual guarantees. He knew what he was against, and that was enough.

The individual American, then, has customarily thought of himself as opposed to restricting institutions – opposed to the Church, or its hierarchy, or its dogmas; against the State, or the party, or the bureaucracy, or (most frequently) the majority; against the company, or its inhibiting organisation; against class, and against conformity. Such individualism hardly constitutes a local phenomenon; as Freud observed, men inevitably form civilisations, and then war with them. But the concept does have particular and unpleasant connections with the American experience, as Freud also remarked:

> The desire for freedom that makes itself felt in a human community may be a revolt against some existing injustice and so may prove favourable to a further development of civilization and remain compatible with it. But it may also have its origin (as it has in America) in the primitive roots of the personality, still un-

fettered by civilizing influences, and so become a source of anta-
gonism to culture.

In the United States, the cry for freedom has been directed not so
much against 'particular forms or demands of culture' as 'against
culture itself', against its limitations upon the freedom of the
individual.

Freedom, certainly, was what the early settlers of Massachusetts Bay were after – freedom from the corruptions of the English
Church, freedom to achieve political and economic and social
success outside the tight boundaries of the English class system.
These vexed and troubled Englishmen were excoriated in their
native land as 'turbulent and factious spirits', in status not gentlemen but tradesmen or lawyers, in religion insisting upon a cleaner
break with popery, in politics a sect, as James I had it, 'ever discontented with the present government and impatient to suffer
any superiority, which maketh their sect unable to be suffered in
any well-governed commonwealth'. In the passage across the
Atlantic, they believed themselves transformed, lifted by God out
of history and into a new Eden.

But they had of course brought their cultural baggage with
them. The founders of New England were seventeenth-century
Englishmen, and perhaps 90 per cent of their ideas and customs
were indistinguishable from those of other seventeenth-century
Englishmen. Based on the conviction that the universe was
orderly and hierarchical and that everyone should occupy his
allotted place in the Divine scheme, the system of Church and
civil government they established closely resembled the one which
they had left behind. In significant ways, however, the philosophy
behind the system was different, and in the differences lay the
origin of the eventual collapse of the Puritan commonwealth.
The settlers of New England bound themselves together by
voluntary covenants, for instance, into congregations; they believed that the conscience of the individual, if he were among the

elect, was the ultimate judge of right and wrong; they believed
that no elaborate apparatus should stand between God and man;
they believed that all were sinners but some might be saved by the
direct infusion of God's grace. As Perry Miller remarks, 'the
Puritan leaders were in grave danger of arousing a revolt against
themselves by their very own doctrines'.

The revolt was not long in coming. God, Mistress Anne
Hutchinson revealed, had told her directly that she was saved, so
that she and her followers no longer needed the comfort and
assurance of other members of the congregation; Roger Williams
insisted that each man might worship as he pleased and pay alle-
giance to whatever government he pleased. Both were banished.
Nathanael Ward, in *The Simple Cobbler of Aggawam* (1646), provided a plain-spoken reason for their banishment. It was part of
true religion, he observed, 'to be all like minded, of one accord'.
If the Antinomians called for liberty, let them 'have free Liberty
to keepe away from us, and . . . the sooner the better'. New
England, love it or leave it.

One year earlier, Governor John Winthrop defended himself
rather more elegantly against a suit brought by the citizens of
Hingham. Eighty-one men of the town protested that Winthrop
had made a decision that went clearly against the majority will, a
point the governor at once conceded. What was more, he acknowledged the possibility that he had made an error; after all, magi-
strates were but human. 'The great questions that have troubled
the country,' he observed, 'are about the authority of the magi-
strates and the liberty of the people.' But, Winthrop pointed out,
he had been called to his office by the very constituents who now
petitioned against him, and in so doing they were attempting to
break a solemn covenant. 'We account him a good servant, who
breaks not his covenant. The covenant between you and us is the
oath you have taken of us, which is to this purpose, that we shall
govern you and judge your causes by the rules of God's laws and
our own, according to our best skill.' He did not challenge the

people's right to elect their rulers, but maintained that once those rulers were elected they should be obeyed.

In this argument, Winthrop also revealed his famous views on the nature of liberty:

> There is a twofold liberty, natural (I mean as our nature is now corrupt) and civil or federal. The first is common to man with beasts and other creatures. By this, man, as he stands in relation to man simply, hath liberty to do what he lists; it is a liberty to evil as well as to good. This liberty is incompatible and inconsistent with authority, and cannot endure the least restraint of the most just authority. The exercise and maintaining of this liberty makes men grow more evil, and in time to be worse than brute beasts . . . The other kind of liberty I call civil or federal, it may also be termed moral, in reference to the covenant between God and man, in the moral law, and the polite covenants and constitutions amongst men themselves. This is the proper end and object of authority, and cannot subsist without it; and it is a liberty to that only which is good, just, and honest. This liberty you are to stand for, with the hazard . . . of your lives, if need be.

Whatever the merits of his argument, Winthrop's tone seems objectionable to the modern reader. He adopts the magisterial 'we', he instructs as from an eminence, he begs the question unmercifully. In 1645, however, this tone would not have seemed at all unusual, for Winthrop wrote in consonance with the Puritan notion that all good writing must teach, even sermonise. As a consequence, Puritan literature tends towards biography and autobiography designed to enlighten by example, or towards historical writing illuminating the sins of the past, or towards symbolism and allegory as devices of instruction. Thus, when a drunk blasphemes on one page of William Bradford's *Historie of Plimouth Plantation*, he is certain to be swept overboard on the next. Like his fellows, Bradford, for thirty years governor of the Plymouth colony, clearly regarded history as a series of cautionary tales.

Puritan poetry as well as prose was designed to convey a moral lesson. Michael Wigglesworth, in his best-selling *The Day of Doom* (1662), committed in thumping rhythms a long, didactic poem depicting in lurid detail the hellish fate awaiting those who did not prepare themselves for judgement. All 1,800 copies of the first edition sold within the year, numerous other editions followed, and schoolchildren were brought up on its 'premonitions of eternal combustion' well into the nineteenth century. Two much better poets of the time were Anne Bradstreet, whose private and often emotional poetry was filched from her to be published in England as *The Tenth Muse Lately Sprung Up in America* (1650), and Edward Taylor, a Puritan minister in Westfield whose metaphysical metaphors, which are quite as startling as any in John Donne or George Herbert, were finally discovered in the Yale University library to surface in *The Poetical Works of Edward Taylor* (1939):

> Who in this Bowling Alley bowld the Sun?

> In this sad state, Gods Tender Bowells run
> Out streams of Grace . . .

and of Christ as advocate,

> He'll plead thy Case, and not accept a Fee.
> He'll plead Sub Forma Pauperis for thee.

As so often in American letters – consider the case of Melville or of Emily Dickinson – the private, silent writer finally basks in the glow of recognition. Unlike Wigglesworth, neither Bradstreet nor Taylor set out to instruct their fellow New Englanders, but three centuries later Bradstreet's simple lyric, 'To my Dear and Loving Husband',

> If ever two were one, then surely we.
> If ever man were lov'd by wife, then thee.

and her sad one, 'Upon the Burning of our House', movingly evoke our sympathy, while Taylor's 'Preparatory Meditations', verses composed before delivering sermons, vividly convey his religious passion.

In prose far more than in poetry, however, the early New Englanders explored the themes which lie at the heart of American culture. No one document better illustrates the point than John Winthrop's distinction between natural and civil liberty, between the licence to behave like the brute beasts and the liberty to perform good, just, and honest acts. Believe as he did that all men are depraved through Adam's fall (though some may be arbitrarily saved), and there can be little quarrel with his conclusion that true liberty must be confined within the bounds of authority; this would seem to be the conclusion, often painfully arrived at, of such writers as Nathaniel Hawthorne, Herman Melville and the later Mark Twain. Believe on the other hand that men stand next to the angels, basically good and potentially perfectible, and Winthrop's discourse seems but another rationale for tyranny; this approximates to the view of such Transcendentalists as Emerson and Thoreau.

Men Better than Towns

Thomas Jefferson, the most philosophical of American statesmen, occupied a liberal position on the issue of the individual's relations with society. Like his colleague and friend James Madison, he acknowledged that government itself constituted 'the greatest of all reflections on human nature. If men were angels, no government would be necessary. If angels were to govern men, neither external nor internal controls on government would be necessary.' Government, then, could not be avoided, but Jefferson, fearing that it might oppress the individual, advocated as little government as possible. If those in power showed an inclination to tyranny, he proposed a violent remedy: 'The tree of liberty,' he observed, 'must be watered from time to time with the blood of patriots and tyrants.' Put to the test, Jefferson believed the rights of the individual, which he classically enunciated as 'life, liberty, and the pursuit of happiness', to be paramount:

> Of liberty then I would say, that, in the whole plentitude of its extent, it is unobstructed action according to our will, but rightful liberty is unobstructed action according to our will within limits drawn around us by the equal rights of others. I do not add 'within the limits of the law', because law is often the tyrant's will, and is always so when it violates the right of an individual.

The French aristocrat Alexis de Tocqueville, whose prophetic *Democracy of America* (1840) has been characterised as 'perhaps the greatest work ever written on one country by the citizen of another', took an opposite tack, describing individualism in the new nation as a sort of disease. 'Selfishness,' he wrote,

> ... blights the germ of all virtue: individualism, at first, only saps the virtues of public life; but in the long run it attacks and destroys all others and is at length absorbed in downright selfishness ... individualism is democratic origin, and threatens to spread in the same ratio as equality of condition.

In his little-read prose, the American poet Walt Whitman elaborated on one symptom of the disease which de Tocqueville, like Jefferson, detected – that is, the tendency to ignore one's obligations to other men and groups:

> One of the problems presented in America these times is, how to combine one's duty and policy as a member of associations, societies, brotherhoods or what not, and one's obligations to the State and Nation, with essential freedom as an individual personality, without which freedom a man cannot grow or expand, or be full, modern, heroic, democratic, American. With all the necessities and benefits of association (and the world cannot get along without it), the true nobility and satisfaction of a man consist in his thinking and acting for himself. The Problem, I say, is to combine the two, so as not to ignore either.

In the very first lines of his epic *Leaves of Grass* (1855), however, Whitman resolves the problem in typically Transcendental fashion:

> One's-self I sing, a simple separate person,
> Yet utter the word Democratic, the word En-Masse.

Confronted with the paradox, Whitman obliterates it simply by giving it expression, a device, along with hyperbole, which he probably learned from Emerson, the acknowledged leader of the Transcendental camp.

A term that defies easy analysis, Transcendentalism never represented a systematic philosophy and serves more conveniently as an historical than a substantive label. Its origins have been traced to the idealism of Kant and Fichte and Swedenborg, to Plato and Plotinus, to the Upanishads, to the English romanticism of Coleridge and Wordsworth, and to a substantial native tradition as well. Its effects were to put mystery back into religion, to exalt the individual over society, and to elevate man, 'a god in ruins', nearly to the stature of the angels. The movement also had a location: in Concord, Massachusetts, slightly west and a good deal to the left of Boston, and a company of practitioners who included Emerson and Thoreau, Amos Bronson Alcott, Margaret Fuller, William Ellery Channing and Jones Very.

In two of his best-known essays, 'The American Scholar' (1837) and 'Self-Reliance' (1841), Emerson spelt out his radical individualism in a series of memorable aphorisms. He must have taken pleasure in delivering, on 31 August 1837, his shocking views on what he called 'Man Thinking' to the newly chosen scholars of Harvard's Phi Beta Kappa chapter. For one thing, he had not been himself honoured as an undergraduate by selection to the prestigious academic fraternity; for another, in his audience that day sat Oliver Wendell Holmes, who later called Emerson's address the nation's 'intellectual declaration of independence';

James Russell Lowell, who referred to the speech as 'an event without any former parallel in our literary annals'; Thoreau, come from Concord to hear his neighbour and mentor; the brightest students of American's oldest college, and finally the Harvard professors themselves, whose ears must have burned in outrage as the young ex-Unitarian minister on the platform (all the Emersons had been clergymen until Waldo came along) argued their redundancy.

'We have listened too long to the courtly muses of Europe,' Emerson said. The past has little to teach us: 'Meek young men grow up in libraries, believing it their duty to accept the views which Cicero, which Locke, which Bacon, have given; forgetful that Cicero, Locke, and Bacon were only young men in libraries when they wrote these books.' We might learn far more through communion with nature: 'Books are for the scholar's idle times.' Above all, he advised his young auditors, be a whole man, a Man Thinking, not a man compartmentalised into roles imposed by society. 'The priest becomes a form; the attorney a statute book' (so much for the ministers and lawyers in the hall). 'The state of society is one in which the members have suffered amputation from the trunk, and strut about so many walking monsters – a good finger, a neck, a stomach, an elbow, but never a man.' The solution is independence. 'We will walk on our own feet; we will work with our own hands; we will speak our own minds . . . The world is nothing, the man is all.'

'Self-Reliance', which enlarges on the same theme, is the most powerful statement for individualism in American literature. Here Emerson argued that each man possesses the potential for genius, indeed, that 'in every work of genius we recognise our own rejected thoughts', rejected because we lack the courage to believe that what is true for us 'is true for all men'. It follows that we should trust ourselves alone: 'Insist on yourself; never imitate,' for, 'No greater men are now than ever were.' Do not be ruled by the law: 'No law can be sacred to me but that of my nature.' Forget the restrictions of the Church: 'Nothing is at last sacred but the integrity of your own mind.' Do not fret over what others may think: 'Whoso would be a man, must be a nonconformist.' If one contradicts oneself, never mind: 'A foolish consistency is the hobgoblin of little minds, adored by little statesmen and philosophers and divines.'

In brief, we should liberate ourselves from the restrictions of society, which has made us 'afraid of truth, afraid of death, and afraid of each other'. Only the individual can improve. 'Society never advances. It recedes as fast on one side as it gains on the other.' Besides, 'Society everywhere is in conspiracy against the manhood of every one of its members.' We must trust ourselves. 'Is not a man better than a town?'

Emerson's greatest disciple, Thoreau, was half a generation younger than the acknowledged dean of American letters whose patronage he enjoyed, whose house he lived in for a time, and whose accomplishments he eventually outstripped. If Emerson was cold, Thoreau achieved social frigidity. 'I find it wholesome,' he announces, 'to be alone the greater part of the time. To be in company, even with the best, is soon wearisome and dissipating. I love to be alone.' He would not talk so much about himself, he ingenuously confessed, if there were anybody else whom he knew as well. Afflicted with perversity ('What demon possessed me that I behaved so well?'), nothing was more typical of the man than his decision to reverse the names bequeathed to him by his parents (he was born David Henry Thoreau). He never married, as a seeming ne'er-do-well served as the butt of village jokes, and took his eventual revenge by writing one of the world's great journals, *Walden*.

As a stylist Thoreau had the gift of bringing basic Transcendental ideas immediately to life. 'Traveling,' Emerson observed, 'is a fool's paradise.' With Thoreau, the generalisation becomes personalised – 'I have traveled a good deal in Concord' – and dramatised – 'It is not worth the while to go round the world to count the cats in Zanzibar.' Hyperbole, an occasional device with Emerson, became his disciple's customary mode of expression. As scholars have demonstrated, although Thoreau preached back-to-nature, he cut off very few of his ties when he went to the woods. Yet one should not complain too much of *Walden*'s disregard for the truth; the book is after all a work of the imagination, exaggeration is its consistent technique, and in its pages young people, particularly, have found inspiration to simplify and economise their existence, aware that 'the possibilities of the close at hand wait in a constant nick of time for the perception of anyone anywhere'. In his advocacy of individualism, Thoreau denied that he wanted anyone to follow his example. 'I would not have anyone adopt my mode of living on any account,' he wrote, 'for . . . I desire that there may be as many different persons in the world as possible; but I would have each one be very careful to find out and pursue his own way, and not his father's or his mother's or his neighbor's instead.' That each person should find 'his own way' represented Thoreau's eternal lesson and, deny it as vigorously as he liked, he none the less indulged his schoolteacher's instincts by instructing through example.

Consider the night he spent in Concord jail. Outraged by the Mexican War and by the continuance of Negro slavery, he declined to pay his taxes and was for the offence incarcerated for one night; a popular though apocryphal anecdote has Emerson passing by the jail next morning and inquiring of his imprisoned friend, 'Why, Henry, what are you doing in there?' which enabled Thoreau to riposte, 'Why, Waldo, what are you doing out there?' The imprisonment is memorialised in Thoreau's influential essay 'Civil Disobedience' (1849), where he proclaimed the superiority of the individual to his government. Ideally, we should have no government at all, he argued, and in time perhaps the State would come 'to recognize the individual as a higher and independent power, from which all its own power and authority are derived', and act accordingly. Meanwhile, he would do what he could to harass and annoy its operation, confident that there was 'but little virtue in the action of masses of men', that any man 'more right than his neighbors constitutes a majority of one', that

> . . . if one thousand, if one hundred, if ten men whom I could name, – if ten honest men only, – ay, if one honest man, in this State of Massachusetts, ceasing to hold slaves, were actually to withdraw from this copartnership, and be locked up in the county jail therefor, it would be the abolition of slavery in America.

'Civil Disobedience' is a powerful plea for anarchy, based on the deep conviction that each person's individual conscience formed the only criterion of what is right and just. Few American writers, after the heyday of Transcendentalism, were able to agree with him, a circumstance that would not have troubled Thoreau for one moment.

The Community of Sinners

Hawthorne and Melville, the two most distinguished writers of fiction in the mid-nineteenth-century period usually called the American Renaissance, shared a distaste for what seemed to them the easy optimism of the Transcendentalists. In the world posited by Emerson and Thoreau, they decided, there was but little room for tragedy. Emerson's essay 'The Tragic' (1844) demonstrates one of the reasons why this was so: his assumption that good predominates over evil. Acknowledging the existence of 'the House of Pain', for 'as the salt sea covers more than two thirds of the surface of the globe, so sorrow encroaches on man in felicity', Emerson none the less insists that one normally lives on the felicitous land. Further, no man is exposed to undue suffering, since 'Nature proportions her defense to the assault' and pain 'is so distributed as not to destroy. That which would rend you, falls on tougher textures.'

It follows, in Emerson's argument, that he who says he suffers does not suffer. A man should remain tranquil, 'rarely giving way to extreme emotion of joy or grief', but those who are tragedy-prone 'treat trifles with a tragic air. This is not beautiful. Could they not lay a rod or two of stone wall, and work off this super-abundant irritability.' (Emerson, clearly, felt an impatience with anyone who sensed the power of darkness, who communicated that 'blackness, ten times more black' that Melville so admired in Hawthorne.) Certainly, tragedy might produce a soft and sweet sorrow, but this was only art, whereas 'higher still than the acti-vities of art', in his mystical formulation, lay 'the intellect in its purity, and the moral sense in its purity', which 'are not distin-guished from each other, and . . . ravish us into a region whereinto these passionate clouds of sorrow cannot rise'.

If men were basically good, the Transcendentalists reasoned, there need be no conflict between the individual and society. Each person should listen to the different drummer within who rapped out his private cadence, and if he marched out of step with his fellows, so be it – no harm would come. But tragedy cannot take place except in the context of a given social order, in conflict with others. Without Iago and Venice, *Othello* would be merely bathos; without Claudius and Denmark, *Hamlet* no more than a histrionic bloodbath. The same is true of Hester Prynne and Boston, Ahab and the whaling community.

Not surprisingly, then, both Hawthorne and Melville employed satirical approaches to dissociate themselves from Emersonian optimism. Melville's *The Confidence-Man*, in fact, is a full-length variation on the theme of human gullibility, while his hapless Bartleby in 'Bartleby the Scrivener' (1853), a lawyer's copy clerk who recalcitrantly 'prefers not' to do whatever is asked of him and finally dies in prison after refusing the offer of food, bears a noticeable resemblance to the Thoreau of 'Civil Disobedience'. Hawthorne's 'The Celestial Railroad', however, constitutes the most effective satire of all.

In another story by Hawthorne, 'Earth's Holocaust', the characters attempt to achieve purity by throwing all emblems of corrupt institutions into a massive bonfire. The reformers burn everything – books, titles, money, liquor, tobacco – in a procedure reminiscent of *Walden*'s injunction to 'simplify, simplify', but the project ends in failure, for, as the devil assures the morose drunk, thief, murderer and hangman, the reformers have forgotten one item which will ensure a return of evil. They have not burned the human heart, 'the little yet boundless sphere wherein existed the original wrong of which the crime and misery of the outward world were merely types'. 'Earth's Holocaust' appeared in *Mosses from an Old Manse* (1846), the Manse in the title referring to a Concord home owned by Emerson and occupied by the Hawthornes from 1842 to 1846. The story provides whatever evidence is needed that the two writers, who lived for a while at the opposite ends of Concord, Massachusetts, remain forever at the opposite poles of American literature. 'Nathaniel Hawthorne's reputation as a writer,' so the unsympathetic Emerson observed, 'is a very pleasing fact, because his writing is not good for anything, and this is a tribute to the man.'

The Scarlet Letter intricately examines the tension that arises, in seventeenth-century Boston, between the competing drives of individual passion and community order. In its imagery, the novel contrasts the wild rose of nature with the black flower of Puritan civilisation, and apparently opts in favour of civilisation. Not that the stern Puritans of Boston emerge as sainted beings, for in visiting an awful penance upon Hester they deny their own sinfulness, and thus, for Hawthorne, their humanity. All men are sinners, and the only salvation lies in admitting membership in a flawed brotherhood. Thus, after the forest scene, Dimmesdale has an intimation that if he does flee his Boston, his ministry, and his responsibilities, he will have committed himself to the service of the devil. Perhaps the lovers will not be reunited in another world, but Dimmesdale dies happily relieved of his burden of false innocence. 'Reunion after isolation,' as Hyatt Waggoner wrote, 'came in Hawthorne's works to be both a symbol of and a literal means to salvation. No writer has ever placed a higher value on communion and community.'

And yet Hawthorne invests most of the book's imagery and rhetoric on the side of escape from the repressive community. 'What we did,' Hester tells Dimmesdale, 'had a consecration of its own,' and it is difficult, considering the hypocrisy of the leading Puritans and the satanic machinations of Roger Chillingworth, Hester's husband who re-emerges in the guise of the black man of the forest, not to share the view that at the very least the lovers have been more sinned against than sinning. As D. H. Lawrence put it, all the classic American writers (he enumerates Hawthorne, Poe, Longfellow, Emerson, Melville) affirmed 'the old morality' with their heads while undermining it with their hearts:

> Therefore they give tight mental allegiance to a morality which all their passion goes to destroy. Hence the duplicity which is the fatal flaw in them, most fatal in the most perfect American work of art, *The Scarlet Letter*. Tight mental allegiance given to a morality which the passional self repudiates. [See below, Chapter 5, pp. 166–7.]

Certainly a similar sort of duplicity operates in Melville's masterpiece, *Moby-Dick*, whose protagonist, Captain Ahab, is a 'grand ungodly godlike man' so fixated on the capture of the White Whale that he takes a shipload of men down to the depths with him. Ahab exerts a charismatic effect upon the crew, expressing himself with the eloquence of a Shakespearean tragic hero, and it is impossible not to admire him. Yet at the same time Melville's hero also serves as a terrifying symbol of destructive individualism. Not only does Ahab possess a damning hubris; he – and those about him – are also victimised by his extreme self-reliance.

Through incident and metaphor Melville illustrates the need for community. As the *Pequod* roams the seas in pursuit of Moby

Dick, for example, she encounters nine other whaling ships; normally, these 'gams' provide an opportunity for exchange of news and convivial conversation among men who are at sea for as long as three years. But the single-minded Ahab puts only one question to passing ships, 'Hast seen the White Whale?' and if the response is negative, will not pause in his mad pursuit to enjoy the benefit of fellowship.

The financial imagery of *Moby-Dick* underscores the message. There are places in the novel where Melville takes a humorous stance towards dollar fiends, and there are others where he regards materialism with satirical bitterness. But there are also instances where Melville uses imagery from the world of corporate finance to suggest the high values of brotherhood and community in a world torn asunder by the heedless individualism of Captain Ahab.

Ahab is of course a man apart, a man unlike other men, very nearly a superman. He is keenly aware of his *distinctness*, his separation from his fellow man. Melville makes the point in Ahab's reflection on the carpenter who has made him an ivory leg: 'Here I am, proud as a Greek god, and yet standing debtor to this blockhead for a bone to stand on! Cursed be that mortal inter-indebtedness which will not do away with ledgers. I would be free as air; and I'm down in the whole world's books.' This passage tells a great deal about Ahab. It demonstrates his scornful attitude towards those lesser beings, blockheads, who jointly occupy the world with him. It indicates his perception that free will, even when exercised by so strong a man as himself, is not likely to be the only or final determinant of events. Most of all, though, the passage represents Ahab's realisation of the community of mankind. Men are terrible blockheads, he thinks, and yet he cannot do without them. In fact, he owes them something; and it is the debtor's state, being down 'in the whole world's books', that tries and burdens him. Ahab struggles to be free, to escape his debts, but only succeeds in proving mankind's inter-indebtedness by taking his men down with him.

Ahab probably uses terminology from the world of accounting – 'ledgers' and 'books' – with a measure of scorn. But Melville obviously does not advocate Ahab's individualistic hubris; in several other instances, the author employs financial imagery to carry the idea of community, without any hint of irony. One particular financial relationship, in fact, is depicted as natural and wholesome, not in the least as artificial. The harpooner Queequeg fishes a drowning sailor out of the sea, and afterwards reflects (so it seems to Ishmael) that, 'It's a mutual, joint-stock world, in all meridians. We cannibals must help these Christians.' The same metaphor is repeated in the chapter concerning the monkey-rope. Ishmael on board ship and Queequeg in the ocean are attached at opposite ends of the monkey-rope, and Ishmael observes that

> . . . my own individuality was now merged in a joint-stock company of two; that my free will had received a mortal wound; and that another's mistake or misfortune might plunge innocent me into unmerited disaster and death . . . I saw this situation of mine was the precise situation of every mortal that breathes; only, in most cases, he, one way or other, has this Siamese connexion with a plurality of other mortals.

Melville invented the idea of linking two men by the monkey-rope, well knowing that such a ligature was not customary on whale ships. This union of Queequeg and Ishmael fits into the author's affirmation of brotherhood and prepares the way for Ahab's most damning blasphemy – his cursing of 'mortal inter-indebtedness'. The monkey-rope connotes mutual danger as well as mutual support: if Queequeg slips, he will bring Ishmael tumbling after him. In this way, this incident prepares for the disastrous end of the *Pequod*, when Ahab brings devastation to all but one on board. The joint-stock company image represents the community of mankind.

Radical Innocents

When Ernest Hemingway commented that all 'modern American literature comes from one book by Mark Twain called *Huckleberry Finn*,' one thing he surely had in mind was Twain's treatment of the theme of innocence. The *Bildungsroman*, the coming-of-age novel, constitutes a sub-genre in all literatures, but there is a measurable distance between, say, Tom Jones and Julian Sorel and such protagonists as Huck Finn and Billy Budd. By contrast with their European cousins, American youths are practically sheathed against experience by their extraordinary naïveté. Significantly, two recent and distinguished books on American literature bear titles reflecting this distinction: Tony Tanner's *The Reign of Wonder* and Ihab Hassan's *Radical Innocence*.

In hitting upon this theme and entrusting his story to the honest vernacular of his boy-hero, Twain wrote what remains the finest portrait of radical innocence in American literature. Huck's 'adventures', like those of such subsequent voyaging innocents as Hemingway's Nick Adams and J. D. Salinger's Holden Caulfield, are traumatic and tremendous. Huck matures enormously on the trip downriver. He achieves a dignity which sets him apart from the cowardly riff-raff, the bloodthirsty aristocrats, and the just plain nasty folks of the river towns. He is a better person than they are, because he has learned to listen to the dictates of his sound heart and ignore the voice of his corrupt social conscience. But his emotions are stripped raw by his journey, and in the end he heads off alone, like Nick Adams and Frederic Henry, safeguarding making his separate peace in a retreat from sensibility.

Huck Finn originally promises not to 'tell on' Jim out of curiosity: he wants to know how and why Jim has run away. It is extremely hard for Huck to keep his vow, which conflicts with conventional morality. Jim is, after all, 'Miss Watson's nigger', running away from his owner. In helping him escape, Huck behaves like a 'low down Abolitionist', that is, like a thief. Some idyllic days and nights slide by on the raft, but Huck's conscience, formed when coming of age in St Petersburg, will not let him alone for long. The thought of being close to freedom makes Jim 'all over trembly and feverish', and that kind of talk makes Huck shiver, too. What troubles him is that he shares the town's belief in the sanctity of property:

> ... I begun to get it through my head that he *was* most free – and who was to blame for it? Why, *me*. I couldn't get that out of my conscience, no how nor no way ... Here was this nigger which I had as good as helped to run away, coming out flat-footed and saying he would steal his children – children that belonged to a man I didn't even know; a man that hadn't ever done me no harm.

As the trip progresses, Jim's loyalty and kindness soften the strength of Huck's materialistic faith. So do the tears of the Wilks girls when the 'king' and 'duke' sell their male slaves away from their families. But Huck does not repudiate the notion that Negroes are property until he elects to suffer the tortures of the damned rather than to betray Jim. Huck refuses to place property rights above human rights, and so separates himself from the good citizens of the South. *That* kind of 'sivilizing' he must escape, even if it means lighting out for the territory alone.

But the innocence he tries to preserve by escaping is a fragile thing, menaced not only by society but by Pap and Pap's attitude towards Negroes. The vigour of his language ('a prowling, thieving, infernal, white-shirted free nigger') makes it clear that Pap recognises a form of humanity in the Negro. But he obviously considers 'niggers' below himself in status. In fact, Huck's father displays the traditional unwillingness of the poor white to regard members of the coloured race as equals. Other whites constantly remind Pap of *his* inferiority, and his ego desperately needs someone to feel superior to. He is outraged when he discovers a Negro allowed to vote:

I was just about to go and vote, myself, if I warn't too drunk to get there; but when they told me there was a State in this country where they'd let that nigger vote, I drawed out. I says I'll never vote agin. Them's the very words I said; they all heard me; and the country may rot for all me – I'll never vote agin as long as I live.

In the course of their journey, Huck Finn succeeds in learning to think of Jim as something more than a plaything, or a mere piece of property, but Pap's example is too strong to overcome. He can never accept Jim as his equal, because he is a Negro. The persistence of this attitude explains the otherwise startling brutality of his dialogue with Aunt Sally. Huck invents an accident aboard ship to explain his late arrival at the Phelps farm:

'We blowed out a cylinder-head.'
'Good gracious! anybody hurt?'
'No'm. Killed a nigger.'
'Well, it's lucky, because sometimes people do get hurt.'

Huck's casual remark helps to give his story verisimilitude; as he has just remarked, Providence 'put the right words' in his mouth when he needed them. A proficient liar, Huck proposes the insignificance of 'niggers' partly because he knows that he is appealing to Aunt Sally's view and because it is the sort of thing that he, now masquerading as Tom Sawyer, would be expected to say. Still, Huck's words come as a shock, immediately following his decision to go to hell on Jim's behalf. Mark Twain cannot have been unaware of this shock, and he must have intended to suggest that Huck had not shed his sense of superiority. To underline the point, Twain permits Huck to pay Jim a final compliment. Jim has agreed to stay with Tom, his now-wounded tormentor, until a doctor can be found. Huck reflects on this act of unselfishness, which seems likely to cost Jim his chance of escape: 'I knowed he was white inside, and I reckoned he'd say what he did say ...' Huck has been moved by Jim's generosity, but the highest compliment he can pay him is to propose that he is 'white inside'. The irony is powerful, for the reader cannot have forgotten how badly almost every white man in the book has behaved.

Despite efforts to 'sivilize' him, Huck Finn is an outcast like his father before him. The difference is that Huck rejects society, whereas society had rejected Pap. Huck has made his choice. He has sloughed aside conventional morality, and he wants nothing more to do with Tom Sawyer's self-dramatisations. Rejecting society, he heads for the territory quite alone.

If anything, the orphaned Billy Budd had still fewer ties to society than Huck Finn. Written in Melville's last years and published posthumously in 1924, *Billy Budd* is usually interpreted in allegorical terms. Impressed and brought aboard the British man-of-war, HMS *Indomitable*, soon after the Nore Mutiny, Billy Budd symbolises absolute innocence, resembling Christ in his cheerful peace-making and Adam before the fall in his prelapsarian ignorance of evil. The master-of-arms aboard the ship, James Claggart, is irrationally driven (as the symbol of evil) to confront and destroy this almost perfect seaman. He falsely accuses Billy of fomenting mutiny, and the young innocent, unable because of his single fault of stammering to defend himself against the accusation, involuntarily strikes a blow which kills Claggart. It rests with Captain Vere to adjudicate the matter, and he agonisingly determines that Billy, though 'an angel of God', must hang as an example to the fleet: in difficult times, hard measures are required. The young sailor calls out 'God bless Captain Vere' as he goes to his death, and discipline is restored on board.

Billy Budd is by no means an unambiguous story, and critical battles rage over its interpretation. Supporters of the view that the short novel represents Melville's 'testament of acceptance' point to the last words of the innocent sailor as a clinching argument; those who regard the tale contrarily as a 'testament of resistance' emphasise that the blessing comes from a totally ignorant source, and that if Billy Budd forgives his hangman there are sufficient reasons why others should not condone the death of any individual on the expedient grounds of the greatest good for the greatest number. The dispute apparently defies resolution, and it may be that Melville left both options open. In any case, the ambiguity only adds to the fascination of the tale.

Moreover, the confrontation of good and evil in *Billy Budd* carries an archetypal appeal which may account for the frequent conversion of Melville's short novel into other literary forms. Benjamin Britten composed a distinguished opera on this theme, Louis O. Coxe and Robert Chapman wrote a successful play (and later motion picture), and W. H. Auden in his poem 'Herman Melville' took *Billy Budd* as evidence that late in life Melville 'sailed into an extraordinary mildness' where he finally saw the simple and inevitable truth:

> Evil is unspectacular and always human,
> And shares our bed and eats at our own table,
> And we are introduced to Goodness every day,
> Even in drawing rooms among a crowd of faults;
> He has a name like Billy and is almost perfect
> But wears a stammer like a decoration;
> And every time they meet the same thing has to happen;
> It is the Evil that is helpless like a lover
> And has to pick a quarrel and succeeds
> And both are openly destroyed before our eyes.

But it is not only the evil Claggart who is helpless; the good Billy Budd is equally unable to control his fate, and falls victim to the judgement of a world he never made.

Of Men as Mice

In the late nineteenth and early twentieth centuries, American writers consistently challenged the prevailing philosophy of social Darwinism. As enunciated by Herbert Spencer, this creed stressed that socially as well as biologically the species was evolving towards higher forms. Progress, then, was inevitable (though politicians of the Progressive era believed the process could be helped along by legislation), and serious writers were distressed by the implication that there was little any individual could do to speed up – or slow down – this evolutionary engine. Some of these writers, notably the ageing and embittered Mark Twain, questioned whether mankind had progressed at all.

In addition to *A Connecticut Yankee in King Arthur's Court* two of the best long stories of Twain's last years demonstrate his deepening misanthropy. The title character of 'The Man that Corrupted Hadleyburg' (1900), for example, achieves his goal simply by relying on the basic dishonesty of individuals living in a town that prided itself on its honesty. The trouble with Hadleyburg, and its citizens, is that they had never put their much-advertised honesty to the test. Even as children, the townspeople had been indoctrinated in the importance of honesty: '... it's been one everlasting training and training and training in honesty – honesty shielded, from the very cradle, against every possible temptation, and so it's *artificial* honesty, and weak as water when temptation comes . . .' Given the opportunity to practice dishonesty without being detected (so the leading citizens think), each of them succumbs to greed and tries to lie his way into money he has not earned. Like the Puritan John Milton, Twain cannot praise 'a fugitive and cloistered virtue'. Like the Puritan John Winthrop, Twain assumes the innate dishonesty of the individual, and concludes that virtue can only be derived from social restraints.

The Mysterious Stranger, published posthumously in 1916, provides a still darker picture of the nature of man. A young angel named Satan descends upon Eseldorf, a medieval Austrian town, forms a friendship with several young boys of the town, and begins to instruct them in his superior knowledge. Their race, he tells the boys, is made up of sheep who follow the noisiest minority; thus when a woman is publicly punished in the centre of town, all sixty-eight people there cast a stone, though sixty-two of them do so with revulsion in their hearts. Such brutality, he explains, is a consequence of 'a large defect in your race – the individual's distrust of his neighbor, and his desire, for safety's or comfort's sake, to stand well in his neighbor's eye'.

Lest it be assumed that the individual might remedy such behaviour, Satan, who is invested with supernatural powers, explains that there is no such thing as free will: 'a child's first act knocks over the initial brick, and the rest will follow inexorably'. No one can alter the chain of events. Men may think that they have a choice of actions, but 'no man ever does drop a link – the thing has never happened! Even when he is trying to make up his mind . . . that itself is a link, an act, and has its proper place in his chain . . .' Twain's is a latter-day, irreligious determinism, however, for God does not preordain matters – they are shaped by each man's circumstances and environment. In such a universe, any individual's pretensions to importance are laughable when they are not contemptible.

The insignificance of the individual formed a central plank in the philosophy of Stephen Crane, whose short but brilliant career produced one exceptional novel and a number of first-rate short stories. Unlike Twain, however, Crane did not abandon all hope for the human race; his characters can be saved, and the path they must follow to their salvation very much resembles that of Nathaniel Hawthorne. Henry Fleming of *The Red Badge of Courage* breaks and runs on the first day of his first battle, but later returns to his companions and redeems himself by submerging his overweening sense of personal importance in the goals of the group. This same process – enlightenment as to one's own insignificance, followed by a 'return to the regiment' and final dignity – occurs frequently in Crane's writing.

In 'The Open Boat' (1897), for example, Crane recasts in fictional form his own experience as survivor of a shipwreck. Adrift in a violent sea in a small boat, the correspondent who is Crane's spokesman is first inclined to rage against his plight: 'When it occurs to a man that nature does not regard him as important, and that she feels that she would not maim the universe by disposing of him, he at first wishes to throw bricks at the temple, and hates deeply the fact that there are no bricks and no temples.' Next, the desperate man may turn to prayer, feeling 'perhaps, the desire to confront a personification and indulge in pleas, bowed to one knee and with hands supplicant, saying, "Yes, but I love myself." ' Still later, as the chances for survival seem to dim, a man may

> . . . see the innumerable flaws of his life, and have them taste wickedly in his mind, and wish for another chance. A distinction between right and wrong seems absurdly clear to him, then, in this new ignorance of the grave-edge, and he understands that if he were given another opportunity he would mend his conduct and his words, and be better and brighter during an introduction or at a tea.

The characteristic irony of the last clause underlines Crane's point: in deepest misfortune man rages, then prays, then begs for another chance, but in each case he stupidly overestimates his own importance. One of Crane's poems neatly sums up the case:

> A man said to the universe:
> 'Sir, I exist!'
> 'However,' replied the universe,
> 'The fact has not created in me
> A sense of obligation.'

Finally, however, the correspondent abandons his solipsistic self-regard, and throws all his energies into a joint effort with the other shipwrecked men, suddenly aware of a brotherhood, a comradeship that he 'knew even at the time was the best experience of his life'. Both the correspondent and Henry Fleming learn of their own human weakness and insignificance, both learn that nature is amoral, both learn the lesson of brotherhood, and both end by making a commitment to the group. This, Stephen Crane believed, is what man must do to be saved.

Though Crane was an avowed follower of Howells's brand of realism and Garland's creed of veritism, he always remained a romantic in his insistence that the individual did have alternatives and could, with the gift of enlightenment, choose the right course. For Crane as for many other American writers at the turn of the century, French naturalism exerted a powerful appeal. Inheritors of the Calvinist tradition, they found congenial the naturalistic idea that men were depraved and their fate predetermined. Certainly, in the society around them – and especially in the sorry spectacle of the robber barons – they found sufficient evidence to support such a view.

But naturalism, like social Darwinism, never took deep root in American fiction, and for the same reason: the pessimistic philosophy, like the optimistic one, so devalued and limited the scope of individual action as to be repellent to writers who were descendants of Roger Williams as well as John Winthrop, Emerson as well as Hawthorne. The consequence was that even men like London and Norris, whose *McTeague* consciously appropriates the techniques of Émile Zola, were unable to achieve the objectivity of approach, the clinical view of mankind, that represented the hallmark of naturalism. With such writers, romanticism consistently impinged on realism. Thus *Martin Eden* (1909), London's most autobiographical novel, emerges as a kind of romance of naturalism. On the one hand, the author's detailed reproduction of segments of life in Oakland, California, and his rhetorical insistence that vast natural forces were at work determining human actions fit the naturalistic code. On the other hand, however, London's protagonist is depicted as a kind of superman who is somehow exempted from those inevitable and impersonal rules which govern the rest of the universe. 'As for myself,' he announces in the first person, 'I am an individualist.'

Escaping History

The early settlers of New England emigrated to America to escape from history, or at least from Church and Crown, English institutions they regarded as damnably corrupt. Their distaste for particular English institutions translated itself, in the course of time, into a national antipathy toward all institutions both for the restraints they imposed on the individual and for their presumed inherent corruptness. (Americans expect the worst from their politicians, which helps to explain a tolerance for chicanery in high places which is remarkable to other lands.) The Founding Fathers, given the task of organising a new nation, therefore attempted to limit the scope of government as much as possible, using the doctrine of separation of powers to preclude any one branch gaining excessive control.

America, then, has proved an extremely poor climate for the growth not only of political and religious but of any and all institutions. In his biography of Hawthorne, Henry James presented this bill of particulars against his native land, which lacked almost all 'items of high civilization':

> No State . . . No sovereign, no court, no personal loyalty, no aristocracy, no church, no clergy, no army, no diplomatic service, no country gentlemen, no palaces, no castles, nor manors, nor old country houses, no parsonages, nor thatched cottages, nor ivied ruins; no great universities nor public schools – no Oxford, nor Eton, nor Harrow; no literature, no novels, no museums, no pictures, no political society, no sporting class – no Epsom nor Ascot! . . . The natural remark, in the light of such an indictment, would be that if these things are left out, everything is left out.

His friend Howells, an occasional overseas traveller but not an expatriate like James, disagreed: despite all these omissions there remained 'simply the whole of human life' – that is, the life of the individual. As far as the novel was concerned, James was right and Howells wrong, for the very stuff of the European novel has been man's inescapable life in society, while classic American novels, by way of contrast, 'have dealt not so much with the lives of men in society as with the life of solitary man' alienated and isolated and finally opting out of social entanglements.

Above all, the American writer has never felt free to satirise his institutions, which pose too great a threat to his independence to be made light of. Rather self-consciously, he has tried instead to define the entire vast nation, and to sum it up as rather less important than any one individual – say, Walt Whitman – simultaneously in love with and hating the restrictions of an abstraction called America. In popular as in canonical literature, the hero takes on an epic, mythic quality, and earns admiration in proportion to his ability to break through social boundaries and establish his self-sufficiency.

Nowhere is this proclivity more evident than in the figure of the frontiersman, path-finder, trail-blazer, pioneer, mountain man, and – on television and in the pulp magazines – seemingly in his final form, the cowboy. Natty Bumppo of Cooper's immensely popular Leatherstocking Tales possesses many of the same woodsman's skills as Robin Hood, but he leads no band of followers. As the introduction to the autobiography of Davy Crockett, himself an embodiment of the pioneer image, proudly comments:

> No other age or time could have produced his like. Europe colonized in clans or tribes; American immigration was individual. Men like [Daniel] Boone and Crockett moved alone, hunted alone, planted alone, and harvested alone – only in time of war against the savage did they come together in fellowship and active cooperation. To have a neighbor within six miles was helpful; to have one within sound of an axe was a nuisance.

The fact that this is nonsense, that even Crockett took his legend and used it for political profit, hardly matters. The myth persists, so that Ernest Hemingway, for example, bred in the suburbs, created for himself certain attractive if wholly fictious solitary adventures in the Michigan wilderness; while each night contemporary American children marvel at the exploits of the ruggedly individualistic cowboy who, if he ever lived, has certainly been dead for several generations.

On the water and in the air as well as on land, the solitary pioneer continues to command the nation's admiration. A roster of such paragons might begin with the Mississippi river pilot, about whose existence Twain wrote ecstatically in *Life on the Mississippi* (1883):

> If I have seemed to love my subject, it is no surprising thing, for I loved the profession far better than any I have followed since, and I took a measureless pride in it. The reason is plain; a pilot, in those days, was the only unfettered and entirely independent human being that lived in the earth. Kings are but the hampered servants of parliament and the people; parliaments sit in chains forged by their constituency; the editor of a newspaper cannot be independent, but must work with one hand tied behind him by party and patrons, and be content to utter only half or two-thirds of his mind; no clergyman is a free man and may speak the whole truth, regardless of his parish's opinions; writers of all kinds are manacled servants of the public . . . In truth, every man and woman and child has a master, and worries and frets in servitude; but, in the day I write of, the Mississippi pilot had *none*.

Twain's approach is nostalgic, and the implication clear that we shall not see the pilot's like again, but he reckoned without yet another frontier – the sky.

When Neil Armstrong in his awkward garb stepped onto the moon, the massive United States space programme reached its moment of fulfilment and simultaneously its glamour began to fade. Certainly, it was magnificent to see the fuzzy pictures of one man standing on the moon, but no one could be under the illusion that Armstrong had done it alone. There were, after all, his two companions on the flight (though their names have all but faded from memory), and the intrepid voyager's historic words, which must have been written by a public relations man with little sense of American mythology, placed the emphasis not on the individual but on the mass: he was taking, Armstrong intoned, 'one small step for a man, one giant step for mankind'.

Perhaps what this means is that contemporary life is so complicated, so technologically complex that one can no longer credit the possibility of individual heroics. If that is true, the last of the epic American pioneers may turn out to have been the taciturn young Minnesotan, Charles Lindbergh, whose solo flight across the Atlantic in 1927 inspired the whole nation to idolatry. Though the pilot himself never said 'I', but always 'we', in referring to his pace-setting flight, the American public celebrated him as a 'lone eagle', and Teddy Roosevelt identified him as the 'lineal descendant' of men like Crockett and Boone who had 'played a lone hand' and won the pot. The suggestion was that America's glory lay somewhere in the past, the lesson of Lindbergh's accomplishment that the nation must look back to a finer, more individualistic time for its guidance.

Perhaps the expatriated James, however, best characterised the pitfalls inherent in American individualism. In a conversation with the worldly Madame Merle, the heroine of *The Portrait of a Lady* (whose name, Isabel Archer, suggesting both the Spanish queen whose patronage led to the discovery of the New World and the chaste Diana of mythology, could hardly have been better constructed), asserts that she cares nothing about the house of her future husband, Gilbert Osmond. Madame Merle maintains that 'every human being has his shell' which must be taken into account, that, 'There's no such thing as an isolated man or woman; we're each of us made up of some cluster of appurtenances . . . one's house, one's furniture, one's garments, the books one reads, the company one keeps – these things are all expressive.' Isabel takes an exactly opposite tack, remarking that 'nothing that belongs to me is any measure of me; everything's on the contrary a limit, a barrier, and a perfectly arbitrary one'. As Tony Tanner observes, Isabel is partly right; we are not what we wear. But in her radical repudiation of any limits, any barriers, she exemplifies as well the unpleasant consequences of a heedless drive for individual freedom.

Henry James presents his heroine as a young woman of unusual potential who is victimised by the passionate desire for total freedom which is her most salient characteristic. So strongly is Isabel in the grip of her ruling passion that she marries Osmond, exactly the wrong man, and is immediately ensconced, like a piece of fine ivory, in his Florentine prison-house. Isabel's perversity drives her to this marriage; she might not have married Osmond, as the perceptive Ralph Touchett knew, if it had not been that others told her not to. Once that happened, however, she was helpless to avoid asserting herself by doing precisely the worst thing.

Isabel's perversity, in short, is her ruin. So long as others understand that she can be bought and sold by an appeal to her hyperactive individuality, they can manipulate her at will. She had not learned the hard lesson, as the sociologist David Riesman put it, that the autonomous person is he who will not be forced to be a nonconformist, who will not be forced to a perverse act of self-reliance. She had not learned a lesson that goes against the grain of American individualism, that the only freedom possible to the individual in an urbanised, industrialised world dominated by the mass media is to live in society.

CHAPTER 5

Freedom and Repression

The Statue of Liberty, given to the American people by the French in 1885, symbolised the once lively, not-yet-dead image of America as the hope and proof of democracy, the nation whose revolution preceded and maybe helped France's own. As the Declaration of Independence phrased it in 1776, America stood for the rights of 'Life, Liberty and the Pursuit of Happiness'; as Abraham Lincoln put it in 1863, America was 'a new nation, conceived in Liberty', Americans a people 'engaged in a great civil war, testing whether this nation or any nation so conceived, can long endure'; a nation whose 'dead shall not have died in vain', and which, 'under God, shall have a new birth of freedom'.

Positing freedom in general, emotional terms was one thing; defining or enacting it another. For example, the Civil War (1861–5) led to the abolition of slavery and the plantation economy and gave the Negro the vote; but there was little alternative employment in the South, and the Negro became a marginal man, a wage slave, while his lack of education made him politically gullible and subject to bribes (in both North and South). The black's vaunted freedom became a new kind of repression. In fiction, too, it proved easier to deplore the presence of repression, to attack caste, capitalism and political corruption than to analyse what constitutes real freedom and how to achieve it. But American literature can boast a substantial, earnest body of fiction which deals with the three major areas where the freedom/repression issue was most poignant: colour, sex and the fate/free-will nexus.

The Civil War was a watershed in the treatment of these three areas. The impassioned moral diatribes of Northern abolitionists and the urbane defences of Southern paternalists gave way to bitter comment on the relationships between white Northerners, white Southerners and blacks. Black writers began to come to the fore. The role and the self-confidence of women also expanded in and after the war, as women who had tasted wartime opportunity saw to it that their daughters became assertive and profession-conscious. Women novelists, themselves among the new women, wrote with increasing authority on the freedom/repression theme, which concerned them as women, Americans and human beings. And of course the new woman became a fictional subject, *par excellence* in Henry James's *The Bostonians*, a memorable satire on women reformers, asexual creatures, 'flushed women with loosened bonnet-strings, forcing thin voices into ineffectual shrillness', who believed that 'all wives are bullied, all mothers stricken, all maidens dishonored'. Many of James's novels suggest the artificial polarisation of mind and body in women; there is a feeling that Isabel Archer and Claire de Cintré, for instance, would have been happier women if they had followed their sexual impulses. But, generally speaking, in the nineteenth century women writers took the lead in analysing their sex's sexuality.

Literary interest in the environment and situation-conditioning burgeoned in post-war years. Industrialisation speeded up the growing contrast between flourishing cities and the depressing, depressed countryside, between the go-ahead North and the sapping, sapped South, thus providing an apt commentary on the bio-sociological theories which fascinated peace-time America: Darwin's biologically based, sociologically applied theory of the way in which species are conditioned by their environment; Herbert Spencer's Darwinistic corollary-cum-slogan, 'the survival of the fittest'. Is freedom possible, or are we all the victims of fate and/or chemistry, asked the realistic novelists? What role did will power play in combating repression and achieving freedom?

Mark Twain explored this question in its widest and most basic senses through the neo-Rousseauesque figure of Huckleberry Finn, a juvenile village pariah with no urge or need to conform or please: an apparently self-sufficient, honestly selfish, unself-conscious nature child, with no sense of his 'eccentricity' in the eyes of others.

> Huck came and went at his own free will. He slept on door-steps in fine weather, and in empty hogsheads in wet; he did not have to go to school or church or call any being master or obey anybody; he could go fishing or swimming when and where he chose, and stay as long as it suited him; nobody forbade him to fight; he could sit up as late as he pleased; he was always the first boy that went barefoot in the spring and the last to resume leather in the fall; he never had to wash, nor put on clean clothes; he could swear wonderfully. In a word, everything that goes to make life precious, that boy had.

But even with this head start, Huck cannot think or act as a totally free individual. He may flee down-river away from his drunken father and the civilising Widow Douglas; but, however unconsciously and vestigially, he has acquired 'principles', he has absorbed beliefs, and he can never act independently of received wisdom, even when he seems to reject it. When he decides not to write a letter turning the escaped Nigger Jim over to the law, he cannot view his inaction with a good and free heart; for he is conditioned to think he is doing wrong – 'All right, then, I'll go to hell' – though he also feels he is doing right. Call it conscience, call it morality, call it law and order, it represses him.

Colour

Race relations in American literature in the period up to 1920 was a three-way affair. Albion Tourgée, in his novel *A Fool's Errand*

(1879), spoke of two nations as powerfully separate and distinct as Disraeli's.

> North and South had been two households in one house – two nations under one name. The intellectual, moral, and social life of each had been utterly distinct and separate from that of the other. They no more understood or appreciated each other's feelings than John Chinaman comprehends the civilization of John Bull.

The South was autocratic, pastoral and believed 'the negro was fit only for slavery'; the progressive North believed 'the negro is a man, and had [sic] equal inherent rights with the white race'. The third nation was the black nation; and if, even in the mid-twentieth century, it still lacked acknowledged leaders and visible unity, its natural desire for an independence which amounted to a 'repression' of the white freedom to enslave was believed in by the Northern white and feared by the Southern white. This desire was articulated by the novelist Harriet Beecher Stowe. 'Is not the *sense* of liberty a higher and a finer one than any of the five?' she asked. 'Who can speak the blessing of that rest which comes down on the free man's pillow, under laws which insure to him the rights that God has given to man?'

Just as the Civil War would not have been fought without the existence of Negro slavery in the South, so the issue of what constituted racial freedom and repression would not have exercised the American novelist without the presence in America of numbers of black-skinned people, visibly and apparently different enough to encourage racial pretensions and definitions. It was just because he was as coarse-grained, impure and inferior as black bread that the Negro was a natural slave, argued the refined, pure and superior whites. He should be as free as his inherent racial attributes warranted, no more and no less. This 'judicious' opinion was satirised by George Washington Cable in *The Grandissimes* (1880), when Agricola, an old-established Southerner, talks to a German immigrant.

'How free,' said Agricola . . . 'how free we people are from pre-judice against the negro!'

'The white people,' said Frowenfeld . . . inquiringly.

'H— my young friend, when we say, "we people", we *always* mean we white people. The non-mention of color always implies pure white; and whatever is not pure white is to all intents and purposes pure black. When I say the "whole community" I mean the whole white portion; when I speak of the "individual public sentiment" I mean the sentiment of the white population. What else could I mean? Could you suppose, sir, the expression which you may have heard me use – "my downtrodden country" – includes black and mulattoes? What is that up yonder in the sky? The moon. The new moon, or the old moon, or the moon in her third quarter, but always the moon! Which part of it? Why, the shining part – the white part, always and only! Not that there is a prejudice against the negro. By no means. Wherever he can be of any service in a strictly menial capacity we kindly and generously tolerate his presence.'

Ante-Bellum Southern literature concurred. Its blacks were cheerful, mischievous, feckless and yet essentially good-hearted, a mixture of childishness and tameable savagery; they were a highly inferior species of human being, a highly superior species of pet animal – like Newfoundland dogs, perhaps. In John Pendleton Kennedy's *Swallow Barn* (1832), the most thoughtful literary defence of slavery in this period, Squire Meriwether, an enlightened, benevolent slave-owner, modelled on Byrd and Jefferson, believes with moral certitude that his galaxy of gay, singing blacks, with few and simple wants, are physically and psychologically fulfilled by hard labour and subservient status. Aunt Chloe of *Uncle Tom's Cabin* (1852) unwittingly acts the stereotype when she says to her mistress: 'Now, Missis, do jist look at dem beautiful white hands o' yourn with long fingers and all a sparkling with rings, like my white lilies when de dew's on 'em; and look at my great black stumpin' hands. Now, don't ye think dat de Lord must have meant me to make de pie-crust, and you to stay in de parlor?' The literature abounds with 'obstopolous' boys and outrageously irresponsible Topsys. The adult black male is the most favourable of the stereotypes: a sermonising, Bible-learned, simple but good man, with some capacity for learning and some powers of leadership: Tourgée's Uncle Jerry, for example.

> Uncle Jerry can not read nor write; but he is a man of strange intelligence and power. Unable to do work of any account, he is the faithful friend, monitor and director of others . . . Everybody seems to have great respect for his character. I don't know how many people I have heard speak of his religion.

But although he is allowed a higher sensibility and a greater potential than the female, the male black is nevertheless a very limited individual, only relatively able, gullible in the extreme. The racist author Thomas Dixon's 'Uncle Aleck' thinks he has bought land from the 'Gubment'; but a white girl reads him his title-deed receipt. '*To Whom It May Concern:* As Moses lifted up the brazen serpent in the wilderness for the enlightenment of the people, even so have I lifted twenty shining plunks out of this benighted nigger! Selah!' Even the liberal Twain depicts Nigger Jim as astonishingly superstitious; and 'Uncle Dan'l' of *The Gilded Age* (1873) also reacts with unmitigated naïveté when, in company with some backwoods white children, he sees his first steamboat. The children cry,

> 'What is it? Oh, what IS it, Uncle Dan'l?'
> With deep solemnity the answer came:
> 'Its de Almighty! Git down on yo' knees!'
> It was not necessary to say it twice. They were all kneeling in a moment. And then while the mysterious coughing rose stronger and stronger and the threatening glare reached farther and wider, the negro's voice lifted up its supplications.

When, soon afterwards, another steamboat comes along, the children quickly lose their sense of wonder and recognise a new kind of boat; Uncle Dan'l still tries to rationalise the appearance of yet another Lord.

Before the Civil War there existed in American literature a

strong sense of the symbolic power of blackness – the dark side of the soul, the diabolism which the Puritans represented as 'the Black Man'. In later literature the menace becomes overtly racial, and takes such shapes as the slaves of Melville's 'Benito Cereno' (1856), who mutiny against a good master and brutalise the white crew and passengers. Every black object in Melville's story seems ominous, be it a black malacca cane, a black mahogany washstand, or the black in his apparently subservient, deferential function, shaving his master.

> Setting down his basin, the negro searched among the razors, as for the sharpest, and having found it, gave it an additional edge by expertly stropping it on the firm, smooth, oily skin of his open palm; he then made a gesture as if to begin, but midway stood suspended for an instant, one hand elevating the razor, the other professionally dabbling among the bubbling suds on the Spaniard's lank neck. Not unaffected by the close sight of the gleaming steel, Don Benito nervously shuddered; his usual ghastliness was intensified in its hue by the contrasting sootiness of the negro's body. Altogether the scene was somewhat peculiar, at least to Captain Delano, nor, as he saw the two thus postured, could he resist the vagary that in the black he saw a headsman, and in the white a man at the block.

And in *The Grandissimes*, Cable anticipates Faulkner's gloomy forecast in *Absalom, Absalom* (1936), that, whatever redress is made for injustices, the black community will hang around white America's neck like an albatross. M. Grandissime says: 'the shadow of the Ethiopian . . . blanches . . . ow whole civilization! . . . It brheeds a thousan' cusses that nevva leave home but jus' flutter-h up an' rhoost.'

The most fanatically anti-black of writers, Thomas Dixon, created the monstrous black Gus to substantiate his claim that America must come to her senses and re-enslave the black through the terror machine of the Ku-Klux-Klan. At the climax of *The Clansman* (1905) Gus and some friends break into a house where there were two white women.

Blanched with horror, the mother sprang before Marion with a shivery cry: 'What do you want?'

'Not you,' said Gus, closing the blinds and handing a rope to another brute. 'Tie de ole one ter de bedpost.'

The mother screamed. A blow from a black fist in her mouth and the rope was tied . . . Again the huge fist swept her to the floor.

Marion staggered against the wall . . . 'We have no money,' . . . she pleaded.

Gus stepped closer, with an ugly leer, his flat nose dilated, his sinister bead-eyes wide apart gleaming ape-like as he laughed: 'We ain't atter money!'

The girl uttered a cry, long, tremulous, heart-rending, piteous.

A single tiger-spring, and the black claws of the beast sank into the soft white throat, and she was still.

Early Southern literature celebrated the white Southern code at its best, admirably feudal, chivalric and paternalistic. Historical romances by such writers as William Gilmore Simms and John Pendleton Kennedy abounded. Augustus Baldwin Longstreet and George Washington Harris depicted poorer whites as homely, happy and fairly good. With the exception of Thomas Nelson Page and John Esten Cooke, who were the most popular of the post-war Southern novelists and who dealt strictly in stereotypes, post-war literature portrayed a good deal more realistically a code-ridden society where the disproportionate emphasis on status and ritual led to duels which seemed to symbolise and anticipate fratricidal conflict. Intolerance and violence were endemic in this society, says John W. De Forest in *Miss Ravenel's Conversion from Secession to Loyalty* (1867). Lillie Ravenel and her doctor father come North from New Orleans which he loathes. When he was mugged in that city he was not in the least surprised.

'Not the least. Oh, it's only an ordinary New Orleans salutation. I knew I was in New Orleans when I was hit, just as the ship-wrecked man knew he was in a Christian country when he saw a

gallows ... How lucky I had on ... a stiff beaver ... A brass hel-
met would be still better. Somebody ought to get up a dress hat
of aluminum for the New Orleans market.'

'It was one of those detestable soldiers,' exclaimed Lillie.

'No, my dear,' said the Doctor. 'It was one of our own excellent
people. They are so ardent and impulsive, you know. They have
the Southern heart, always fired up.'

Lillie maintains her preference for the Southern heart, and,
against her father's wishes, marries a Southern gentleman,
Colonel Carter, whom De Forest characterises as a fundamentally
kind, good man, fatally corrupted by a society which encouraged
laziness, self-indulgence and authoritarianism. After his death
Lillie marries again; her second husband is a Northern man, the
gentle, egalitarian Colbourne, and she soon comes to realise that
the South is not the best breeding-ground for good men – hus-
bands or fathers.

American fiction also dealt with the threat to freedom posited
not by black tyranny, but by an inflexible white Southern frame of
mind which at very least would uphold the slavery that no legislation can abolish – the slavery of caste. It seemed to some writers
that the South was permanently addicted to slavery in one form
or another. Tourgée's Comfort Servosse tried not to think so. He
moved South in the belief that immigration by Northerners would
transform that society. Northern whites without prejudice towards the Negro, Southern Negroes without prejudice towards
Northern whites would demonstrate their mutual tolerance, their
similarity, their equality. But Servosse had not taken into account
that this demonstration would look like the exclusion and repression of Southern whites. Soon he was writing to newspapers and
influential people that emancipation did not mean, or breed,
freedom; on the contrary, Southern whites now genuinely felt
that they were the slaves. Nothing had been done to liberate the
mind of the South. And could anything be done when the ethos
and techniques of enslaving the black were being enacted by the

Klan as if nothing had changed? Servosse became deeply pessimistic when he first saw a sample of the Klan's work.

> Great furrows were plowed in the black integument, whose greenly-livid lips were drawn back, while the coagulated fibrine stretched across, and mercifully protected the lacerated flesh . . . Apparently, after having cut the flesh with closely laid welts and furrows . . . the operator had changed his position and scientifically cross-checked the whole. That he was an expert whose skill justified Bob's remark – 'Nobody but an ole everseer ebber dun dat, Kunnel' – was evident.

Uncle Tom's Cabin is nineteenth-century America's most discerning and powerful description of the gamut of repression which stems from the impact of the institution of slavery and which involves the repression of black by black and white by white. Mrs Stowe details not only the bestiality of such white slave-owners as Simon Legree, whose heavy fist, the size of a blacksmith's hammer, had 'got as hard as iron knocking down niggers', but the equally immoral conduct which the contamination of slavery produced in Sambo and Quimbo, two blacks trained by Legree as hard, cruel overseers, repressing their better selves as well as others, and which it produced in 'an average kind of man, good natured and kindly', like Tom's first master, Mr Shelby. By plantation standards Mr Shelby is a good master, who regards his servants as charming children, encouraging them to eat, drink and be merry, but never to think. But he would sooner sell Tom than lower the standard of living to which his 'immoral' earnings have accustomed him. Tom and other slaves are sold and separated from their wives and children, but this does not matter, thinks Shelby, because Tom's wife Chloe isn't fully human, so she can't miss him, though Mrs Shelby thinks differently.

Not that Mrs Stowe sees women as necessarily more tolerant than men; for one of the monstrous characters of the book is Mrs St Clare, who argues the equality issue with her liberal sister-in-law, Ophelia.

'Don't you believe that the Lord made them of one blood with us?' said Miss Ophelia, shortly.

'No, indeed, not I! A pretty story, truly! They are a degraded race . . . As to putting them on any sort of equality with us, you know, as if we could be compared, why, it's impossible! Now, St Clare really has talked to me as if keeping Mammy from her husband was like keeping me from mine. There's no comparing in this way. Mammy couldn't have the feelings that I should . . . As if Mammy could love her dirty little babies as I love Eva!'

Even the liberal St Clare, to whom Tom is first sold, has neither the effective will nor the application to free his slaves. He dies promising and intending to free them, a promise that his auto-cratic wife fails to redeem. Mrs Stowe's moral is that there is no such thing as a good slave-owner; and that anything short of active abolitionism deserves her lash. She even attacks Ophelia, the liberal Northerner, who is intellectually committed to aboli-tionism but physically repelled by blacks.

Mrs Stowe's picture of the black race is of a race in no sense generically inferior to the white race. Uncle Tom is firmly for freedom.

'Well, Tom,' said St Clare . . . 'I'm going to make a free man of you; – so, have your trunk packed, and get ready to set out for Kentuck.'

The sudden light of joy that shone in Tom's face as he raised his hands to heaven, his emphatic 'Bless the Lord!' rather discom-posed St Clare: he did not like it that Tom should be so ready to leave him.

'You haven't had such very bad times here, that you need be in such a rapture, Tom,' he said drily.

'No, no, Mas'r! 'tan't that, – it's bein' *a free man*! That's what I'm joyin' for.'

'Why, Tom, don't you think, for your own part, you've been better off than to be free?'

'*No, indeed*, Mas'r St Clare,' said Tom, with a flash of energy. No, indeed . . . I'd rather have poor clothes, poor house, poor everything, and have 'em *mine* than have the best, and have 'em any man's else, – I had *so*, Mas'r; I think it's natur, Mas'r.'

But Tom never attempts to escape; he shows a passivity which Mrs Stowe draws so strongly as to label it a racial characteristic. Blacks are equal and different. George and Eliza reject America precisely because they are different. Freedom in America? Says George: '*I do not want it*; I want a country, a nation of my own. I think that the African race has peculiarities, yet to be unfolded in the light of civilization and Christianity, which, if not the same with those of the Anglo-Saxon, may prove to be, morally, of even a higher type.' Mrs Stowe agrees with George, and pays the black the highest compliment she can, by affirming not only a different and equal culture – 'life will awake . . . with a gorgeousness and splendor of which our cold western tribes faintly have conceived' – but by attributing 'the highest form of the peculiarly *Christian* life' to the Negro.

The insidious corruption and repression of racism, affecting its practitioners as well as its victims, the way in which the slightest tinge of colour altered relationships, are movingly described by the Creole writer Kate Chopin. 'Desirée's Baby' (1894) tells of a wonderful marriage between Desirée Valmoldée, a shy girl, and the imperious Armand Aubigny. She grows in confidence and poise, he in a tenderness which is extended to his normally abused slaves; they both mature and flower with each day of marriage. But three months after the birth of their daughter, Desirée realises that her husband has become cold to her and cruel to the slaves.

> She sat in her room, one hot afternoon, in her peignoir, listlessly drawing through her fingers the strands of her long, silky brown hair . . . The baby, half naked, lay asleep . . . One of La Blanche's little quadroon boys – half naked too – stood fanning the child slowly with a fan of peacock feathers. Desirée's eyes had been fixed absently and sadly upon the baby, while she was striving to penetrate the threatening mist that she felt closing about her. She looked from her child to the boy who stood beside him, and back again, over and over.

Armand spells out the relationship for her: 'the child is not white . . . you are not white.'

Essentially Desirée is unchanged. But the hint of colour changes the attitude of society, her husband, even her mother, who urges her to accept the inevitable and leave her husband. 'I want you to go,' Armand tells Desirée, and she does, drowning herself and her baby in the bayou. The story ends on an even more tragic note. Armand sits at home, burning the layette, the wedding dress, everything to do with Desirée; and in the back of a drawer where she kept her letters, he finds one from his mother to his father. 'But, above all,' she wrote, 'night and day, I thank the good God for having so arranged our lives that our dear Armand will never know that his mother, who adores him, belongs to the race that is cursed with the brand of slavery.'

Kate Chopin does not spell out whether Desirée was ashamed of her blood; but a character in Howells's *An Imperative Duty* (1893) who discovers she is an octoroon is repressed by the received image of blackness. She looks at herself in the mirror, and thinks: 'my mother was darker and my grandmother darker, and my great-grander like a mulatto, and then it was a horrible old negress, a savage stolen from Africa, where she had been a cannibal.' Twain's moral to Kate Chopin's tale could have been quite different. What a fuss when colour makes no difference in personality, type or ability, he says in *Pudd'nhead Wilson*. In that novel a white-looking black baby and a truly white baby are switched in their cradles. As a result the black baby behaves like a white and vice versa. Environment and upbringing make them what they are, not their genes.

In a somewhat different way the black writer Paul Laurence Dunbar was at pains to point out the equality of blacks and whites – they were equally fallible! Blacks like whites were capable of exploitation; for instance, Mr Solomon Ruggles, who is president, treasurer and founder of the Colonial American Investment Company, 'organised for the encouragement and benefit of the struggling amongst us of African descent': at least, so says his advertisement, and so does Mr Ruggles.

> 'Gent'men,' he said, 'my fellow colo'ed brotheren, I jest want to say this to you, that we Af-Americans been ca'yin a leaky bucket to the well too long. We git the stream from the ground, an' back to the ground it goes befoah we kin git any chance to make use o' what we've drawed. But, not to speak in meterphers, this is what I mean. I mean that we work for the white folks for their money. All they keer about us is ouah work, an' all we keer about them is their money; but what do we do with it when we git it? I'll tell you what we do with it; we take an' give it right back to the white folks fu' somef'n or other we want, an' so they git ouah labour, an' ouah money too. Ain't that the truth?

The truth about Mr Ruggles is that he is a trickster who absconds with his investors' funds.

American literature is rich in descriptions of the physical difference of Negroes, with 'their flat wide nostrils and noses, their great rolled thick lips'. Mrs Stowe apart – for even Mark Twain uses such phrases as 'white inside' to suggest Nigger Jim's potential – the great evocation of blackness in this period is by blacks and, except for the powerful short fiction of Charles Chesnutt, takes the form of the autobiographies of Booker T. Washington, James Weldon Johnson and W. E. B. Dubois (it was comparatively rare for the post-Civil War black to feel he could afford the luxury of fiction or poetry). In the mid-twentieth century Richard Wright, Chester Himes, Ralph Ellison, Claude MacKay and James Baldwin have all created memorable black characters; before 1920 the palm goes to the part-black heroine of Gertrude Stein's *Melanctha* (1909), which surpassed both Thomas Nelson Page ('Marse Chan', 1887) and Joel Chandler Harris (*Uncle Remus*, 1880) in capturing the idiomatic, laconic-expansive black speech which has become an element in today's white American speech.

Made up of a little of her white mother and a lot of her black father, Melanctha seems to be a new and remarkable kind of person: exceptionally versatile, subtle and intelligent, adventurous and honest, refined and passionate, educated and instinctive, a loner and a joiner, a pupil and a master. But her specialness and independence fit her badly for society. For instance, when the young mulatto doctor she has been heavily dating makes it clear he wants coloured people to be like the whites, to be quiet, orderly and restrained, not gay, extrovert and physical, Melanctha tells him frankly:

> All you are always wanting Dr Campbell, is just to talk about being good, and to play with people just to have a good time, and yet always to certainly keep yourself out of trouble. It don't seem to me Dr Campbell that I admire that way to do things very much. It certainly ain't really to me being very good.

And when her suddenly bankrupt fiancé Jem genuinely cites masculine pride as a reason for not letting her marry into his poverty, she cannot understand his reasoning. She outgrows and outdistances her menfolk, who want her on their terms, in their images. She is surrounded by characters of social and intellectual stature; but they are pygmies beside the truly emancipated Melanctha. What sets her above and apart is miscegenation: the fusing of colours and the disappearance of prejudice in the fused individual. She symbolises the true freedom that Gertrude Stein thinks will only come when all men are, in some sense, physical and/or psychological, one. In practice, the Melancthas of this world are at one only with themselves; they are as much the victims of society as the blackest black. Melanctha was gloriously and dreadfully unique. She died of real and symbolic consumption. Her best friend, Rose, could write her epitaph even before Melanctha's death.

> No, I am always real sorry for Melanctha, she never was no just common kind of nigger, but she don't never know not with all the time I always was telling it to her, no she never no way could learn, what was the right way she should do. I certainly don't never want no kind of harm to come bad to Melanctha, but I cer-

tainly do think she will most kill herself some time, the way she always say it would be easy way for her to do. I never see nobody ever could be so awful blue.

Sex

An archetypal American woman has passed into sociology and mythology; and whether she takes the shape of Calamity Jane, the pistol-packin' mama, or the Puritan Matron, she is an assertive and dominant woman, whose conspicuous consumption and parade of luxuries and labour-saving devices overcompensates for the real (and exaggerated) frontier privations which she and her ancestors suffered. The archetype is literary too, and the first of American literature's repressed women determined to find a freedom which at the very least meant equality with the American male is Hawthorne's Hester Prynne. A married woman, with an illegitimate child by the local bachelor minister, she has chosen to keep the father's name secret and to accept, externally, the community's judgement – a spell in jail, virtual ostracisation and the need to wear the letter A for 'adulteress' for the rest of her life. She lives apart, as if agreeing that she is evil, contaminating; she confines her luxurious womanhood in sexless clothes. There was 'nothing in Hester's form, though majestic and statue-like, that Passion would ever dream of clasping in its embrace . . . Some attributes had departed from her, the permanence of which had been essential to keep her a woman.' But the repressed 'isolatoe' has in fact added intellectual freedom to her physical licence, '[A] question often rose into her mind, with reference to the whole race of womanhood. Was existence worth accepting, even to the happiest among them?'

Her philosophising leads her to reject conventional concepts of guilt, sin, morality and marriage. She equates happiness with justice, and justice with freedom. Her rightful mate, she believes, is Minister Dimmesdale; while the Christian marriage ceremony between herself and Roger Chillingworth cannot make good a relationship which lacks love and passion. She ends her life as a kind of radical prophetess, to whom come women of all sorts – wounded, wasted, wronged, misplaced, erring 'or with the dreary burden of a heart unyielded, because unvalued and unsought', anxious to hear Hester's assurance that one day 'a new truth would be revealed', establishing 'the whole relation between man and woman on a surer ground of mutual happiness'.

Hester was a revolutionary, and the same might be said of Hawthorne; for there was nothing in American literature to touch his bold and sympathetic treatment of extra-marital sex and real freedom for women until Kate Chopin's *The Awakening*, which anticipates D. H. Lawrence in its beautiful, uninhibited treatment of female sexuality, appeared in 1899. *The Awakening* is about the flowering of physical and spiritual selfhood in Edna Pointellier, twenty-eight, a cold wife and an averagely caring mother of two children. Vacationing on the Louisiana coast, she learns to live fully through her contacts with a local beau, Robert Lebrun, and with the sea.

> She was like the little tottering, stumbling, clutching child, who of a sudden realizes its powers, and walks for the first time alone, boldly and with over-confidence. She could have shouted for joy. She did shout for joy, as with a sweeping stroke or two she lifted her body to the surface of the water.
>
> A feeling of exultation overtook her, as if some power of significant import had been given her to control the working of her body and her soul. She grew daring and reckless, overestimating her strength. She wanted to swim far out, where no woman had swum before.

She revels in the physical liberation of being able to swim, in the sensation of the waves on her body and in the new physical response to her lover, Robert. She decides to live as and for herself, no longer sacrificing to her children, no longer trapped by furniture and clothes which repressed her personality and therefore her freedom. While her husband is away on a long business trip she moves from their impressive, showy house to a small, soft, feminine, feline cottage. Robert, for a variety of personal and social reasons, comes to feel the relationship cannot continue; but Edna, determined to remain herself, takes another road to liberation. She goes back to the Gulf holiday house, and finds her old bathing-suit.

> She put it on, leaving her clothing in the bath house. But when she was there beside the sea, absolutely alone, she cast the unpleasant, pricking garments from her, and for the first time in her life she stood naked in the open air, at the mercy of the sun, the breeze that beat upon her, and the waves that invited her.
>
> How strange and awful it seemed to stand naked under the sky! how delicious! She felt like some new-born creature, opening its eyes in a familiar world that it had never known.
>
> The foamy wavelets curled up to her white feet, and coiled like serpents about her ankles. She walked out. The water was chill, but she walked on. The water was deep, but she lifted her white body and reached out with a long, sweeping stroke. The touch of the sea is [sic] sensuous, enfolding the body in its soft, close embrace.
>
> She went on and on.

If her action seems escapist, this is society's misinterpretation, Mrs Chopin indicates. Edna is giving herself to the freedom of continuing to be honest. Like Whitman, she equates body and soul; to obey one is to obey the other. She cannot live a lie – she loves Robert, and if their love cannot continue openly, the only freedom available to her is the deathly embrace of her original liberator.

Mrs Chopin is not so unsubtle as to equate sexual freedom and total freedom, but she does suggest that in most women the physical being predominates and cannot necessarily be confined to marriage. Self-assertion is for her the crucial key to freedom, as is seen in 'The Story of an Hour', where a woman who loves her husband is nevertheless exalted when she hears of his death in a train accident.

She did not stop to ask if it were or were not a monstrous joy that
. . . there would be no one to live for her during those coming
years, she would live for herself. There would be no powerful will
bending her in that blind persistence with which men and women
believe they have a right to impose a private will upon a fellow-
creature. What could love, the unsolved mystery, count for in face
of this possession of self-assertion which she suddenly recognised
as the strongest impulse of her being!

'Free! Body and soul free!' she kept whispering.

When her husband, who has not after all been killed, returns, she
collapses and dies of a heart attack: 'the joy that kills', Mrs Chopin
dualistically phrased it.

Chopin and Hawthorne apart, American novelists explored the
role of woman in society less radically but, within their limits,
with critical frankness. New Englanders and Southerners alike
write voluminously on unhappy marriages, but usually allow
their heroines to remarry happily after a disastrous first marriage.
They question less the institution than the pitfalls of the traditional
interpretation that women and men put on marriage.

There is remarkable restraint and fine frankness in the way in
which the New England writers Mary Wilkins Freeman and
Sarah Orne Jewett put their argument for spinsterhood. Neither
introduces male villains or stereotypes; both make effective statements for the kind of personality that is happier, more fulfilled in
remaining single. In Jewett's *A Country Doctor* (1884) the heroine,
Nan, an orphan, brought up by a widowed doctor, decides to
train in medicine. George Gerry, a potential suitor, is repelled by
the career woman in Nan. He sees an alarming demonstration of
Nan's medical skills on a river trip when they are hailed by a
farmer's wife to fetch the doctor for her injured husband. Before
George could set off

. . . Nan pushed the spectators into the doorway of the kitchen,
and quickly stopped and unbuttoned her right boot, and then
planted her foot on the damaged shoulder and caught up the hand
and gave a quick pull, the secret of which nobody understood;

but there was an unpleasant click as the bone went back into its socket, and a yell from the sufferer, who scrambled to his feet. 'I'll be hanged if she ain't set it,' he said, looking quite weak and very much astonished. 'You're the smartest young woman I ever see.'

Like the farmer, George overcomes his prejudice, and he proposes. Nan likes him, physically and mentally; but she has something in life which she prefers, and she is sure she does right to prefer it, she tells Dunport's social arbiter, Mrs Fraley.

> I won't attempt to say that the study of medicine is a proper vocation for women, only that I believe more and more every year that it is the proper study for me. It certainly cannot be the proper vocation of all women to bring up children, so many of them are dead failures at it; and I don't see why all girls should be thought failures who do not marry. I don't believe that half those who do marry have any real right to it, at least until people use common sense as much in that most important decision as in lesser ones.

Mary Freeman pokes truly liberated fun at the stereotype of the frustrated spinster in her ironically titled short story 'A New England Nun' (1891), the story of Louisa Ellis, whose fiancé, Joe Dagget, returns to marry her after spending fourteen years making his fortune in Australia. Louisa's mildly sensual impulses have been channelled elsewhere in Joe's absence – into the love of embroidery, fine china and home-grown redcurrant preserves. She

> ... had almost the enthusiasm of an artist over the mere order and cleanliness of her solitary home. She had throbs of genuine triumph at the sight of the window-panes which she had polished till they shone like jewels. She gloated gently over her orderly bureau-drawers, with their exquisitely folded contents redolent with lavender and sweet clover and very purity.

Her nature is incompatible not with marriage but with Joe Dagget's type of masculine presence. On a typical visit, when Dagget rose to go,

. . . he stumbled over a rug, and trying to recover himself, hit Louisa's work-basket on the table, and knocked it on the floor . . .

When Joe Dagget was outside he drew in the sweet evening air with a sigh, and felt much as an innocent and perfectly well-intentioned bear might after his exit from a china shop. Louisa, on her part, felt much as the kind-hearted, long-suffering owner of the china shop might have done after the exit of the bear.

Fortunately for their respective integrity, they agree not to marry; they find freedom and fulfilment in not marrying each other.

For Freeman and Jewett freedom lies in being authentic, in being oneself, in being liberated from conventions and inherited viewpoints. Each generation, each individual must inaugurate his and her own Lincolnian 'new birth of freedom'. No one excels Ellen Glasgow in the ability to analyse and evoke the ruinous and repressive preconceptions of the woman reared to believe that not to marry meant misery and disgrace for herself and her family. When Gabriella, of *Life and Gabriella* (1916), thinks her fiancé may jilt her because she insists that her mother should come and live with them in New York (her mother's refusal is to solve the matter), she imagines the alternative, spinsterhood, to be 'an unendurable life'.

It was as absurd to think that she could love again as that a flower could bloom afresh when its petals were withered. No, without George there was only loveless old age . . . The possibility was so agonizing that she rose blindly from her chair and turned from the window as if the quiet street, filled with the dreamy sunshine of October, had offered an appalling, an unbelievable sight to her eyes. If he had ceased to love her, she was helpless; and this sense of helplessness awoke a feeling of rage in her heart. If he did not come back, she could never go after him. She could only sit and wait until she grew . . . old and . . . ugly . . . While the minutes, which seemed hours, dragged away, she wept the bitterest tears of her life.

The innocent Gabriella's eyes are quickly and cruelly opened to the reality of marriage. Her father-in-law appals her; he is the type of husband who adores his wife as an ideal but ignores her as a person. Her mother-in-law has always neglected her husband for her children. And so, at the end of a month, Gabriella finds herself less free than ever before as the wife of a man who has always had his own way. She has had to discipline her fearless directness; 'she had learned not to answer back when she knew she was right; she had learned to appear sweet when her inner spirit demanded a severe exterior'. And so, when George, who proves to be a layabout and a drunken libertine, finally and flauntingly sets up his mistress in an apartment, Gabriella feels not affronted but liberated.

> The embittering memories of her life with George were submerged in the invigorating waves of energy that flooded her being. Her inert body responded to the miraculous restoration of her spirit; and, while she walked swiftly from the door to the window, she had a sensation of lightness and ease as if she had just awakened from a refreshing sleep . . . She was free from George. She had escaped from the humiliating bondage of her marriage.

With her divorce Gabriella dissociates herself from the creed that the only comfortable and dignified way for a woman to make her living is to marry; that a man is the only satisfactory means of livelihood, whether it is alimony or allowance he provides. She finds comfort, dignity, freedom, happiness and livelihood as an overworked, underpaid saleswoman in a *haute couture* salon. She articulates a new philosophy: 'I want to be happy, but it depends on myself.' Freedom is not status, convention or refinement, but truth.

Freedom is also flexibility, not rigidity; this is a lesson Ellen Glasgow's Virginia cannot learn. Virginia believes fervently that a woman's role is in the home, and is passive.

> She thought of the daily excitement of marketing, of the perpetual romance of mending his clothes . . . She saw herself waiting – waiting happily – but always waiting. She imagined the thrilling expectancy of the morning waiting for him to come home to his supper; the blissful expectancy of fearing that he might be late.

This traditional concept of marriage drives her own marriage onto the rocks. She overwhelms her husband, a struggling playwright, with things domestic: he cannot write in peace, for the full involvement of the husband and father in the home, when he is at home, is part of the tradition. But Oliver too is at fault in his concept of marriage. He has been brought up to believe that a sweet, docile little woman is the ideal wife for every man; whereas he clearly needs someone more his intellectual equal, someone much less bland, someone who does not think it is immoral to want the solitude to write; someone who, unlike Virginia, does not instinctively do the maternal, wifely, dogmatic, wrong thing – right in the hoary folklore of marriage, wrong in the changing circumstances and pragmatic demands of marriage in practice.

Virginia has a moral-fraught ending. Oliver divorces his wife and marries an actress, but, ominously, 'his ideal woman still corresponded to the type he had first chosen for his mate'; this hide-bound thinking seems likely to wreck his second marriage. Nor will Virginia admit the sense of her elder daughter's philosophy, her belief in the crying need for women's 'education in life, sex and psychology', and the need for growth after marriage. Virginia's younger daughter rightly repulses Virginia when that lady protests against the elderly widower this daughter has decided to marry. 'Mother, dear, you must allow me to decide what is for my happiness . . . After all, you know so much less of life than I do. How can you advise me?' Virginia is left in her lonely Southern mansion waiting for her son to come home and comfort her; this conventional reliance is as unlikely to run true to theory as did her conventionally conceived marriage.

Consistently, but with varying degress of compassion, women writers explore and expose those 'weaknesses' of their sex which amount to self-repression. Nowhere is this more subtly and feelingly explored than in the attractive if irritating personality of Edith Wharton's Lily Bart. Brought up with expensive tastes, the beautiful Lily finds it hard to adjust to life without much money when her father goes bankrupt, and when, orphaned, she is given a small allowance by a puritanical aunt. She needs to find a rich husband; and she goes to great lengths to woo many such men, only to ruin her chances by going off to do what she says, and perhaps thinks, she enjoys – walking alone, or with Lawrence Selden, an insufficiently wealthy lawyer whom she likes very much. They both lack money, they both regret their lack of it. He wants more books and envies his friends their trips abroad, he tells her.

> She drew a sympathetic breath. 'But do you mind enough – to marry to get out of it?'
> Selden broke into a laugh. 'God forbid!' he declared.
> She rose with a sigh, tossing her cigarette into the grate. 'Ah, there's the difference – a girl must, a man may if he chooses.' She surveyed him critically. 'Your coat's a little shabby – but who cares? It doesn't keep people from asking you to dine. If I were shabby no one would have me; a woman is asked out as much for her clothes as for herself. The clothes are the background, the frame, if you like: they don't make success, but they are a part of it. Who wants a dingy woman? We are expected to be pretty and well-dressed till we drop – and if we can't keep it up alone, we have to go into partnership.'

But how honest is Lily being? Is fate to blame – or the constitutional weakness she admits to? 'Her whole being dilated in an atmosphere of luxury; it was the background she required, the only climate she could breathe in.'

Living beyond her income, in fast sets; losing her inheritance when her aunt hears of her gambling debts; cast off by society, unable to hold down a job, eventually committing suicide – Lily's life and death seem equally the responsibility of society and herself. Her idea of success is social: other-regarding and repressive; Selden's definition of success strikes the authentic note. 'My idea of freedom,' he said, 'is personal freedom – from money, from poverty, from ease and anxiety, from all the material accidents . . . [Freedom is] to keep a kind of republic of the spirit.'

With a commendable lack of either male or female chauvinism, American novelists of both sexes attribute the repression of women less to society than to women themselves. In *Zury, the Meanest Man in Spring County* (1887) Joseph Kirkland suggests that any kind of tyranny is largely the fault of the victim. Why was Zury so mean, so dominant, his successive wives such drudges, his 'colleagues' so subordinate? Because they knuckled under to him and played traditionally submissive roles. The exception was Anne Sparrow, a New England schoolmistress who acts very freely when Zury, chairman of the school board and everything else, fills in the details on her appointment form.

'Sex?'

'Unfortunately, female.'

'Age at 'pintment?'

'Oh, what do they want to know that for? Do they expect a woman to tell her age?'

'Wal, they 'xpect her t' tell some age or other; 'n' one old enough to shew she comes within the statit – over eighteen and under seventy.'

'Oh, well, I'm old enough to vote if women had their rights.'

'Put ye daown a hundred, then; women 'd oughter to be voters; just as they touch th' even hundred, 'n' not a minute before.'

'Well, I'm twenty-one, and if I don't know more than the average voters' –

Accustomed as he is to a world where women are bought and sold and used like cattle, the self-possessed Anne Sparrow elicits from Zury the remark: 'Gee Rusalem! I wouldn't care if she never milked a cow in her life.' Eventually he works to become a state senator, and marries her.

Anne and Zury come to share a level of education; and, adds Frank Norris, writing of the Jadwins in *The Pit* (1903), no relationship is free and equal unless all things are shared, business as well as pleasure. It was wrong that men passed

... a life in which women had no part, and in which, should they enter it they would no longer recognise son or husband, or father or brother. The gentle-mannered fellow, clean-minded, clean-handed, of the breakfast or supper table was one man. The other, who and what was he? Down there in the murk and grime of the business district raged the Battle of the Street, and therein he was being transformed, case hardened, supremely selfish, asking no quarter; no, nor giving any.

In this marriage, as in Virginia's, both partners are at fault. Traditionally, reflexively, Curtis Jadwin keeps his wife in ignorance of his attempt to corner wheat on the Chicago Exchange; traditionally she puts him on a pedestal, has no wish to know about, no pretensions to understand, his work; and their mutual ignorance nearly proves disastrous for their marriage when the agony of Jadwin's widely predicted defeat coincides with Laura's birthday and she, ignorant of his agony, behaves like a virago because he has forgotten the anniversary.

Norris is despondent about the capacity for and usefulness of self-knowledge, and other kinds of knowledge, in either men or women. Theodore Dreiser argues 'know yourself, accept yourself, and act accordingly'. He makes this point in the course of writing about the primacy of sex in men. There is nothing wrong with the urge, if it is recognised, acknowledged and followed. Restrained, repressed, it will lead to multiple injuries. Dreiser's book *The Genius* (1915) shows just how wrong a man can go if he is forced into social conventions that do not accord with his sexual or temperamental proclivities. Eugene Witla 'could never stop with mere kissing and caressing . . . if not persistently restrained. It seemed to him natural that love should go on.' Yet when he has made love to his girl-friend Angela in her father's house, he feels guilty.

> The atmosphere of the house after this night seemed charged with reproach to Eugene although it took on no semblance of reality in either look or word. When he awoke in the morning and looked through the half closed shutters to the green world outside he felt a sense of freshness and of shame. It was cruel to come into such a home as this and do a thing as mean as he had done. After all, philosophy or no philosophy, didn't a fine old citizen like Jotham, honest, upright, genuine in his moral point of view and his observance of the golden rule, didn't he deserve better.

Governed by this reflex action to convention, Eugene marries Angela. But in spite of apparently doing the right thing he is neither happy nor convinced he *has* done the right thing. He only feels honest when he exercises the persistent impulse to respond to 'the sheer animal magnetism of beauty, that when it came near him in the form of a lovely girl of his own temperamental inclinations, he could not resist it'. Why should he resist (he does not) Stella, Margaret, Ruby, Angela, Christine and Freida? Why shouldn't he be himself? He was, *par excellence*, a realist, as his painting showed, with its

> . . . raw reds, raw greens, dirty gray paving stones – such faces! Why this thing fairly shouted its facts. It seemed to say: 'I'm dirty, I am commonplaae, I am grim, I am shabby, but I am life.' And there was no apologizing for anything in it, no glossing anything over. Bang! Smash! Crack! came the facts one after another, with a bitter, brutal insistence on their so-ness.

By the time Angela dies, in childbirth, and also of sorrow, Dreiser has created such sympathy for Eugene's right to be himself that it is difficult to see her as wronged, difficult to blame Eugene. He is the kind of man who should not have married, as Angela finally understands. 'I know what it is with you, Eugene,' she said, after a time; 'it's the yoke that galls. It isn't me only; it's anyone. It's marriage. You don't want to be married . . . You want [and need] your freedom, and you won't be satisfied until you have it.'

In novels of Balzacian detail, Dreiser presents a galaxy of promiscuous heroes whom he considers to be admirably selfish. Lester Kane in *Jennie Gerhardt* recognised that 'of course the conjugal state was an institution. It was established. Yes, certainly. But what of it? The whole nation believed in it. True, but other nations believed in polygamy.' Frank Cowperwood of *The Titan* (1914) and *The Financier* (1912) asked 'how had it come about that so many people agreed on this single point, that it was good and necessary to marry one woman and cleave to her until death?

He did not know. It was not for him to bother;' and though he marries twice, he never contracts or cleaves for life.

In 1920, in *Miss Lulu Bett*, Zona Gale made a statement about women's freedom which was as radical as anything Dreiser had to say. At first the story looks like a classic case history of vicious and unwarranted male domination. Whenever Lulu breaks out of her role as a drudge spinster she is crushed by her brother-in-law Dwight Deacon. If she buys flowers, that is bad housekeeping. The bunch of flowers, retrieved from the woodpile, symbolises the development of the story as Lulu develops the capacity to throw off a quite unnecessary repression (she becomes a wage earner at a bakery), the desire for total freedom and selfhood, the ability to be always the animated good company she is away from the Deacons. Her chance comes when Dwight's brother Ninian arrives for a visit, likes Lulu, flatters her personality and gives her confidence. Their attraction is not primarily a sensual one, though it does involve a short-lived marriage. Lulu's physical unattractiveness is, in fact, emphasised. The day she marries

> She wore the white waist which she had often thought they would 'use' for her if she died. And really, the waist looked as if it had been planned for the purpose, and its wide, upstanding plaited lace at throat and wrist made her neck look thinner, her forearm sharp and veined. Her hair she had 'crimped' and parted in the middle, puffed high – it was so that hair had been worn in Lulu's girlhood.
> 'Well!' said Ina [her sister], when she saw this coiffure, and frankly examined it, head well back, tongue meditatively teasing at her lower lip.

Although the 'marriage' breaks up – Ninian is in fact already married – Miss Lulu Bett has been liberated. Ninian's mistress has become mistress of herself, making her own choices, leading her own life.

Fitzgerald's *This Side of Paradise*, also published in 1920, articulates a philosophy akin to Zona Gale's. For a woman, success, happiness, fascination and freedom are not dependent on conventional or unconventional relationships; what matters is doing as the widowed Clara, facing facts honestly. Freedom comes from integrity, as her cousin Amory Blaine recognises.

> Her steely blue eyes held only happiness; a latent strength, a realism, was brought to its fullest development by the facts that she was compelled to face. She was alone in the world, with two small children, little money, and, worst of all, a host of friends. He saw her that winter in Philadelphia entertaining a houseful of men for an evening, when he knew she had not a servant in the house except the little colored girl guarding the babies overhead. He saw one of the greatest libertines in that city, a man who was habitually drunk and notorious at home and abroad, sitting opposite her for an evening, discussing girls' boarding-schools with a sort of innocent excitement.

But Amory discovers that the freedom to be oneself is by no means fulfilling unless one is an exceptional being, and he is not. Huckleberry Finn's dilemma is reversed. Freedom is possible, thinks Amory, but is it desirable?

Fate and Free-will

In Chapter 132 of *Moby-Dick* Captain Ahab cries: 'What is it, what nameless, inscrutable, unearthly thing is it; what cozening, hidden lord and master, and cruel remorseless emperor commands me . . . Is it I, God, or who, that lifts this arm?' Melville called *Moby-Dick* a hell-fired book; and it is just that in the sense that its hero, Ahab, in challenging the authority of what might rule the world, posits that force in deific or diabolically deific terms. The relative power of men, nature and God is an implicit consideration in the larger part of Melville's and Hawthorne's writings (see above, Chapter 3, pp 102–7), though the fate/free-will nexus was probably major only in *Moby-Dick*. In the post-Civil War years it was the fatal determinism of the environment which took the literary fancy and became an explicit and primary theme in fiction.

Against the ironic background of an America supposedly at one, at peace and able to move forward to a great and manifest destiny, the American novelist looked round, at city and country, at North, South, East and West, and found that all was not good. Mark Twain, Bret Harte and Jack London found that the Far West of the Golden Gate and the goldfields produced a terrifying toughness and materialism; Southern writers anticipated Faulkner's treatment of a South which bore down on its inhabitants just as the Spanish moss tree bore down on the rest of the vegetation; where 'the climate was too comfortable, the soil too rich'; where there was too much lushness and fecundity; where 'the land was an inverted firmament of flowers'. The writers who left the rural Midwest because they thought it was stagnant and narrow-minded found themselves embarking on a love/hate relationship with cities like Chicago, which were more various, more fascinating, more corrupting, and more enslaving. (See above, Chapter 2, pp 62, 75–9.) Writers tended to assume, a little vaguely, that environmental determinism was proven; but their passionate sense of restriction in an increasingly conformist and fenced-in society led them to make scapegoats of their environment.

The feeling that even New England was puritanical in the pejorative senses of that word and cripplingly genteel gained increasing currency as the century advanced. Sarah Orne Jewett, who loved working and writing and living in the region, had to admit that, Boston excepted, New England, the first settled and first civilised part of the country and once the flower of America's culture, no longer represented cultural advantage but cultural deprivation. In *The Marsh Island* (1885) Dick Dale, a city-dweller, reacts enthusiastically to Maine's wide-open spaces – 'this is like a bit of freedom' – only to find that the lack of options, of varied stimuli and facilities made the freedom only physical, and otherwise illusory and vacuous. Even the seemingly self-sufficient characters of *The Country of Pointed Firs* (1896), Mrs Todd and

Mrs Blackett, a mother and daughter of great country lore and philosophical outlook, emerge as repressed. At a rare family reunion the narrator, a lodger of Mrs Todd's, who thought she knew her well, noted:

> As the feast went on, the spirits of my companion steadily rose. The excitement of an unexpectedly great occasion was a subtle stimulant to her disposition, and I could see that sometimes when Mrs Todd had seemed limited and heavily domestic, she had simply grown sluggish for lack of proper surroundings. She was not so much reminiscent now as expectant, and as alert and gay as a girl. We who were her neighbors were full of gayety, which was but the reflected light from her beaming countenance. It was not the first time that I was full of wonder at the waste of human ability in this world, as a botanist wonders at the wastefulness of nature, the thousand seeds that die, the unused provision of every sort. The reserve force of society grows more and more amazing to one's thought. More than one face among the Bowdens showed that only opportunity and stimulus were lacking, – a narrow set of circumstances had caged a fine able character and held it captive.

Fictional images of the rural Midwest were even more depressing, perhaps because in a region of great cities the contrast hit hard. At least Sarah Orne Jewett's characters respond with appreciation, however parochial, to their startlingly beautiful surroundings; they love their solitude and their difference from the urban mainstream; but the inhabitants of Hamlin Garland's windswept prairies have lost this capacity. A son who gets out of this environment succeeds because he gets out; the mother and brother and friends who stay behind fail because they stay. In 'Up the Coulé' (1891) Howard McLane, whose vivid imagination made him leave home and work his way up to become a successful actor, is appalled when, ten years later, he visits home, and finds his brother still milking scraggy cows.

> They stood and looked at each other. Howard's cuffs, collar, and shirt alien in their elegance showed through the dusk, and a glint of light shot out from the jewel of his necktie as the light from the

house caught it at the right angle . . . Grant stood there, ragged, ankle-deep in muck, his sleeves rolled up, a shapeless old straw hat on his head.

But after feeling guilty about having neglected his family, Howard becomes impatient with their attitude of discontent and inaction; an inaction so extraordinary, a discontent so passively expressed that only the power of their environment can explain it. Howard heard Grant say:

Farmin' ain't so free a life as it used to be. This cattle-raisin' and butter-makin' makes a nigger of a man. Binds him right down to the grindstone and he gets nothin' out of it – that's what rubs it in. He simply wallers around in the manure for somebody else. I'd like to know what a man's life is worth who lives as we do? How much higher is it than the lives the niggers used to live?'

'That's the God's truth, Grant,' said young Cosgrove, after a pause.

'A man like me is helpless,' Grant was saying. 'Just like a fly in a pan of molasses. There ain't any escape for him. The more he tears around the more liable he is to rip his legs off.'

'What can he do?'

'Nothin'.'

This, for Garland, is the regular pattern of life in the Midwest. 'Mainly it is long and wearyful'; and if a man has the initiative to move he merely exchanges 'a dull little town at one end' for 'a life of toil at the other'. In Garland's post-Civil War America the small man believed himself the helpless victim of the unequal distribution of first, money and, second, of fruitful and pleasant surroundings.

An equally strong indictment of the Midwestern environment occurs in E. W. Howe's semi-autobiographical *Story of a Country Town* (1883). When Howe, alias Ned Westlock, thinks of the years he lived in high, bleak Fairview, he thinks of a place more depressing than anything depicted by Thomas Hardy, where the sun never shone, where the damp black church and its wind bell cast the shadows and sounds of doom over the village, where a barren landscape bred barren thoughts, where a small town bred small minds, where his father, a clergyman, preached that life was a misery to be endured on earth that a reward might be enjoyed after death, and where religion was masochistically perverted into a belief in the presence of evil and the existence of hell. 'The men pretended to believe that their associates were great libertines, and many of the women were scandalized in an unjust and cruel manner. The men rather took a pride in reputations of this sort, for they never had any other, and, although pretending to deny it, they really hoped the people would continue to accuse them.' Whether in the town or on the farms, it seemed to Ned that the people were miserable and discontented. 'The place . . . made all the men surly and rough and the women pale and fretful.' The tone of the community was such that the Reverend John Westlock finally runs away with a local woman – driven to adultery by the physical and psychological Midwestern environment, as he incoherently explains to Ned, his son.

> My health is good, my business prosperous, my family everything that a reasonable man could desire, but in spite of this I am so nervous, restless and unreasonable that the sight of my home, the sight of and the greetings of people I meet, fill me with desperation and wickedness. I believe that were I compelled to remain here another week, I should murder somebody – I don't know who – anybody – and for no other reason than that I cannot control myself. I have carefully investigated my own mind, fearing I had lost my reason, but my brain is healthy and active.

He wonders he held out as long as he did.

Forty-two years after Howe's book, in 1915, the stagnation of the rural Midwest was still a strong theme in American literature, and formed the substance of Edgar Lee Master's fine collection of poems, *Spoon River Anthology* (which inspired Dylan Thomas's *Under Milk Wood*); and as late as 1919 Sherwood Anderson made his literary debut with a collection of stories about the dull, hypocritical, unprivate, worthless majority in that now famous one-horse town, Winesburg, Ohio. (See above, Chapter 2, pp 61–3.)

Social Darwinism involved not only the concept of the all-powerful environment but the power of biology and heredity. Influenced by the doubts which the evolutionary theory cast on biblical truth and traditional morality, artists as well as scientists gave secular and physical explanations for such phenomena as 'the poor ye have always with ye'. Inequalities existed because people were genetically unequal. Chemistry was inescapable, and so was chance. 'We all know that life is unsolvable – we who think,' wrote Theodore Dreiser. 'The remainder imagine a vain thing, and are full of sound and fury signifying nothing.' Trina, the miserly, vicious anti-heroine of Frank Norris's *McTeague*, says, 'I can't help myself': and nearly all the realistic and naturalistic novelists of post-Civil War literature crave indulgence for their characters on the same grounds. There is no such thing as freedom, just existence. We are governed by the accidents and facts of geneticism, as Dreiser demonstrated when he has Jennie Gerhardt meet Lester Kane for the first time.

'I like you. Do you like me? Say?'

She looked at him, her eyes wide, filled with wonder, with fear, with a growing terror.

'I don't know,' she gasped, her lips dry.

'Do you?' He fixed her grimly, firmly with his eyes.

'I don't know.'

'Look at me,' he said.

'Yes,' she replied.

Though she could not explain her own emotions, she belonged to him temperamentally and he belonged to her. There is a fate in love and a fate in fight. This strong, intellectual bear of a man, son of a wealthy manufacturer, stationed, so far as material conditions were concerned, in a world immensely superior to that in which Jennie moved, was, nevertheless, instinctively, magnetically, and chemically drawn to this poor serving maid. She was his natural affinity, though he did not know it – the one woman who answered somehow the biggest need of his nature.

This is not immorality, this is fate: and there is a new morality in following fate, argues Dreiser. By becoming Lester's mistress, Jennie is able to help her desperate, poverty-stricken parents, brothers and sisters. Stephen Crane too argues that matter dominates mind, and that it may be all to the good, through Henry Fleming, the hero of *The Red Badge of Courage*. Before battle he wonders if he will have the courage to face the fire; he finds himself fleeing and argues from the physical to the intellectual.

> He had fled, he told himself, because annihilation approached. He had done a good part in saving himself, who was a little piece of the army. He had considered the time, he said, to be one in which it was the duty of every little piece to rescue itself if possible. Later the officers could fit the little pieces together again, and make a battle front. If none of the little pieces were wise enough to save themselves from the flurry of death at such a time, why, then, where would be the army? It was all plain that he had proceeded according to very correct and commendable rules. His actions had been sagacious things. They had been full of strategy. They were the work of a master's legs.

He equates matter with mind at its best; physical weakness with mind at its worst. This is a far cry from Conrad's Lord Jim, though Crane and Conrad admired each other tremendously.

Increasingly the imagery of the novelists becomes animal. The top Chicago financiers, says Norris, had 'eyes and jaws which varied from those of the tiger, lynx and bear to those of the fox, the tolerant mastiff and the surly bulldog'. The Chicago Stock Exchange becomes the Pit, the railroad taking over California the Octopus. It is from watching the battle between a squid and a lobster in a tank that Dreiser's Frank Cowperwood formulates his philosophy.

> The incident made a great impression on him. It answered in a rough way that riddle which had been annoying him so much in the past: 'How is life organized?' Things lived on each other – that was it. Lobsters lived on squids and other things. What lived on lobsters? Men, of course! Sure, that was it! And what lived on

men? he asked himself. Was it other men? . . . That was it! Sure, men lived on men.

The most animalistic of all the characters in American literature of this period is Frank Norris's McTeague,

> . . . a young giant, carrying his huge shock of blond hair six feet three inches from the ground; moving his immense limbs, heavy with ropes of muscle, slowly, ponderously. His hands were enormous, red, and covered with a fell of stiff yellow hair; they were hard as wooden mallets, strong as vises, the hands of the old-time car-boy. Often he dispensed with forceps and extracted a refractory tooth with his thumb and finger. His head was square-cut, angular: the jaw salient, like that of the carnivora.

McTeague represents man in the process of evolution, conscious of his animality, trying to fight it and to let his rational impulses rule. When the beautiful Trina comes to him as a patient – he is a dentist – and is under the anaesthetic he is sexually aroused, and wants to rape her. He manages to control himself; yet still Norris holds out no hope for him; because 'below the fine fabric of all that was good in him ran the foul stream of hereditary evil, like a sewer. The vices and sins of his father and of his father's father [drunkards and debauchees] to the third and fourth and five hundredth generation, tainted him.'

But while Dreiser in *Sister Carrie* thought that man would be refined genetically, Norris thought it immaterial whether heredity could be bred out when an individual is always likely to be confronted with other uncontrollable, brutalising forces – the impact of wealth, for instance, as seen in the transformation of the purely bred, delicate, scrupulous Trina McTeague into a selfish, sluttish miser. Norris traces the process of her corruption from her winning $5,000 in a lottery, just before her marriage. Money becomes her baby, her husband, her sensuous and intellectual life.

> At times, when she knew that McTeague was far from home, she would wash the gold, draw the heap lovingly toward her and bury her face in it, delighted at the smell of it and the feel of the smooth,

cool metal on her cheeks. She even put the smaller gold pieces in
her mouth, and jingled them there . . . She would plunge her small
fingers into the pile with little murmurs of affection, her long,
narrow eyes half closed and shining, her breath coming in long sighs.

When McTeague, out of work, and barely kept by Trina, steals
her money, Trina behaves like Electra out of Balzac.

Her grief was terrible. She dug her nails into her scalp, and
clutching the heavy coils of her thick black hair tore it again and
again. She struck her forehead with her clenched fists. Her little
body shook from head to foot with the violence of her sobbing.
She ground her small teeth together and beat her head upon the
floor with all her strength.

Her hair was uncoiled and hanging a tangled, dishevelled mass
far below her waist; her dress was torn; a spot of blood was upon
her forehead; her eyes were swollen; her cheeks flamed vermilion
from the fever that raged in her veins.

This is a modern tragedy. To such a pass has materialism brought
the animal–human species.

And so the giant Ahabs who bestrode American literature,
seeking and challenging the forces that govern the universe, give
way to the early-twentieth-century pygmies who refuse to recognise either their insignificance or their part in the inexorable chain
of being. Ahab admits he is pulling down the crew of the *Pequod*
with him; Curtis Jadwin of *The Pit* refuses to admit that by exer-
cising his freedom as an individual to speculate he is causing a
million men's repression by starvation – the effect of his attempt
to corner wheat on the poorer areas of Europe. Blind to the forces
of greed and power-lust which govern him, he is sucked into the
pit, financially and spiritually ruined by the urban jungle symbolised in the Board of Trade building, 'black, monolithic,
crouching on its foundations like a monstrous sphinx'. The
building also represents the elemental forces of supply and demand; forces which, if not inanimate, are inhuman, defying
human or humane control.

Few American novelists of the first water expressed the belief that it was possible to redeem man from this slavery. Men and women were merely straws in the prevailing winds, insects in the urban jungle; humanism seemed unrealistic. Some socialist writers like Jack London and Upton Sinclair felt that the repressive force was capitalism, the liberating force socialism; London's *Martin Eden* and Sinclair's *The Jungle* (1906) argue that laws and political systems can be changed and the socialist millenium could come. The only major American writer of this period with an optimistic view of man's capacity to create and change was Willa Cather, whose *œuvre* constitutes a fine humanistic statement of mind over matter. In *O Pioneers!* (1913) she wrote of land not as a geographical or geological master but as 'the material out of which countries are made'. How are they made? 'The history of every country begins in the heart of a man or woman,' and Alexandra Bergson is such a creative woman, who believes that 'forces' must be co-operated with, and that mankind alone can fully activate these forces. 'It fortified her to reflect upon the great operations of Nature, and when she thought of the law that lay behind them, she felt a sense of personal security.' In a mystical but practical way, Alexandra tames the land by working it with faith, will and love, without which 'the record of the plough was insignificant, like the feeble scratches on stones left by prehistoric races'.

The general tendency to shrug off the idea of any possibility of freedom, or of individual responsibility for freedom, and then to blame a prevailing creed or life-style was to take on an increasing sophistication in the 1920s, with the cynicism of Fitzgerald's lost, disillusioned generation and the politically passionate writing of John Dos Passos. The environmental settings of the 1920s novels were often exotic and European; but Dick and Nicole Diver in Cannes proved no more effectively responsible than Carrie Meeber and George Hurstwood in New York. They floundered. Hemingway's heroes occasionally deluded themselves that they were masters of their fates and their situations; but ultimately, like the other protagonists, they did not form, they were formed.

189

CHAPTER 6

Religion and Irreligion: God and Mammon

A Man and His Calling

The most important English settlement in the New World was not the most famous one, that of the *Mayflower* Pilgrims who landed at Plymouth Rock in 1620. Nor was it the first one, the Virginia Company settlers brought to Jamestown aboard the *Sarah Constant* in 1607. No, neither of these settlements – partly because both, small to begin with, were rapidly decimated by the ravages of hostile Indians and bitterly cold weather – bulks as large in the course of American culture as the one at Massachusetts Bay, where the *Arbella* deposited John Winthrop and his Puritan followers at Salem and Boston in 1630.

The Bay Colony prospered from the start; by the end of its initial year 2,000 English settlers were in residence. Furthermore, unlike the Pilgrims who had emigrated first to Holland before venturing to the New World, the Puritans were not Separatists, but loyal if disaffected Englishmen of some education and prominence. The Plymouth settlement was basically 'a small and feeble enterprise . . . necessarily and always limited by the slender resources of the poor and humble men who originated it'. The Bay Colony, on the other hand, was led by men of substance and

190

standing who shaped the culture of New England, and since until recently New England has been the source of most American ideas, customs and institutions, the Bay Colony leaders – men like Governor Winthrop and John Cotton – inevitably left their mark on American thought.

The Puritans had been granted a remarkable royal charter, like most others in providing for proper government of the Massachusetts Bay Company but quite unlike them in omitting the usual clause that company business must be conducted in England. As a consequence, Puritan leaders among the company soon took control of their own affairs in the New World. As Samuel Eliot Morison has observed, their goals were threefold – 'patriotic, commercial, and religious' – though not necessarily in that order. 'I am not so simple to think,' the explorer and promoter Captain John Smith had written in his *Description of New England* (1616), 'that ever any other motive than wealth, will ever erect there a commonweale; or draw companie from their ease and humours at home, to stay in New England'. But Smith was mistaken, for not one but five commonwealths were eventually established in New England, at least partly on religious grounds, and the Bay Colony, in particular, was consciously directed from the beginning towards the building of a great Puritan state, a city set upon a hill as a beacon to all mankind. Winthrop and his fellow settlers brought with them not only an extraordinary royal charter, but a still more solemn and binding covenant with God to create a New Jerusalem in the New World.

The relationship between religion and commerce, always a curiously close one in American culture (indeed, the concept of the sanctity of the business contract can clearly be traced to the regal charter and holy covenant), had by the end of the nineteenth century undergone a sea change into the rich and strange form variously called the gospel of wealth or the religion of success. Under either rubric, the philosophy was called upon to justify the activities of the great American robber barons, to give legitimacy to the Gilded Age, to explain and condone the process by which the colonists' dream of a New Jerusalem had become transformed, so Henry Adams believed, into something 'a good deal like the stampede of hogs to a trough'.

To put this unholy gospel into perspective, one must go back to the origins of American thought, and specifically to a sermon preached by the distinguished Puritan minister John Cotton in 1641. Choosing as his subject 'A Christian Calling', Cotton exhorted his listeners – the entire community, since no one was exempt from attending church services, though only the elect could be full members of the congregation – to persevere in their work. A man of God, he pointed out, will not rest until he finds his calling. This occupation must be one that serves the public good, not merely one's private gain. By serving our fellow man, we also serve God, and so should not be concerned with acquisitiveness. Cotton's emphasis was on future reward: the true Christian 'doth not so much look at the world as at heaven', seeking eternal salvation rather than temporal success. God provides each man with adequate gifts to perform his calling, Cotton went on, and hence he should stick to his warranted task, no matter how dirty (cleaning the stables) or how dangerous (fighting Indians) it might be. If he succeeds, he should not puff himself up with vanity; if he fails, he should not despair. If he does his work honestly and well, he will be comforted.

It is reasonable to speculate that Cotton's sermon was prompted by grumbling within the ranks of the settlers, complaints that the choice jobs and rewards were being unequally and arbitrarily distributed. Obviously, building a New Jerusalem in the wilderness required massive effort, creating too many tasks to be performed by the number of labourers available. Strict discipline was required, and to maintain it, Cotton invested the grubbiest tasks with the halo of sanctity. One should not heap up goods; one must work at whatever calling, low or high, for the greater glory of God. His sermon presents an early and powerful case for the continuing worship of work (and the accompanying distrust of any leisure class) in the United States.

The sermon or the reflective journal written for purposes of instruction characterised American literature during the first colonial generations. Poetry, too, was didactic; Michael Wigglesworth's popular *The Day of Doom* (1662), for example, conjured up terrible visions of the hell-fire awaiting those who had not prepared for the separation of sheep and goats at Judgement Day. Following the Biblical precedent, Wigglesworth situated the humble, Heaven-bound sheep at the right hand of the Lord, where they join in judgement upon the whining goats, some of whom have been assured of a trip to the Other Place by their covetousness. This metaphor, in Wigglesworth's treatment, is handled with the high seriousness that pervades his long jeremiad. Half a century later, however, as Sarah Kemble Knight's journal of 1704 reveals, a more worldly attitude had become dominant, and men (as well as a few exceptional women like herself) were engaged in the pursuit of wealth, not for the sake of fulfilling their Christian calling, but for its own sake.

This change in attitude is implicit in Madame Knight's account of her visit to Fairfield, Connecticut. There were, she wrote, many sheep thereabouts (real ones, not metaphorical ones), and a good profit could be turned simply by renting out flocks to fertilise fields with dung. So good were the profits, in fact, that the 'litigious' inhabitants had taken to paying their minister in sheepdip, and begrudging him even that unsavoury salary. Finally, she recounted the anecdote of the scoundrel who rented the sheep for their nightly droppings, and then sheared them instead. Madame Knight's tone is jaunty, bantering; she writes to entertain, not to point a moral lesson, and the sense of high seriousness has disappeared entirely. She is either unaware of or untroubled by the biblical association of sheep and goats with Judgement Day; her irreverent comments about Connecticut sheep and men, which point forward to the literary tradition of the Yankee trickster, would certainly have shocked the author of *The Day of Doom*.

In *The Autobiography of Benjamin Franklin* (1771) the desire to teach nicely blends with pragmatic wisdom, as Franklin makes explicit:

> Having emerged from the poverty and obscurity in which I was born and bred, to a state of affluence and some degree of reputation in the world, and having gone so far through life with a considerable share of felicity, my posterity may like to know [about the events of my life], as they may find some of them suitably to their own situations, and therefore fit to be imitated.

The energetic Franklin had completed but two of his three remarkable careers – first as successful businessman, second as brilliant inventor and scientist, finally as witty and effective statesman – when he set down the record of his life in the 1750s, and the *Autobiography* deals almost exclusively with the question of getting ahead.

Like Cotton, Franklin extolled the benefits of work, but the benefits, he believed, should accrue in this world, not the next. The individual should prosper so that he might then, as Franklin himself did, devote himself to the betterment of the community, the nation, mankind. He is relentlessly practical and outspoken in his advice, cautioning his readers, for example, 'not only to be in *reality* industrious and frugal, but to avoid all appearances to the contrary' and conceiving of marriage as a good thing since, when as a young man he had put it off,

> . . . that hard-to-be-governed passion of youth hurried me frequently into intrigues with low women that fell in my way, which were attended with some expense and great inconvenience, besides a continual risque to my health by a distemper which of all things I dreaded, though by great good luck I escaped it.

This tone can offend twentieth-century ears. Thus D. H. Lawrence refers to Franklin as 'snuff-coloured . . . cunning little Benjamin', insists on his freedom *not* to work, and observes of

Franklin's posited religion that 'if Mr Andrew Carnegie, or any other millionaire, had wished to invent a God to suit his ends, he could not have done better'.

Two aphorisms in the *Autobiography* – which might as easily have come from *Poor Richard's Almanack* (1733–57), an annual compilation put out by Franklin in his role as printer and publisher – illustrate his view of the relationship between wealth and virtue. The first of these, 'Nothing so likely to make a man's fortune as virtue,' proposes the strong probability that the good man will be rewarded with wealth. The second, 'It is hard for an empty sack to stand upright,' states the obverse proposition that the poor man will probably succumb to vice. In these two sayings, as Lawrence understood, lay the foundations for the religion of success which flourished a century later in the heyday of Andrew Carnegie, John D. Rockefeller and the other great entrepreneurs.

The Popular Success Story

By the late nineteenth century, Franklin's tentative suggestions had become virtually unchallenged cultural givens. The successful man *was* virtuous, and the virtuous man successful. The poor man *was* vicious, and the vicious man poor. In its passage through romanticism, American thought had appropriated all of Franklin's pragmatism and half of Emerson's double-edged idealism. In exalting the self, Emerson and the Transcendentalists had provided the incredible burst of industrial and commercial energy which succeeded the American Civil War with a widely accepted rationale. As Van Wyck Brooks observed, 'if the logical result of a thorough-going, self-reliant individualism in the world of the spirit is to become a saint . . . the logical result of a thorough-going, self-reliant individualism in the world of the flesh is to become a millionaire. And in fact,' Brooks added, 'it would be hard to say whether Emerson more keenly relished saintliness or shrewdness.'

The Gilded Age, in effect, made no distinction between the saintly and the successful, despite the rise of the robber barons, whose methods of assembling wealth usually involved squeezing competitors until they were reduced to poverty, creating monopolies, and then overcharging a public left without alternative sources of supply. *Caveat emptor*, and the public be damned. Here, as so often in American history, the empirical America did not coincide with the imagined one; myth was at odds with reality. Perhaps the most famous expression of this dominant cultural myth came from a man named Horatio Alger, Jr, who lived from 1832 to 1899, wrote 119 books, and died plaintively wondering, 'Am I, dear God, a failure?'

By his own lights, he was. Indeed, Alger's life, when contrasted with his incredibly optimistic tales, sadly illustrates the gulf between myth and reality.

In a typical version of the myth, as Alger disseminated it to the nation's youth, 'Ragged Dick' (1867) or 'Mark the Match Boy', a virtuous young man from the country, comes to the city where he shines shoes to such a gloss that he is noticed favourably by a business tycoon. Subsequently, the lad rescues the tycoon's daughter from a runaway horse-carriage, for which he is, first, rewarded with the hand in marriage of the daughter, who is, as always beautiful with long blonde curls, and, second, placed in full charge of the tycoon's vast business holdings, becoming an instant millionaire.

The balloon begs to be punctured. How many shoeshine boys become millionaires? How many have the opportunity – not to mention the skill and courage and desire – to halt runaway carriages? Alger stresses that his heroes must be virtuous, but clearly, in order to succeed, they must be amazingly lucky as well. Yet his were very popular books, acting out a fantasy in the truth of which nearly every American boy wanted to believe – that he too, if he were diligent and clean-living, might taste the fruits of success, that he too could find his reward in this world, and not the next.

It was a myth Alger himself passionately believed in, though his own existence hardly served to confirm the belief. He began badly, being born on a Friday the 13th. He was still less fortunate in coming into the world as the child of Horatio Alger, Sr, a Unitarian minister who devoted himself to training his first son to succeed him in the pulpit. The boy was subjected to a stern upbringing, allowed few friends, and dressed so like a little clergyman that he was soon called 'Holy Horatio'. Rarely permitted to play, he was allowed to build a snowman, since when it melted his father had an opportunity to discourse to him on the permanence of God's works and the ephemeral nature of those of man. By and large, however, the father was disappointed with his son, who seemed dull and unresponsive, at least until Horatio, Jr, at the age of thirteen, produced his first published piece entitled 'A Race Up the Hill':

A boy was waiting at the bottom of the hill for someone to come and play with him. Soon he heard whistling and was happy because he thought a friend of his was coming. The whistling came from the wind which was blowing about the fields and at first the boy was ready to weep because he had no one to play with. The wind kept whistling and the whistle seemed to say, 'Come, little boy, *I* will play with you.' The boy listened hard and was sure he heard the words. This new companion made him full of joy even if he could not see it.

So he jumped about and ran merrily about the trees with the wind singing and chasing after him. The fact that the boy ran ahead of the wind pleased him very much. He was proud and challenged the wind to a race up hill. 'Well, well,' cried the wind, 'let us start.' The boy ran as fast as he could run. The wind was close behind him. 'I win,' said the boy as he stopped. 'I beat the wind.' The wind grew angry at hearing the boast and whistled by him and did not come back to play.

Rarely has a pre-adolescent so poignantly portrayed his loneliness as in this tale of the friendless boy who offends even his inanimate imaginary companion, the wind. But the Reverend Alger did not see it that way at all; the story, he proudly proclaimed in the local newspaper, was in reality a sermon which said, 'Thou shall not set thyself against the word of the Lord.'

Indeed, Horatio Alger, Sr, carefully guarded his son against any relationships which might hinder his future career. Sent off to Harvard, young Horatio fell in love with a girl, named Patience Stires, who reciprocated his feeling. But his father, learning of the liaison, wrote to Patience that 'a woman who truly loved would scarcely think of shattering the career of her loved one'. Soon after, the son reported home sadly that 'the young lady I hoped to marry seems to have changed her mind'; but he never learned of his father's intervention, and he never married anyone at all. Dutifully, he plunged ahead with his studies, finishing theology school but lasting only eighteen months as a minister before abandoning the profession. Ever after, in the eyes of his father, he was a failure.

He left the church to pursue literature; pathetically, he wanted to write a great book. As Herbert Mayes, his biographer, reports, Horatio was constantly seeking time to turn out a novel that would 'find a place in the company of fine writing'. As soon as he found a proper theme, he remarked in 1871, he would separate himself 'from juvenile fiction long enough to write a lasting work'. On his deathbed in 1899, he vowed not to die because there was a book he had left unwritten; his sister consoled him, 'You've written enough, Horatio,' and so, posterity would agree, he had.

In the later years of his life Alger became a famous man. Clergymen made it a point to look him up in New York, the mayor appointed him to the anti-vice commission, newsboys thronged to hear his inspirational talks, and all American boys growing up for another generation (Scott Fitzgerald and Ernest Hemingway among them) avidly read his potboilers. But his own life was a luckless affair – a lonely bachelor, he fulfilled neither his father's dream nor his own. However wide his public fame, Horatio Alger knew his books were trash, and that they lied.

If Alger wrote for boys, the Reverend Russell Conwell, a Baptist minister and the founder of Temple University in Philadelphia, preached to men. He preached the same sermon, in fact, more than 6,000 times on the Chatauqua circuit which took him and his message to nearly every city and hamlet in the country. The sermon was called 'Acres of Diamonds'; it was printed first in 1888 and in dozens of editions thereafter, and its method was instruction by anecdote, followed by a pointed moral.

Conwell began, then, by telling the story of Ali Hafed, an ancient Persian who owned a very large farm, had money at interest, and 'was a wealthy and contented man. He was contented because he was wealthy, and wealthy because he was contented.' One day, however, Ali Hafed 'heard all about diamonds, how much they were worth, and went to his bed that night a poor man. He had not lost anything, but he was poor because he was discontented, and discontented because he feared he was poor.' The next day, he sold his farm and set out on a long and hopeless search for diamonds. Finally, 'in rags, wretchedness, and poverty', he flung himself into a great tidal wave that 'came rolling in between the pillars of Hercules' and 'sank beneath its foaming crest, never to rise in this life again'.

Meanwhile, back in Persia, Ali Hafed's successor 'noticed a curious flash of light from the white sands of the stream' that ran through the farm, and pulled out a black stone that reflected 'all the hues of the rainbow'. Thus, Conwell insisted, 'was discovered the diamond-mine of Golconda, the most magnificent diamond-mine in all the history of mankind'.

In case anyone missed the moral of the story, he then spelt it out: 'Had Ali Hafed remained at home and dug in his own cellar, or underneath his own wheat-fields, or in his own garden, instead of wretchedness, starvation, and death by suicide in a strange land, he would have had "acres of diamonds".' Furthermore, what was true for Ali Hafed remained true for everyone. 'I say to you,' Conwell hammered away, 'that you have "acres of diamonds" in Philadelphia [or Keokuk, or Lexington, or Minneapolis, or wherever he was lecturing] right where you now live.' The opportunity to get rich, to attain unto great wealth, he went on, 'is here in Philadelphia now, within the reach of almost every man or woman who hears me speak tonight, and I mean just what I say'. Only in a land of comparative plenty could such hyperbole be imaginable, and of course Conwell's claim was blatantly exaggerated. Yet certain men in America *had* managed to create great fortunes out of small beginnings and if the great majority constituted the plundered, the individual within that majority might still see himself as one day achieving rank as a plunderer.

Conwell saw nothing wrong with the accumulation of wealth. On the contrary, he told his listeners, 'you ought to get rich, and it is your duty to get rich'. The wealthy were good and honest. 'If you will take me out to the suburbs of your city, and introduce me to the people who own the fine homes there, I will introduce you to the very best people in character as well as in enterprise in our city, and you know I will.' Money does good. 'Money printed your Bible, money builds your churches, money sends your missionaries, and money pays your preachers, and you would not have many of them, either, if you did not pay them.' Therefore, get money: 'it is your Christian and godly duty to do so'.

In his talk, Conwell disposed of objections by raising and dismissing them himself. Did he not sympathise with the poor? Of course he did, or else he would not have been lecturing all these years. Still, 'While we should sympathize with God's poor – that is, those who cannot help themselves – let us remember there is not a poor person in the United States who was not made poor by his own shortcomings, or by the shortcomings of someone else. It is all wrong to be poor, anyhow.' In their radical equation of poverty with lack of merit, the words almost defy belief. Did his listeners think Conwell heartless? Did he not know that there were some things more important than money?

Of course I do, but I am talking about money now. Of course there are some things higher than money. Oh yes, I know by the grave that has left me standing alone that there are some things in this world that are higher and sweeter and purer than money . . . Love is the grandest thing on God's earth, but fortunate the lover who has plenty of money.

Finally, Conwell disposed of one last objection. Did the Bible not teach that money was the root of all evil? Indeed not, money honestly acquired and rightly used was a very good thing indeed. It was 'the love of money' that lay at the root of evil.

Conwell's talk gave a strong moral sanction to the process of acquisition; getting rich, he made clear, amounted to the most virtuous occupation imaginable. And as a Baptist minister, his words carried a weight that those of Alger, who was enormously popular but still a hack writer, could not. Still more influential, perhaps, was the widely disseminated advice of Andrew Carnegie, the son of a poor Scots immigrant who amassed one of the world's great fortunes in the steel industry. Late in life, Carnegie attained a reputation for benevolence by giving away much of his wealth (as did Conwell), in his philanthropy proving that 'few sights are more moving than the generosity of those who have climbed to success over the bloody and dying bodies of their would-be competitors'.

Carnegie's best-selling book was titled, appropriately, *The Gospel of Wealth and Other Timely Essays* (1900). In that book, as in his 'A Talk to Young Men' (1885), the industrialist set forth his version of Herbert Spencer's 'survival of the fittest'. In an admonition reminiscent of John Cotton's, he advised his listeners not to be too proud to begin at the beginning. Many leading businessmen, he pointed out in an attempt at humour, had 'had a very serious responsibility thrust upon them at the very threshold of their career. They were introduced to the broom, and spent the first hours of their business lives sweeping out of the office.' The burden of Cotton's message, however, was that the sweeper should stick to his broom no matter what; as Nathanael Ward expressed it in *The Simple Cobbler of Aggawam*,

> The upper world shall Rule,
> While Stars will run their race
> The nether world obey,
> While People keep their place.

Carnegie, on the other hand, advised young men to aim high: 'Say each to yourself, "My place is at the top." *Be king in your dreams*.' The opportunity for mobility along social and economic lines was probably not much more available in 1885 than in 1645, but expectations had altered radically. Do not expect too much, Cotton proposed. Expect the moon, Carnegie advised.

To realise these grandiose expectations, Carnegie added, one must be honest, truthful, fair-dealing and live a pure, respectable life. Above all, one should avoid 'three of the gravest dangers' which blocked one's 'upward path'. The first and most seductive of these was drink. Hard liquor ruined men, and it was best not to take it at all, but in any event the young businessman should 'resolve never to touch it except at meals' and 'be far too much of a gentleman ever to enter a bar-room'. The second great danger was speculation, and again Carnegie drew his argument on pragmatic grounds; in his experience, 'Gamesters die poor'. Finally, he cautioned his audience against acting as financial guarantors, even for friends. Friendship was one thing, and business another: 'Before you indorse at all, consider indorsements as gifts, and ask yourselves whether you wish to make the gift to your friend and whether the money is really yours to give and not a trust for your creditors.' It was far better to save money oneself, because 'for every hundred dollars you can produce as the result of hard-won savings, Midas, in search of a partner, will lend or credit a thousand; for every thousand, fifty thousand.'

The man who followed Carnegie's programme might not achieve success himself, but there can be no doubt that he would make a solid, thrifty, hard-working employee. Indeed, instead of the question, 'What must I do for my employer?' Carnegie proposed, 'What can I do?' To get ahead, the rising man should accomplish not merely what was expected of him, but something exceptional. 'HE MUST ATTRACT ATTENTION.' Furthermore, Carnegie stressed, the 'prime condition' of success was a concentration of 'energy, thought, and capital' upon one business: ' "Don't put all your eggs in one basket" is all wrong. I tell you "put all your eggs in one basket, and then watch that basket".' In summary, he invoked Ralph Waldo Emerson, the patron saint of business enterprise as well as of private meditation: 'be not impatient, for, as Emerson says, "no one can cheat you out of ultimate success but yourselves".'

Reactions to the Myth

These three then – Alger, Conwell and Carnegie – articulated (in what seemed, at least in the last case, to be useful advice) one of the dominant cultural myths of late-nineteenth-century America: the intimate relationship between virtue and wealth. But was this a peculiarly American myth? Max Weber, in *The Protestant Ethic and the Spirit of Capitalism*, attempted to show how Protestantism led to the growth of capitalism, and it is possible to see how John Cotton's Calvinist views were transformed, once they lost their other-worldly orientation, into Franklin's practicality and eventually the professedly hard-headed but actually romantic 'dreams-come-true' pronouncements of the Gilded Age. But there are many Protestant countries, and Weber's proposition, however useful as a model, has not successfully borne close examination. A more persuasive argument for the uniqueness of American concentration upon personal wealth comes from Alexis de Tocqueville, whose perceptive *Democracy in America* pointed out that in democratic countries, where all men were presumably equal, one permissible way of distinguishing oneself from the mass of men was to become demonstrably rich.

But it remained for W. H. Auden, that half-Americanised Englishman, in his essay 'The Almighty Dollar' (printed in *The Dyer's Hand and Other Essays*, 1963), to draw the essential distinction between European and American attitudes towards gaining wealth. Europeans took it for granted, Auden wrote, that the only ways of obtaining a fortune were by inheritance or by exploitation of others' labour, and hence getting rich did not necessarily redound to one's favour – if anything, quite the opposite. In America, on the other hand, it had been true until the mid-twentieth century that each man had an excellent chance of making more money than his father had, and not to do so was not only an indication of lack of virtue, but even of lack of manliness. It was not that the possession of money itself was important in America: indeed, as Henry Adams had remarked in *The Education of Henry Adams* (1907), 'the American mind had less respect for money than the European or Asiatic mind, and bore its loss more easily; but it had been deflected by its pursuit til it could turn in no other direction'. The money itself – especially if it was inherited – did not matter; its successful pursuit, the proven ability to make it, counted for everything.

The literary demonstration of the peculiar American tendency to confuse God and Mammon came not only in the success literature of Horatio Alger and Russell Conwell, who have found their modern avatars in Dale Carnegie and Norman Vincent Peale (authors, respectively, of *How to Win Friends and Influence People* and *The Power of Positive Thinking*), but in the persistence of this theme in serious American writing, where the concept of monetary success is viewed from a more critical perspective, and in the literature of the social gospel which followed hard upon, but did not supplant, the gospel of wealth.

The books and articles of the reformers and trust-busters and muckrakers of the Progressive era (the late nineteenth and early twentieth centuries) cracked down on the robber barons, and reaffirmed Cotton's emphasis on service to the community. By far the most influential book of this sort was *Looking Backward: 2000–1887* (1888), written by Edward Bellamy. In terms of popularity, *Looking Backward* was, after *Uncle Tom's Cabin* and *Ben-Hur*, the most popular book at the turn of the century, circulating in many millions of copies in the United States and translated into more than twenty languages. Even more significantly, Bellamy's vision of a utopian Boston in the year 2000 inspired a political movement, as 165 groups called variously 'Bellamy Clubs' or 'Nationalist Clubs' sprang up between 1890 and 1891.

Bellamy, a sincere and intelligent socialist, presented his brave new society without a hint of satire, comparing the competitive, and therefore lamentable, present with the co-operative, and therefore admirable, future in two central metaphors. The first was that of a giant umbrella, which covered the entire city of Boston when it rained, and in affording to all equal protection from the elements represented an improvement upon the nineteenth-century custom of individual umbrellas. The second, more elaborate and more telling metaphor was that of the coach. As Dr Leete, the wise spokesman for the author, propounded it, the society of 1887 could best be compared to

> . . . a prodigious coach which the masses of humanity were harnessed to and dragged toilsomely along a very hilly and sandy road . . . Despite the difficulty of drawing the coach at all along so hard a road, the top was covered with passengers who never got down, even at the steepest ascents. These seats at the top were very breezy and comfortable . . . and the competition for them was keen, every one seeking as the first end in life to secure a seat on the coach for himself . . . By the rule of the coach a man could leave his seat to anyone whom he wished, but on the other hand there were so many accidents by which at any time it might at any time be wholly lost.

The driver of the coach was Hunger, and he permitted no lagging among the multitude required to pull it. When it was necessary to mount very steep hills,

... the desperate straining of the team, their agonized leaping and plunging under the pitiless lashing of hunger, the many who fainted at the rope and were trampled in the mire, made a very distressing spectacle, which often called forth highly creditable displays of feeling on the top of the coach. At such times, the passengers would call down encouragingly to the toilers of the rope, exhorting them to patience, and holding out hopes of possible compensation in another world for the hardness of their lot, while others contributed to buy salves and liniments for the crippled and injured. It was agreed that it was a great pity that the coach should be so hard to pull, and there was a sense of general relief when the specially bad piece of road was gotten over. This relief was not, indeed, wholly on account of the team, for there was always some danger at these bad places of a general overturn in which all would lose their seats ... If the passengers could only have felt assured that neither they nor their friends would ever fall from the top, it is probable that, beyond contributing to the funds for liniments and bandages, they would have troubled themselves extremely little about those who dragged the coach.

Here the whole programme of heedless individualistic pursuit of wealth was summed up and condemned. But the popularity of Bellamy's book may have derived as much from public interest in glamorous collective Utopias as from the ideas couched in metaphor, for most Americans were reluctant to part with the still more glamorous Alger-ian fairy tales of individual success. For every Bellamy there were a dozen who, like Elbert Hubbard, inquired, 'If men will not act for themselves, what will they do when the benefit of their effort is for all?' For every man who, like Thorstein Veblen in *The Theory of the Leisure Class* (1899), deplored 'conspicuous consumption' and 'invidious waste', there were several, such as William Graham Sumner, to counter that the dire alternative to survival of the fittest was the survival of the unfittest. Theodore Roosevelt, purportedly a Progressive reformer, said to the muckraking socialist Upton Sinclair, the author, in *The Jungle*, of an excoriating attack upon conditions in the Chicago stockyards, 'Really, Mr Sinclair, you must keep your head.' Almost everyone agreed with another president and Progressive, Woodrow Wilson, that there was nothing fundamentally wrong with America. Not even Bellamy's widow, in fact, seemed to have understood him. She told an interviewer in 1950, 'I am sure he was haunted by thoughts of other people's problems, especially the poor. And that's something that fills me with wonder. Why did he feel such things so deeply when he himself had been comfortably raised and had never wanted?'

For their own reasons, not usually associated with political reform, most of America's canonical writers have also felt deeply the crippling effects of the gospel of wealth. Popular writing, according to James D. Hart, flourishes when it answers certain needs of a culture; he lists 'clarification of ideas already in circulation' and 'emotional statement of feelings that people are prepared to accept' as two of those needs. More serious and longer-lasting writing, on the other hand, places such ideas under close examination and usually finds them wanting. Where the merely popular book *reflects* the culture, the important one *reacts* against it.

In their attack on the pursuit of wealth, writers like Melville and James emphasised how that activity tends to dehumanise people and to devalue artistic endeavour. In 'The Tartarus of Maids', for example, Melville condemned the sterility of an industrial system which effectively de-sexed its female labourers. Similarly, in 'Bartleby the Scrivener', he found the profit motive as insidiously at work in a Wall Street office as in the frigid paper-factory near Woedolor Mountain. *Moby-Dick* illustrates the writer's further conviction (especially through Ahab's use of a symbolic doubloon to entice his crew towards blind pursuit of the White Whale and his accompanying reflection that the 'permanent constitutional condition of the manufactured man . . . is sordidness') that men can be easily manipulated by money.

Such manipulation, of course, is rife in the work of Henry James, who visits damning moral judgements on the manipulators. The Jamesian international theme usually confronted a restless, morally spontaneous, indisputably innocent and actually or potentially rich American with a complicated, morally ambiguous representative of the Old World. Unlike his friend Howells, who in such early novels as *The Lady of the Aroostock* (1879) condemned Venetian society as immoral, James achieved a certain persuasiveness by usually making his villain–manipulators Americans more or less permanently transplanted to Europe. Thus both Madame Merle and Gilbert Osmond, who combine to separate Isabel Archer from her freedom and inheritance, are American by birth but European by inclination and in their way of life.

In *The American* during conversations between Christopher Newman and the Bellegardes, James brilliantly demonstrated his sensitivity to the problem posed by American worship of monetary success. His very poverty, Valentin de Bellegarde tells Newman, is his capital:

> Being an American, it was impossible you should remain what you were born, and being born poor—do I understand it?—it was therefore inevitable that you should become rich. You were in a position that makes one's mouth water; you looked round you and saw a world full of things you had only to step up to and take hold of.

His own case, M de Bellegarde went on, was quite different. Wherever he looked, signs said 'Hands off!' As a Bellegarde he could not make money or go into politics or even marry a rich girl, because no Bellegarde had ever done so.

But this presumed freedom was, of course, imaginary; as Valentin himself observed, it was 'inevitable' that Newman should become rich. He had if anything less choice in the matter than Bellegarde, the bonds of democracy holding him in check quite as firmly as the bonds of aristocracy limited Bellegarde. As Newman laments to Mme de Cintré, 'You think of me as a fellow who has had no idea in life but to make money and drive sharp bargains. That's a fair description of me, but it is not the whole story.' If it had been the whole story, Newman ('that new man, the American') would hardly have come to Europe in middle life to acquire – he knew not what – something to give his life flavour or resonance. 'A man ought to care for something else,' he goes on, 'though I don't know exactly what. I cared for money-making, but I never cared particularly for the money. There was nothing else to do, and it was impossible to be idle.' (See above, Chapter 1, pp 9–46.)

In this speech, Newman the businessman expresses in inchoate form the dilemma facing the artist in American culture: an indifference to his product and scorn for his financially unrewarding profession. 'Dollars damn me,' Melville passionately summed up his plight in a letter to Hawthorne. 'What I feel most moved to write, that is banned, – it will not pay. Yet altogether, write the *other* way I cannot . . . and all my books are botches.' In a burst of bravado, Edwin Arlington Robinson sarcastically addressed the 'Dear Friends' who might be perusing his first book of poems (1896),

> The shame I win for singing is all mine,
> The gold I miss for dreaming is all yours.

By the twentieth century, such defensive laments turned into more open defiance. Thus in *Green Hills of Africa* (1935) Ernest Hemingway singled out incessant questing after money as the shortcoming that ruined most American authors, and in the posthumously published *A Moveable Feast* (1964) he made the accusation more vivid and personal, suggesting that it was the rich who had destroyed his idyllic and artistically productive first marriage:

> When you have two people who love each other, are happy and gay and really good work is being done by one or both of them, people are drawn to them as surely as migrating birds are drawn at night to a powerful beacon . . . Those who attract people by their happiness and their performance are usually inexperienced.

O 209

They do not know how not to be overrun and how to go away. They do not always learn about the good, the attractive, the charming, the soon-beloved, the generous, the understanding rich who have no bad qualities and who give each day the quality of a festival and who, when they have passed and taken the nourishment they needed, leave everything deader than the roots of any grass Attila's horses' hooves have ever scoured.

A number of other works still more clearly depict the distressing consequences of equating virtue with wealth. In self-justification, Captain Ahab reflects that even the Crusaders looted and stole on their holy mission, and Hank Morgan asked to go along on a sixth-century crusade, turns down the proposal when he discovers that there is no profit in it: 'Well, I should smile.' In the same book, Twain wonderfully punctured the religion of success in his portrayal of the blacksmith, Dowley, a self-made man (he has married the boss's daughter) who calls his mundane trade 'the mystery'. Twain, speaking through his protagonist, comments about Dowley: 'Self-made man, you know. They know how to talk. They do deserve more credit than any other breed of men, yes that is true; and they are the very first to find it out, too.'

Sherwood Anderson explores a similar theme in his portrait of Jesse Bentley in 'Roots'. Though he had originally intended to become a missionary, Bentley comes back to Winesburg upon the death of his father to take over his farm, and through unstinting effort manages to accumulate a good deal of land and to wring the utmost profit from it. In his relations with other people, Jesse is less successful. Jesse is so consumed with his financial goals, in fact, that he drives his wife to her death and turns his daughter into a misanthrope. None the less, Jesse remains convinced that the Lord has a special mission for him to perform, and after his grandson David comes to live with him, he takes the lad and a lamb he intends to offer as a sacrifice in quest of a sign from heaven. The boy, terribly frightened, stuns his grandfather with a stone, and runs away. Jesse, when he recovers his wits, continues his joint pursuit of wealth and holiness, with the first endeavour taking precedence:

> There were two influences at work in Jesse Bentley and all his life his mind had been a battle ground for these influences . . . While he worked night and day to make his farms more productive and to extend his holdings of land, he regretted that he could not use his own restless energy in the building of temples, the slaying of unbelievers and in general in the work of glorifying God's name on earth.

This confusion of virtue (or happiness) with wealth constitutes a central theme in the work of Fitzgerald. In a memorably sacrilegious story, 'The Diamond as Big as the Ritz' (1922), Fitzgerald creates a fantasy world of incredible luxury in the Rocky Mountains presided over by the corrupt and amoral Braddock Washington. The continued existence of this Xanadu depends upon its remaining undiscovered by the federal government, which would want taxes paid, or by other adventurers after its fantastic wealth. As a matter of security, the infrequent guests to the mountain hideaway are quietly done away with. But in the end, the diamond mountain is discovered, and as the aeroplanes circle preparing to drop bombs, Washington offers a gigantic diamond as a bribe to God, doubting only 'whether he had made his bribe big enough. God had His price, of course. God was made in man's image, so it had been said: He must have His price.' The sacrifice, like Jesse Bentley's, fails; the mountain is wiped away in a massive eruption. God has become hopelessly and fatally indistinguishable from Mammon.

CHAPTER 7

Religion and Irreligion: Doubts and Certainties

All the Answers

One of the most striking things about the early settlers of New England was their religious certainty. They *knew*, by way of Calvinist doctrine, that man was inherently sinful and guilty, because, 'In Adam's fall/We sinnéd all.' They *knew* that they had been divinely directed to build a New Jerusalem. They *knew* the truth, and they knew the truth was simple. The Word was revealed in the Book: 'The Scripture saith, there is nothing makes free but Truth, and Truth saith, there is no truth but One.' As Perry Miller commented, the 'Puritan thought the Bible . . . was the word of God from one end to the other'. Paradoxically, however, though the truth was simple and could be found in the Bible, one of the first steps the settlers of New England took was to establish Harvard College, where young men might learn to interpret the Word. Plain and explicit though it might be, the Bible revealed its truth only to those equipped with the proper education and skilled in the proper rules of deduction.

Read the Bible right, they believed, and it laid down a divinely given set of laws covering not only theology, but also 'ethics, costume, diplomacy, military tactics, inheritances, profits, marriages, and judicial procedure'. Trained to think in terms of correspondences, the early New Englanders were certain that everything that happened in this world had its symbolic significance. During a sermon before the synod of Cambridge, John Winthrop wrote in his journal, a snake appeared behind the pulpit and was killed by one of the elders. Winthrop's comment on the incident exemplified the Puritan's emblematic habit of thought:

> This being so remarkable, and nothing falling out but by divine providence, it is out of doubt, the Lord discovered somewhat of his mind in it. The serpent is the devil; the synod, the representative of the churches of Christ in New England. The devil had formerly and lately attempted their disturbance and dissolution; but their faith . . . overcame him and crushed his head.

It is 'out of doubt' that his interpretation is correct, that the serpent *is* the devil. With astounding assurance, Winthrop converts metaphorical fancy into fact. Emerson nowhere better reflected his Calvinist ancestry than in adopting the doctrine of correspondences, the belief that every natural fact is a sign of a spiritual fact.

'Operating from such a position, reading the book of the world along with the Bible,' so Roy Harvey Pearce observed, 'the Puritan intellectual might work out the pattern of his culture.' It was a logical pattern, and the world it contemplated rested in orderly stasis. How sure the Puritans were! There is an anecdote about a famous twentieth-century judge who, when asked about his controversial decisions, remarked, 'We are often wrong, but we are never in doubt.' Like the judge, the early settlers of New England were never in doubt; unlike him, they did not concede that they could have been wrong. The consequence was an overriding intolerance toward views that conflicted with their own: let dissenters be banished to the Indians and wolves, let wrongthinkers by punished.

This cruel intolerance is strikingly portrayed in the fiction of Hawthorne. As has been mentioned earlier, he was a descendant of Judge John Hathorne, one of the judges at the notorious Salem witch trials of 1693, and he was given to sarcastic references to, for example, the 'fines, imprisonments, and stripes, liberally distributed by our pious forefathers'. Both in *The Scarlet Letter* and in 'The Gentle Boy' (1837) he vividly portrayed the way in which absolute certainty made monsters of even the youngest and most innocent children. The gentle boy is a Quaker lad named Ilbrahim, who, after he is abandoned by his mother, lives in a Puritan household and makes friends with a boy who has been temporarily laid up at home. Once this child has recovered and they go out to frolic with the other Puritan children, however, his companion at once repudiates Ilbrahim as a Quaker and joins with the other youngsters, 'baby fiends', in stoning the gentle boy. Hawthorne's target here is not simply Puritanism but religious fanaticism in any form, for if Ilbrahim's mother had not deserted him in order to pursue Quaker missionary work, he would not have been subjected to such physical and psychological violence.

Even aside from the issue of intolerance, the Puritans' very sense of certainty begged for contradiction and inspired dissenting views. Thus one great theme in American literature has been what Pearce calls 'the impulse toward antinomianism', the rejection of received values in favour of answers arrived at independently and with difficulty. 'I want to know,' Henry James's naïve young heroine Daisy Miller insists: 'I want to know why,' cries the adolescent narrator in one of Sherwood Anderson's best stories (1918), and they are not alone.

The Age of Belief

By the nineteenth century, the Puritans' dream of a New Jerusalem still shone brightly, but their complementary belief in the essential depravity of man had quite faded away. As Philip Freneau expressed it in his Princeton commencement poem, *The Rising Glory of America* (1771),

> Paradise anew
> Shall flourish, by no second Adam lost,
> No dangerous tree with deadly fruit shall grow,
> No tempting serpent to allure the soul
> From native innocent.

The children of the new nation were not 'baby fiends', but native innocents inhabiting an Eden without serpents and without 'dangerous' apples.

The quarter century from 1830 to 1855 witnessed a remarkable series of attempts to recreate the Garden on American soil. Reformers guaranteed perfect health for those who would eat only wholemeal flour or bathe in pure waters; they embraced temperance and deplored prison conditions; they discovered God in blinding personal visions and unearthed golden plates that his emissaries had left in upstate New York; they founded communitarian settlements from which all agents of the devil were excluded. 'What a multitude of projects,' the iconoclastic Emerson remarked, 'for the improvement of the world!'

But belief in the perfectibility of man, such as that preached by the charismatic John Humphrey Noyes, the founder of the most successful Utopian colony at Oneida, was impervious to common sense. The case of William Miller amply illustrates the point. An eloquent and convincing speaker, Miller calculated, and announced to his followers, that the world would end in 'about 1843', and that they had better prepare for the millenium. The appearance of Halley's comet in that year intensified the religious excitement, but 1843 passed without further incident and, fining down his calculations, Miller decided that the latest possible date for the Second Advent was 21 March 1844. Perhaps 250,000 converts to Millerism waited through the night for the millenium. When it did not come, Miller serenely commented that if he had it to do all over again, he would do the same, for, 'I still believe that the day of the Lord is near, even at the door; and I exhort you, my brethren, to be watchful, and not let the day come upon you unawares.' He had simply miscalculated; the organ of the Millerites published yet another farewell number with the message: 'At 3 o'clock in the morning, 22nd October, he will surely come. Child, believe it.' Miller's children believed, and after yet another disappointment many continued to believe. Perhaps, they reasoned, the end had come in heaven if not upon earth, and the names of those who had not attended to the millenial prophecy had been stricken from Gabriel's book.

Such gullibility moved Poe, in whose writing the supernatural mingled with the ratiocinative, to scornful comment:

> The world is infested, just now, by a new sect of philosophers, who have not yet suspected themselves of forming a sect . . . The only common bond among the sect, is Credulity: – let us call it Insanity at once, and be done with it. Ask any one of them *why* he believes this or that, and, if he is conscientious (ignorant people usually are), he will make you very much such a reply as Talleyrand made when asked *why* he believed in the Bible. 'I believe in it first,' said he, 'because I am Bishop of Autun; and secondly; *because I know nothing about it at all.*'

Hawthorne was still more sceptical, adopting a philosophy of uncertainty both in his private life and in his fiction. In 'an odd and incomprehensible world', he wrote in *The House of the Seven Gables*, 'a man's bewilderment is the measure of his wisdom'. Unlike the Transcendentalists, Hawthorne actually spent some time at Brook Farm, one of the most prominent of communistic colonies, but soon gave up the experiment after discovering that a hard day's labour in the fields left him with neither the ability nor the inclination to write. In *The Blithedale Romance*, a novel based on his experience at Brook Farm, he condemned the tendency of reformers to let an *idée fixe* undermine their human sympathies. In 'Ethan Brand' also the single-minded pursuit of any one belief is seen to have a debilitating effect on personality. For Sherwood Anderson too, 'It was the truths that made the people grotesques . . . The moment one of the people took one of the truths to himself, called it his truth, and tried to live his life by it, he became a grotesque and the truth he embraced a falsehood.'

For his own part, Hawthorne constantly saw both sides of the question, and 'ingrained and inherent doubt incapacitated him from following any course vigorously'. Upon observing a slave ship in the harbour in Liverpool, where he was serving as consul during the 1850s, he first considered warning the Negroes (who had not been enlightened as to their fate) that they would be sold into bondage and then considered whether they might be able to achieve a livelihood if they were freed. While he was reflecting, the boat sailed. His mind, in short, was essentially dualistic. Was his child Una (the model for Pearl in *The Scarlet Letter*) angel or devil? She

> . . . seems at times to have but little delicacy, and anon shows that she possesses the finest essence of it; now so hard, now so tender; now so perfectly unreasonable, soon again so wise. In short, I now and then catch an aspect of her in which I cannot believe her to be my own human child, but a spirit strangely mingled with good and evil, haunting the house where I dwell.

This dualistic habit of mind markedly influenced Hawthorne's writing, where ambiguity reigns. His fiction demonstrates not only the ambiguity inherent in language and the ambiguity of human motivation, but also a more startling ambiguity of external action. Thus in a story such as 'Young Goodman Brown' (1835) there is substantial doubt as to what has happened, even on the literal level.

Brown, a young man brought up in the pious ways of seventeenth-century Puritanism, leaves his wife Faith one evening to keep an appointment in the forest. There his senses are bedazzled by a series of encounters. He meets his guide, whose staff 'bore the likeness of a great black snake, so curiously wrought that it might almost be seen to twist and wriggle itself like a living serpent'. But this phenomenon, 'of course, must have been an ocular deception, assisted by the uncertain light'. Of course? Hardly, for young Goodman Brown can be sure of nothing else during his visit to the forest. It seems to him, 'were such a thing possible, that he recognized the voices of the minister and Deacon Gookin' en route to the Witches' Sabbath. Once at the unholy meeting, he 'could have well-nigh sworn that the shape of his own dead father beckoned him to advance . . . while a woman, with dim features of despair, threw out her hand to warn him back. Was it his mother?'

Most troublesome of all, he fancies that he detects the voice of his own wife Faith and, as he ponders this possibility, a pink ribbon which he remembers having seen in Faith's hair flutters down into his grasp. Even this seemingly concrete evidence is ambiguous, however, for as Hawthorne queries, 'Had Goodman Brown fallen asleep in the forest and only dreamed a wild dream of a witch-meeting?' Such ambiguities, variously characterised by critics as 'the formula of alternative possibilities' and 'the device of multiple choice', leave Brown muddled and in despair. He returns home after his trauma uncertain of anyone's piety and distrustful of his wife, with his faith forever shaken.

Hawthorne's friend Melville was beset with similar doubts. 'We incline to think,' he wrote in a burst of impiety, 'that God cannot explain His own secrets, and that He would like a little information upon certain points Himself.' Certainly He did not reveal these secrets to Melville. Hawthorne commented after the two had talked away a long afternoon near Liverpool,

> Melville, as he always does, began to reason of Providence and futurity, and of everything that lies beyond human ken, and informed me that he had 'pretty much made up his mind to be annihilated'; but still he does not seem to rest in that anticipation; and, I think, will never rest until he gets hold of a definite belief. It is strange how he persists – and has persisted ever since I knew him, and probably long before – in wandering to-and-fro over these deserts, as dismal and monotonous as the sand hills amid which we were sitting. He can neither believe, nor be comfortable in his unbelief; and he is too honest and courageous not to try to do one or the other.

The Search for Faith

America returned from World War I, Scott Fitzgerald wrote, to find all gods dead and all faiths shaken. The old standards did not apply, and each person faced alone the burden of constructing a valid religious and moral universe. The impact of post-World War I disillusionment on an entire generation can hardly be exaggerated; yet the search for faith which that generation was forced to undergo had tried and troubled individual American writers for three-quarters of a century before Johnny came marching home.

Emily Dickinson, like Melville, could neither quite believe nor be comfortable in her disbelief. Her personal difficulty was the more galling in that she was brought up, in strict Calvinist orthodoxy, in a religiously conservative town, Amherst, Massachusetts. Biennially, revivals awakened the fervent faith of her friends and even, late in life, of Edward Dickinson, her father, whom she fearfully worshipped. But no such revelation came to her, and its lack, she felt, betrayed a want of grace on her part. She wrote to a school friend at seventeen,

> *I* am one of the lingering bad ones, and so do I slink away, and pause and ponder, and ponder and pause, and do work without knowing why, not surely, for this brief world, and more sure it is not for heaven, and I ask what this message *means* that they ask for so very eagerly; *you* know of this depth and fulness, will you try to tell me about it?

In her poetry, she frequently brought up such questions, considering herself a 'creature of transition' between belief and disbelief:

> 'Faith' is a fine invention
> When Gentleman can *see* –
> But *Microscopes* are prudent
> In an Emergency.

The brief poem sets up the contest between religion and science, and suggests that neither can provide sufficient answers to dismiss doubt. For faith, minimised by the quotation marks, can hardly be seen and cannot, except ironically, be invented like the spinning-wheel or cotton-gin. Furthermore, she stands aloof from the Church establishment of Gentlemen ('This quiet Dust was Gentlemen and Ladies'). Yet there is irony too in the suggestion that microscopes might prove useful in verifying what is not merely minuscule but quite invisible. Unable to participate in the religious life of her time and place, Dickinson rejects Walt Whitman's affirmation that the smallest creature 'is miracle enough to stagger sextillions of infidels' on the grounds of practical scepticism.

Twain's Huckleberry Finn regards religion from a still more practical point of view. Huck is unable to see any advantage in conventional worship if its goal is to be no more rewarding than eventual joint occupancy of heaven with Miss Watson. Her Calvinism implies a natural depravity that fits Huck's experience, but its stern restrictions chafe. Dinner turns cold if grace takes too long. The Widow Douglas's 'inner light' Protestantism assumes an optimistic view of mankind which is incontestably refuted by Huck's experience. He prays for fishing equipment, and gets a line with no hooks.

Huck finds his only viable religious belief in a set of folk superstitions derived from Pap. Nigger Jim shares the same superstitions, and learned them as Pap and Huck did – by word of mouth. These superstitions developed as a way of rationalising man's conflict with his environment, and were especially useful in explaining why things went wrong, as they usually did. If there is a death in the family, it comes of burning a spider or breaking a mirror or looking at the new moon over your left shoulder. Huck Finn's is a terrible world, one of kidnapping and murder and snakebite and robbery and fraud and money-grubbing and simple inhumanity. As he puts it, 'Human beings *can* be awful cruel to one another.' Superstition helps him rationalise this nightmare world, for almost all superstitions predict the onset of *bad*, not good, luck. Prayers do not work out, superstitions do, for to look at the new moon over the left shoulder is to invite some sort of disaster.

In later years, Mark Twain himself became progressively less enchanted with conventional religion. In essays like 'To the Person Sitting in Darkness' and 'The War Prayer', he further elaborated on the way in which religion sanctioned bloodthirsty aggression. And in several stories of his last decade, Twain demonstrated his anti-faith by blaming mankind's ills on its possession of a moral sense.

The sectarian schisms – many of the sects being revivalistic and enthusiastic, strict and old-fashioned – which sprang up in the nineteenth century represented another challenge to religious orthodoxy. As far back as Johnson J. Hooper's *Some Adventures of Captain Simon Suggs* (1846), in which his clever frontier rascal adopted the motto, 'It is good to be shifty in a new country,' revivalism had come in for satirical treatment. Howells, in *The Leatherwood God* (1916), presented a fictional portrayal of one Joseph Dylks, an actual Ohioan who could not be clapped in jail because his only offence was 'claiming to be the Almighty; he pleads guilty to that, and he could be fined and imprisoned if there was any law against a man's being God'. Sinclair Lewis took up a similar theme, though less sympathetically, in *Elmer Gantry* (1927), his novel about a revival-leading charlatan.

The best American novel on a religious theme, however, is *The Damnation of Theron Ware* (1896), the work of Harold Frederic, who was at the time a correspondent in London for *The New York Times*. Set in upstate New York where he had grown up, Frederic's novel depicts the downfall of Reverend Ware, an extraordinarily innocent and susceptible young Methodist minister who is unable to cope with the threats to his faith posed by contemporary life.

In his new pastorate at Octavius, where his deacons advise him to stick to fire and brimstone in his sermons instead of 'traipsin' after strange gods like some people that call themselves Methodists in other places', Theron Ware meets several people whose manner of thinking and depth of education quite bewilder him. The free-thinking Catholic priest, Father Forbes, casually refers in polite conversation to 'this Christ-myth of ours'. The rationalist Dr Ledsmar introduces Theron to the heartless methods of laboratory science: he simultaneously conducts experiments on his lizards and his Chinese manservant. The attractive and rich Celia Madden befuddles Theron's senses by playing Chopin and burning incense for him in her dim-lighted apartments.

The hapless Ware, who would like nothing better than to acquire the degree of knowledgeable sophistication he admires in this trio, might yet have avoided his damnation, however, had he not fallen victim to the plain-spoken, commonsense views of Sister Soulsby, a fund-raiser who comes to town to clear up his church's debts. She first wins Theron's confidence by demonstrating that she admires his mind and has his financial interests at heart, and then persuades him to engage in an underhanded charade that cheats one member of his board for the greater benefit, as she argues, of the church in general and Theron in particular. Her rationale for this activity is that there is good and evil in each of us, that the sheep will not be separated from the goats until Judgement Day, and that the Reverend Theron Ware should take what profit he could in the meantime.

To a young minister brought up in fundamentalist Methodism, her doctrine becomes insupportable. He had thought all men good, or potentially so; with her teaching in mind, he discovers all men to be evil. In consequence he imagines the worst of his kind and faithful wife Alice, suspects Celia Madden and Father Forbes of an illicit liaison, and in his hubris fancies himself a master manipulator who is inherently superior to the members of his old-fashioned congregation.

The Epistemological Obsession

Theron Ware, like Young Goodman Brown, fell from grace because he was unable to conceive of a dualistic moral universe. Despite Ware's fundamentalism and Brown's Puritanism, each of them carried in his mind an ideal picture of the world which ill suited with reality. In short, they were both romantics clinging to the myth that pious church members must be basically good. When that ideal model collapsed, they constructed the opposite one: if men were not good, then they must be evil.

No one in American literature inveighed against idealism more passionately than Howells, the apostle of realism. Let fiction cease to lie about life, he advised,

> . . . let it portray men and women as they are . . . let it leave off painting dolls and working them by springs and wires; let it show the different interests in their true proportions; let it forbear to preach pride and revenge, folly and insanity, egotism and prejudice, but frankly own these for what they are, in whatever figures and occasions they appear; let it not put on fine literary airs; let it speak the dialect, the language, that most Americans know – the language of unaffected people everywhere – and there can be no doubt of an unlimited future, not only of delightfulness but of usefulness, for it.

From his position as the dean of late-nineteenth-century letters, Howells inspired the movement towards realism reflected in the work of Hamlin Garland and E. W. Howe, Sarah Orne Jewett and Kate Chopin, Stephen Crane and Frank Norris, Theodore Dreiser and Sherwood Anderson. All these writers did their best not to lie about life, but they found it far more difficult to know the truth.

For a Transcendentalist like Thoreau, the process had seemed simplicity itself. 'How much virtue there is in simply seeing!' he wrote. 'We are what we see.' By 'seeing' Thoreau meant nothing complicated: simply opening up one's intuitions, one's Reason in

Coleridge's term, to nature's transparent messages. 'What I need,' he observed, 'is not to look at all, but a true sauntering of the eye.' Analysis and thought played no part in his programme of perception. 'I must walk more with free senses. It is as bad to *study* stars and clouds as flowers and stones. I must let my senses wander as my thoughts, my eyes see without looking.' Confidently, he spoke of 'the advantages of ignorance'.

But the knowledge Thoreau gleaned so effortlessly quite eluded his contemporary Melville. Thus the opaque picture hanging in the Spouter Inn, whence the whalers will go off to sea, stands as a metaphor for the difficulty of ascertaining the truth:

> A boggy, soggy, squitchy picture truly, enough to drive a nervous man distracted. Yet was there a sort of indefinite, half-attained, unimaginable sublimity about it that fairly froze you to it, till you involuntarily took an oath with yourself to find out what that marvelous painting meant.

His long story 'Benito Cereno' was, like much of Melville's fiction, based on documentary evidence, in this case *A Narrative of Voyages and Travels in the Northern and Southern Hemispheres* (1817) by Amasa Delano, whose name is appropriated for the central figure in the story. What Melville conspicuously adds is a sense of the mysterious and the sinister, with the focus on Captain Delano as he helplessly attempts to untangle what is going on aboard the becalmed *San Dominick*. In this story, as in others in *The Piazza Tales* (1856), Melville's interest lies in man's inability to perceive.

The same topic virtually obsessed Henry James, most obviously in his masterful tale of psychological aberration, *The Turn of the Screw*, but in many other stories and novels as well. As Tony Tanner has commented, one of James's main concerns 'is epistemological. How – when confronted with the task to any degree – do people assimilate, construe and interpret experience? . . .' In his fiction, though correct interpretations can be made only with difficulty, the failure to make them invariably leads to dire consequences. Winterbourne misconstrues and destroys Daisy Miller;

the governess at Bly hallucinates and frightens poor Miles to death; John Marcher waits for the beast in the jungle to spring and lets the love of his life escape him; Isabel Archer miscalculates her man and shuts herself up in Osmond's prison-house. Part of the excitement in reading James's work stems from this theme of perception: one must play the detective to catch up the Jamesian character as he or she makes a tragic mistake or miscalculation. The hints are always there on the page, but they are by no means always immediately apparent, for James asks of his readers what too few of his characters bring to bear: not less than their entire attention.

Stephen Crane like James stresses the unfortunate effects that await lack of perception. An unreal picture of the world leads Maggie to her downfall and eventual suicide. Similarly, the Swede in 'The Blue Hotel' is condemned to death more as a consequence of his fantastic notions of the wild, wild West than through the agency of any other character. The Swede, who has been reading dime novels, is convinced that men are casually killed in Western bar-rooms and, in a beautiful example of the self-fulfilling prophecy, he manoeuvres exactly such a fate for himself.

Bereft of Calvinistic certainties and unable to credit Transcendental intuition, American writers have almost obsessively sought answers to hard questions in their fiction. The process, according to D. H. Lawrence's *Studies in Classic American Literature* (1923), has not only been futile but also morally damaging. Lawrence, who consistently exalted feeling above thinking, argues that Adam and Eve had surely cohabited before the 'apple episode', and that, 'It didn't become "sin" till the knowledge-poison entered . . . They wanted to KNOW. And that was the birth of sin. Not *doing* it, but KNOWING about it.'

Not surprisingly, then, Lawrence directed his criticism at the American writer's concentration on knowledge. Of Crèvecoeur and his *Letters from an American Farmer*, for example, Lawrence commented: 'He hates the dark, pre-mental life, really. He hates the true sensual mystery. But he wants to "know". To KNOW. Oh, insatiable American curiosity!' It is one thing to know *about* people, Lawrence observes in discussing Poe, but quite another to try to *know* them mentally. 'It is the temptation of a vampire fiend, is this knowledge.' 'These terribly conscious birds, like Poe and his Ligeia, deny the very life that is in them; they want to turn it all into talk, into *knowing*. And so life, which will *not* be known, leaves them.' In Lawrence's philosophy, 'KNOWING and BEING are opposite, antagonistic states. The more you know, exactly, the less you *are*. The more you *are*, in being, the less you know.'

Perhaps the most conspicuous example of early-twentieth-century seekers after such knowledge was Gertrude Stein. Trained in medical science, Stein attempted in *The Making of Americans* (1925) nothing less than a classification of all Americans. The goal, of course, eluded her. 'I can never really be knowing all the ways there are of feeling living,' she confessed. Furthermore, reality would not stand still, but kept changing, so that what knowledge she did possess constantly slipped away from her. Stein has been widely misread and misunderstood because of her critics' lack of understanding that epistemology consumed her, that her goal was 'to get a fingerhold on the slippery world around her.'

If Stein is the early-twentieth-century American writer who is most obsessed with the problem of knowledge, Fitzgerald is the writer who most effectively conveys how the hard edges of reality obscure vision. His fiction is full of images of blindness. The eyes of Dr T. J. Eckleburg, for example, peer down on the ash heaps between Long Island and Manhattan from a billboard:

> They look out of no face, but, instead, from a pair of enormous yellow spectacles which pass over a non-existent nose. Evidently some wild wag of an oculist set them there to fatten his practice in the borough of Queens, and then sank down himself into eternal blindness, or forgot them and moved away. But his eyes, dimmed a little by many paintless days under sun and rain, brood over the solemn dumping ground.

In *The Good Soldier* (1915) Ford Madox Ford, as an English writer, brilliantly depicts this characteristic American blindness. The narrator of the novel is 'that absurd figure, an American millionaire, who has bought one of the ancient haunts of English peace'. In tracing his obtuseness about human relationships (he is trying to understand among other things how his wife could have carried on an affair with an Englishman who seemed the very image of propriety, inasmuch as he did not tell dirty stories in mixed company), Ford lets the American discourse on his own ignorance and lack of awareness, qualities which he not only admits but seems to take pride in. 'Don't you see?' his wife asks. 'Don't you see what's going on?' He does not, and will not. He has spent nine years in Europe, and emerged with nothing whatever to show for it:

> Not so much as a bone penholder, carved to resemble a chessman and with a hole in the top through which you could see four views of Nauheim. And, as for experience, as for knowledge of one's fellow beings – nothing either . . . After forty-five years of mixing with one's kind, one ought to have acquired the habit of being able to know something about one's fellow beings. But one doesn't.

In spite of its satirical approach, Ford's novel captures the characteristic American obsession with epistemology. In Howells's *The Landlord at Lion's Head* (1897) Jeff Durgin, a brash young man, tells the painter Westover that his painting-in-progress does not much resemble the mountain which is its subject. Unruffled, Westover comments, 'Perhaps you don't know,' and when Jeff insists, 'I know what I see,' the painter replies, 'I doubt it.' The truth is not easy to discover. The artist attempts to see what the Durgins and Gatsbys cannot, but even the artist makes out only the shadows in the cave and must blink back tears on emerging into the light. Robert Frost expressed the continuing dilemma:

> We dance round in a ring and suppose,
> But the Secret sits in the middle and knows.

Authors and Works Discussed

*Note: This section includes works consulted but
not necessarily cited in the text*

Chapter 1   The New World and the Old World

Cahan, Abraham. *The Rise of David Levinsky* (1917)
Cather, Willa. *My Antonia* (1918)
Cooper, James Fenimore. *The Pioneers* (1823)
———. *The Prairie* (1827)
———. *Home as Found* (1838)
———. *Homeward Bound* (1838)
———. *The Pathfinder* (1840)
Hawthorne, Nathaniel. *Mosses from an Old Manse* (1846)
———. *The House of the Seven Gables* (1851)
———. *The Blithedale Romance* (1852)
———. *The Marble Faun* (1860)
———. *Our Old Home* (1863)
Howells, William Dean. *Venetian Life* (1866)
———. *Italian Journeys* (1867)
———. *Indian Summer* (1886)
———. *The Landlord at Lion's Head* (1897)
Irving, Washington. *History of New York* (1809)
———. *The Sketch Book of Geoffrey Crayon, Gent* (1820)
———. *Bracebridge Hall* (1822)
James, Henry. *A Passionate Pilgrim and Other Tales* (1875)
———. *Roderick Hudson* (1876)
———. *The American* (1877)
———. *The Europeans* (1878)
———. *The Portrait of a Lady* (1881)
———. *A Little Tour in France* (1885)
———. *The Wings of the Dove* (1902)

———. *The Golden Bowl* (1904)
———. *English Hours* (1905)
———. *Italian Hours* (1909)
Melville, Herman. *Omoo* (1847)
———. *Mardi* (1849)
———. *Redburn* (1849)
———. *Moby-Dick* (1851)
Pound, Ezra. 'Hugh Selwyn Mauberley' (1920)
Twain, Mark. *Innocents Abroad and The New Pilgrim's Progress* (1869)
———. *The Adventures of Huckleberry Finn* (1884)
———. 'The Diary of Adam and Eve' (1893; 1905)
———. *Pudd'nhead Wilson* (1894)
Wharton, Edith. *The Custom of the Country* (1913)
———. *The Age of Innocence* (1920)

Chapter 2   City and Country

Adams, Henry. *The Education of Henry Adams* (1907)
Anderson, Sherwood. *Marching Men* (1917)
———. *Winesburg, Ohio* (1919)
Brown, Charles Brockden. *Arthur Mervyn* (1800)
Cooper, James Fenimore. *The Prairie* (1827)
———. *The Deerslayer* (1841)
Crane, Stephen. *Maggie* (1893)
Crèvecœur, Hector St John de. *Letters from an American Farmer* (1782)
Dickinson, Emily. 'I Like to See It Lap the Miles' (c 1862)
Dreiser, Theodore. *Sister Carrie* (1900)
Garland, Hamlin. *A Son of the Middle Border* (1917)
Howells, William Dean. *A Hazard of New Fortunes* (1890)
———. *Criticism and Fiction* (1891)
Jefferson, Thomas. *Notes on the State of Virginia* (1784)
Marquis, Don. *archy and mehitabel* (1927)
Melville, Herman. *Moby-Dick* (1851)
———. 'The Tartarus of Maids' (1855)
Mencken, H. L. 'The Husbandman' (1924)
Stratton-Porter, Gene. *The Harvester* (1911)
Thoreau, Henry David. *Walden* (1854)
Twain, Mark. *The Adventures of Huckleberry Finn* (1884)
———. *A Connecticut Yankee in King Arthur's Court* (1889)
Wright, Frank Lloyd. *An Autobiography* (1932)

Chapter 3   Dreams and Nightmares

Alcott, Louisa M. *Little Women and Good Wives* (1869)
Bierce, Ambrose. *Tales of Soldiers and Civilians* (1891)
——. *Can Such Things Be?* (1893)
Cooper, James Fenimore. *The Monikins* (1835)
——. *The Pathfinder* (1840)
Fitzgerald, F. Scott. *The Great Gatsby* (1925)
Hawthorne, Nathaniel. *Mosses from an Old Manse* (1846)
——. *The Scarlet Letter* (1850)
——. *The House of the Seven Gables* (1851)
——. *The Blithedale Romance* (1852)
Howells, William Dean. *The Shadow of a Dream* (1890)
Irving, Washington. *History of New York . . .* (1809)
——. *The Sketch Book of Geoffrey Crayon, Gent* (1820)
——. *Bracebridge Hall* (1822)
James, Henry. 'A Curious Dream' (1876)
——. *The Turn of the Screw* (1898)
——. 'The Third Person' (1900)
——. *The Sacred Fount* (1901)
——. 'The Friends of Friends' (1908)
——. 'The Jolly Corner' (1908)
Lewis, Sinclair. *Main Street* (1920)
——. *Babbitt* (1922)
London, Jack. *The Iron Heel* (1907)
Melville, Herman. *Mardi* (1849)
——. *Moby-Dick* (1851)
——. *Pierre* (1852)
——. *The Confidence-Man* (1857)
Poe, Edgar Allan. 'The Narrative of Arthur Gordon Pym' (1838)
——. *Tales of the Grotesque and Arabesque* (1840)
——. *Tales of Adventure, Mystery and Imagination* (1845)
Porter, Eleanor. *Pollyanna* (1913)
Porter, Gene Stratton. *The Harvester* (1911)
——. *Freckles* (1914)
Twain, Mark. *Roughing It* (1872)
——. *The Gilded Age* (1873)
——. *The Adventures of Tom Sawyer* (1876)
——. *The Prince and the Pauper* (1882)

——. *A Connecticut Yankee in King Arthur's Court* (1889)
——. *The Mysterious Stranger* (1916)
Wiggin, Kate Douglas. *Rebecca of Sunnybrook Farm* (1903)
Wister, Owen. *The Virginian* (1902)

Chapter 4   Individual and Society

Boyd, Julian (ed). *The Papers of Thomas Jefferson*, Vol 12 (1955)
Bradford, William. *Historie of Plimouth Plantation* (1656)
Bradstreet, Anne. *The Tenth Muse Lately Sprung Up in America* (1650)
Crane, Stephen. *The Red Badge of Courage* (1895)
——. 'The Open Boat' (1897)
Crockett, David. *A Narrative of the Life of David Crockett* (1834)
Emerson, Ralph Waldo. 'The American Scholar' (1837)
——. 'Self-Reliance' (1841)
——. 'The Tragic' (1844)
——. 'Earth's Holocaust' (1846)
——. *The Scarlet Letter* (1850)
James, Henry. *Hawthorne* (1879)
——. *The Portrait of a Lady* (1881)
Melville, Herman. *Moby-Dick* (1851)
——. *Billy Budd* (1924)
Taylor, Edward. *The Poetical Works of Edward Taylor* (1939)
Thoreau, Henry David. 'Civil Disobedience' (1849)
——. *Walden* (1854)
Tocqueville, Alexis de. *Democracy in America* (1840)
Twain, Mark. *Life on the Mississippi* (1883)
——. *The Adventures of Huckleberry Finn* (1884)
——. 'The Man That Corrupted Hadleyburg' (1900)
——. *The Mysterious Stranger* (1916)
Ward, Nathaniel. *The Simple Cobbler of Aggawam* (1646)
Whitman, Walt. *Leaves of Grass* (1855)
——. *Democratic Vistas* (1871)
Wigglesworth, Michael. *The Day of Doom* (1662)
Winthrop, John. *Winthrop's Journal* (1908)

Chapter 5   Freedom and Repression

Cable, George Washington. *The Grandissimes* (1880)
Cather, Willa. *O Pioneers!* (1913)

——. *The Song of a Lark* (1915)
Chopin, Kate. *The Awakening* (1889)
——. *Bayou Folk* (1894)
——. *A Night in Acadie* (1897)
Dixon, Thomas. *The Clansman* (1905)
Dreiser, Theodore. *Jennie Gerhardt* (1911)
——. *The Financier* (1912)
——. *The Titan* (1914)
——. *The Genius* (1915)
Dunbar, Paul Laurence. *Folks from Dixie* (1898)
Fitzgerald, F. Scott. *This Side of Paradise* (1920)
——. *Tender Is the Night* (1934)
Forest, John W. De. *Miss Ravenel's Conversion from Secession to Loyalty* (1867)
Freeman, Mary Wilkins. *A New England Nun and Other Stories* (1891)
Gale, Zona. *Miss Lulu Bett* (1920)
Garland, Hamlin. *Main-Travelled Roads* (1891)
Glasgow, Ellen. *Virginia* (1913)
——. *Life and Gabriella* (1916)
Hawthorne, Nathaniel. *The Scarlet Letter* (1850)
Howe, E. W. *The Story of a Country Town* (1883)
Howells, William Dean. *An Imperative Duty* (1893)
James, Henry. *The Bostonians* (1886)
Jewett, Sarah Orne. *A Country Doctor* (1884)
——. *The Marsh Island* (1885)
——. *The Country of Pointed Firs* (1896)
Kennedy, John Pendleton. *Swallow Barn* (1832)
Kirkland, Joseph. *Zury, the Meanest Man in Spring County* (1887)
Melville, Herman. *Moby-Dick* (1851)
——. 'Benito Cereno' (1856)
Norris, Frank. *McTeague* (1899)
——. *The Pit* (1903)
Stein, Gertrude. *Three Lives* (1909)
Stowe, Harriet Beecher. *Uncle Tom's Cabin* (1852)
Tourgee, Albion. *A Fool's Errand* (1879)
Twain, Mark. *The Gilded Age* (1873)
——. *The Adventures of Tom Sawyer* (1876)
——. *The Adventures of Huckleberry Finn* (1884)
——. *Pudd'nhead Wilson* (1894)
Wharton, Edith. *The House of Mirth* (1905)

Chapter 6   Religion and Irreligion: God and Mammon

Alger, Jr., Horatio. *Ragged Dick* (1867)
Anderson, Sherwood. *Winesburg, Ohio* (1919)
Auden, W. H. 'The Almighty Dollar' (1962)
Bellamy, Edward. *Looking Backward* (1888)
Carnegie, Andrew. 'A Talk to Young Men' (1885)
Conwell, Russell. *Acres of Diamonds* (1888)
Cotton, John. 'A Christian Calling' (1641)
Fitzgerald, F. Scott. 'The Diamond as Big as the Ritz' (1922)
——. *The Great Gatsby* (1925)
Franklin, Benjamin. *The Autobiography of Benjamin Franklin* (1771)
James, Henry. *The American* (1877)
Knight, Sarah Kemble. *The Journal of Madame Knight* (1825)
Melville, Herman. *Moby-Dick* (1851)
Smith, Captain John. *Description of New England* (1616)
Twain, Mark. *A Connecticut Yankee in King Arthur's Court* (1889)
Wigglesworth, Michael. *The Day of Doom* (1662)

Chapter 7   Religion and Irreligion: Doubts and Certainties

Bellamy, Edward. *Looking Backward* (1888)
Crane, Stephen. 'The Blue Hotel' (1899)
Dickinson, Emily. ' "Faith" Is a Fine Invention' (c 1860)
Fitzgerald, F. Scott. *The Great Gatsby* (1925)
Ford, Ford Madox. *The Good Soldier* (1915)
Frederic, Harold. *The Damnation of Theron Ware* (1896)
Freneau, Philip. *The Rising Glory of America* (1771)
Hawthorne, Nathaniel. 'The Gentle Boy' (1837)
——. 'Ethan Brand' (1846)
——. 'Young Goodman Brown' (1846)
——. *The Blithedale Romance* (1852)
Howells, William Dean. *Criticism and Fiction* (1891)
——. *The Landlord at Lion's Head* (1897)
——. *The Leatherwood God* (1916)
James, Henry. *The Portrait of a Lady* (1881)
——. *The Turn of the Screw* (1898)
Melville, Herman. 'Benito Cereno' (1856)
Stein, Gertrude. *The Making of Americans* (1925)
Twain, Mark. *The Adventures of Huckleberry Finn* (1884)
Winthrop, John. *Winthrop's Journal* (1908)

Selected Critical and
Historical Works

Adams, Grace, and Hutter, Edward. *The Mad Forties*. New York and London, 1942

Ahnebrink, Lars. *The Beginnings of American Literary Naturalism*. New York, 1961

Bewley, Marius. *The Eccentric Design*. London, 1959

Brooks, Van Wyck. *America's Coming of Age*. New York, 1915

——. *The Flowering of New England*. New York, 1936

Cady, Edwin F. *The Road to Realism*. Syracuse, NY, 1956

Cash, Wilbur J. *The Mind of the South*. London, 1971

Chase, Richard. *The American Novel and Its Tradition*. London, 1958

Cunliffe, Marcus. *The Literature of the United States*. Harmondsworth, Middx, 1954

Curti, Merle, *et al*. *American Issues: The Social Record*. Chicago, Ill, and Philadelphia, Pa, 1941

Feidelson, Charles S. *Symbolism and American Literature*. Chicago, Ill, 1953

Fiedler, Leslie A. *Love and Death in the American Novel*. London, 1967; New York, 1970

Freud, Sigmund. *Civilization and Its Discontents*. London and New York, 1930

Geismar, Maxwell. *Rebels and Ancestors: The American Novel, 1890–1915*. Boston, Mass, 1953

Guttmann, Allen. *The Conservative Tradition in America*. New York, 1967

Hart, James D. (ed). *The Oxford Companion to American Literature*. New York and London, 1941

Hart, James D. *The Popular Book*. New York, 1950

Hassan, Ihab. *Radical Innocence*. Princeton, NJ, 1961

Herzberg, Max J. (ed). *The Reader's Encyclopedia of American Literature*. London, 1963

Hofstadter, Richard. *The Age of Reform*. New York, 1955

Howard, Leon. *Literature and the American Tradition*. New York, 1960

Hubbell, Jay B. *The South in American Literature, 1607–1900*. Durham, NC, 1954

Jones, Howard Mumford. *O Strange New World*. New York, 1964

——. *The Age of Energy: Varieties of American Experience, 1865–1915*. New York, 1971

Kazin, Alfred. *On Native Grounds*. New York, 1942

Lawrence, D. H. *Studies in Classic American Literature*. London, 1924

Levin, Harry. *The Power of Blackness*. New York, 1958

Lewis, R. W. B. *The American Adam*. Chicago, Ill, 1955

Martin, Jay. *Harvests of Change: American Literature, 1865–1914*. Englewood Cliffs, NJ, 1967

Marx, Leo. *The Machine in the Garden*. New York, 1964

Matthiessen, F. O. *American Renaissance*. New York, 1941

Maxwell, D. E. S. *American Fiction: The Intellectual Background*. London, 1963

May, Henry F. *The End of American Innocence*. New York, 1959

Miller, Perry (ed). *The Puritans*. New York and Cincinnati, Ohio, 1938

Miller, Perry. *Errand in the Wilderness*. Cambridge, Mass, 1956

Morison, Samuel Eliot. *Builders of the Bay Colony*. Boston, Mass, and New York, 1930

Morris, Wright. *The Territory Ahead*. New York, 1968

Mumford, Lewis. *The Golden Day*. New York, 1926

——. *The Brown Decades*. New York, 1931

Noble, David W. *The Eternal Adam and the New World Garden*. New York, 1968

Parrington, Vernon L. *Main Currents in American Thought*. London, 1960

Pearce, Roy Harvey. *The Continuity of American Poetry*. Princeton, NJ, 1961

Pizer, Donald. *Realism and Naturalism in Nineteenth Century American Literature*, Carbondale, Ill, 1967

Rourke, Constance. *American Humor*. New York, 1931

Smith, Henry Nash. *Virgin Land*. Cambridge, Mass, 1950

Spiller, Robert E. *et al*. *Literary History of the United States*. New York, 1948

——. *The Cycle of American Literature*. New York, 1955

Straumann, Heinrich. *American Literature in the Twentieth Century*. New York, 1968

Tanner, Tony. *The Reign of Wonder*. Cambridge, 1965

Thistlethwaite, Frank. *The Great Experiment*. Cambridge, 1955

Wager, Willis. *American Literature*. London, 1969

Walcutt, Charles Child. *American Literary Naturalism: A Divided Stream*. Minneapolis, Minn, 1958.

Weber, Max. *The Protestant Ethic and the Spirit of Capitalism*. London, 1930

Wecter, Dixon. *The Hero in America*. New York, 1941

Wilson, Edmund. *The Shock of Recognition*. London, 1958

——. *Patriotic Gore*. New York, 1962

Winters, Yvor. *In Defense of Reason*. Denver, Colo, 1947

Ziff, Larzer. *The American 1890's*. New York, 1966

Index

Early Reader Level 3

WITHDRAWN

PRAIRIE FRIENDS

by Nancy Smiler Levinson

pictures by Stacey Schuett

HarperCollins*Publishers*

For Anne Hoppe, who shared my vision of a prairie story,

and Marianne Wallace, who helped the lost friends find their way

—N.S.L.

For Sofia, who knows the value of a good friend

—S.S.

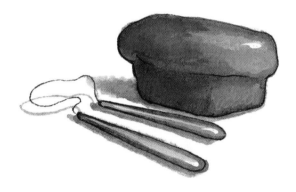

HarperCollins®, 🐾®, and I Can Read Book® are trademarks of HarperCollins Publishers Inc.

Prairie Friends
Text copyright © 2003 by Nancy Smiler Levinson Illustrations copyright © 2003 by Stacey Schuett
Printed in the U.S.A. All rights reserved. www.harperchildrens.com

Library of Congress Cataloging-in-Publication Data
Levinson, Nancy Smiler.
  Prairie friends / story by Nancy Smiler Levinson ; pictures by Stacey Schuett.
    p.   cm. — (An I can read book)
  "An I can read book."
  Summary: When Betsy learns that a new family is coming to the Nebraska prairie, she hopes they
have a daughter who will be her friend.
    ISBN 0-06-028001-8 — ISBN 0-06-028002-6 (lib. bdg.)
  [1. Friendship—Fiction.   2. Frontier and pioneer life—Nebraska—Fiction.
3. Nebraska—History—Fiction.]   I. Schuett, Stacey, ill.   II. Title.   III. Series.
PZ7.L5794 Pr 2003   2002020538
[E]—dc21

    1 2 3 4 5 6 7 8 9 10   ❖   First Edition